ai Plan    2    30/3/09

# HEALTHY &
## delicious

Reader's Digest

# HEALTHY &
# delicious

How to eat
**5** vegetables a day
the easy way!

Published by the Reader's Digest Association Limited
London • New York • Sydney • Montreal

# contents

# the rewards
## of vegetables

# an easy way to **5** a day

Vegetables are the perfect food to give you energy, prevent disease and help you to lose weight – and as if that were not enough, they also taste delicious. Yet many of us do not make the most of the abundance of varieties available or the benefits they offer.

Vegetables have crunch and colour, distinctive flavours and aromas. They pair well with one another and with meats, seafood, fish and poultry. They team with pasta, pulses and rice, and their flavours are complemented and enhanced by herbs, spices, sauces and other flavourings. Better still, they are inexpensive and easy to prepare. Best of all, you can eat generous amounts of vegetables thanks to their low-calorie, high-fibre and high-nutrient content.

The wide range of recipes in this book will show you how to make vegetables a greater part of your daily diet. Some meals are classics that use traditional ingredients and cooking methods. Others are modern variations of old favourites that have been reworked to incorporate ingredients from different cuisines around the world that are a feature of our modern culinary life. Even more introduce healthier cooking techniques that retain optimum flavour and texture.

The book has been developed to benefit people at all stages of health and all levels of cooking expertise. Vegetable-only main meals sit alongside recipes that are designed to accompany or incorporate meat, fish, poultry and seafood. You'll find vegetable inspirations for breakfast, appetisers, main courses for lunch or dinner, side dishes and desserts, too. Each and every one of them is made with at least one vegetable. The green circles that appear with the recipes indicate how many portions of your five vegetables a day you will get with each serving.

With this book as inspiration, you'll find it easy to eat five servings of vegetables a day and you may find you're eating even more – and loving it.

**2**
of your
**5 a day**

## key to **recipes**

Recipes in this book are marked as follows.

| • QUICK RECIPE | • MAKE AHEAD | • HEART HEALTHY |
|---|---|---|
| The recipe can be prepared in 30 minutes or less, from start to finish. | The dish can be made in advance and reheated. Or just one small step is needed to complete it. | Less than a third of the calories in the recipe come from fat. |

**How to use nutrition guidelines** Compare the nutritional analysis at the end of each recipe with the following guidelines established by experts to design daily menus that are within healthy limits.

| daily nutrition guidelines | | | | | | |
|---|---|---|---|---|---|---|
| | calories | protein | total fat | saturated fat | salt | fibre |
| **women** | 2000 | 45 grams | 70 grams | 20 grams | 6 grams | 24 grams |
| **men** | 2500 | 55.5 grams | 90 grams | 30 grams | 6 grams | 24 grams |

# what's in a serving?

Health experts and nutritionists recommend eating at least five servings of vegetables or fruit every day and as many as nine, if possible. Each of the following can be counted as a serving of vegetables.

| Vegetable | Portion equivalent to 80g |
|---|---|
| artichokes (globe) | 2 globe hearts |
| asparagus: fresh<br>: canned | 5 spears<br>7 spears |
| aubergine | 1/3 aubergine |
| beans<br>: black eye, broad,<br>  butter, cannellini,<br>  kidney<br>: french, runner | 3 heaped tablespoons<br><br><br>4 heaped tablespoons |
| bean sprouts: fresh | 2 handfuls |
| beetroot | 3 'baby' whole, or 7 slices |
| broccoli | 2 spears |
| brussels sprouts | 8 Brussels sprouts |
| cabbage | 1/6 small cabbage or 2 handfuls sliced |
| carrot<br>: cooked, canned<br>: shredded | 3 heaped tablespoons<br>1/3 cereal bowl |
| cauliflower | 8 florets |
| celery | 3 sticks |
| chick peas | 3 heaped tablespoons |
| chinese leaves | 1/5 head |
| courgettes | Half a large courgette |
| cucumber | 5cm piece |
| curly kale | 4 heaped tablespoons |
| leeks | 1 leek (white portion only) |
| lentils | 3 tablespoons |
| lettuce | 1 cereal bowl |
| mange-tout | 1 handful |
| mushrooms<br>: fresh<br>: dried | 14 button or 3 handfuls of slices,<br>3-4 heaped tablespoons<br>2 tablespoons or handful porcini |
| okra | 16 medium |
| onion | 1 medium onion |
| parsnips | 1 large |
| peas: fresh, canned, frozen | 3 heaped tablespoons |
| pepper: fresh, canned | half a pepper |
| raddish | 10 raddishes |
| spinach<br>: cooked<br>: fresh | 2 heaped tablespoons<br>1 cereal bowl |
| spring greens | 4 heaped tablespoons |
| spring onion | 8 onions |
| sugersnap peas | 1 handful |
| swede | 3 heaped tablespoons |
| sweetcorn<br>: baby<br>: canned or frozen<br>: on the cob | 6 baby corn<br>3 heaped tablespoons<br>1 cob |
| tomatoes<br>: canned plum<br>: fresh<br>: sundried | 2 whole<br>1 medium, or 7 cherry<br>4 pieces |

# vegetables, the
# real health superstars

You may have thought that five servings of vegetables each day were enough. But research indicates that an even larger number of servings may be advisable. Here are five compelling reasons why you should eat more vegetables.

## 1 rich in fibre

Fibre is the material in a plant that your body cannot digest. On the surface, it would seem that fibre would provide little benefit, as it passes undigested through your body. But the opposite is true. There are two types of fibre – soluble and insoluble – and each has unique benefits.

'Soluble' refers to something that dissolves in water. Soluble fibre mixes with water and food in the digestive tract to form a gooey gel that slows digestion and makes blood sugar enter the bloodstream more gradually; this is particularly useful for people who have Type 2 diabetes. This gel also binds with fats and cholesterol, making it beneficial for the heart.

Insoluble fibre has many benefits as well. It creates a feeling of fullness, which is helpful if you are trying to lose weight; it helps to bulk up stools, preventing constipation; it cleans the digestive tract as it passes through, which doctors believe may help to prevent gastrointestinal diseases such as colon cancer and diverticulosis. Whole grains and vegetables are excellent sources of fibre. Cauliflower and green beans are especially rich in the fibre your body needs to function smoothly.

## 2 virtually fat-free

Reducing your total fat intake reduces the risk of heart disease, certain cancers and other chronic diseases. Some of the dietary fats that are considered most healthy are oils from vegetable sources such as olives and corn. These fats help to keep blood cholesterol levels down, while fats from animal sources tend to raise cholesterol and total fat in the blood.

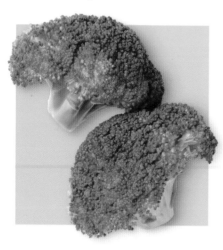

# 3 help with weight loss

Vegetables are the perfect food for weight loss. Most vegetables – particularly leafy greens – are low in calories. As a result, they can be eaten in large quantities and are an excellent source of nutrients.

Then there's the fibre in vegetables, which makes you feel full more quickly, and which binds with fats on its way through the digestive tract. Vegetable carbohydrates are mostly complex, meaning that they provide great fuel, that is released in healthy, steady ways. Even starchy plant foods such as grains, pulses, sweet potatoes, corn and pumpkin have a place in a weight-loss programme. While not especially low in calories, they are high in fibre and nutrients, and can be very filling in small amounts.

# 4 supply crucial nutrients

To function properly, your body needs proteins, fats and carbohydrates for fuel and cellular growth. Other essential requirements are vitamins, minerals and a host of other important substances that are used for the manufacturing of hormones, the creation of immune cells, the functioning of the brain and nervous system. Your body also needs a range of vital minerals. These include calcium and magnesium for building and maintaining strong bones and teeth, and iron and potassium for keeping the blood healthy.

Vegetables are an outstanding source of all these nutrients. Plants are densely packed with the minerals, vitamins and important chemicals you need to function.

# 5 help to prevent disease

For untold centuries, many human cultures have used food as part of the healing process. But only in the past 20 years or so have scientists properly investigated the precise science of phytochemicals and explored why vegetables, fruit and grains have such healing powers.

Phytochemicals are natural chemicals in plants that are beneficial to human health. Technically, vitamins and minerals in vegetables are phytochemicals, but the term is used for a whole group of ingredients with complicated names and specific uses. For example, broccoli, cabbage and other types of green vegetables are rich in chemicals called glucosinolates that can be useful in protecting and fighting against cancers. Garlic and onions are rich in sulphur compounds such as allicin that also battle cancer and cholesterol. Peppers contain bioflavonoids, which help to neutralise free radicals in the bloodstream.

A single plant food can contain many hundreds of these disease-fighting nutrients. These nutrients give vegetables their brilliant colours, distinctive flavours and appetising aromas. They protect the plants from insects, bacteria, viruses, UV light and other environmental threats. In the human body, their benefits are similarly broad. They help the body to dispose of potentially hazardous substances such as carcinogens and free radicals. They stimulate the body's immune cells and infection-fighting enzymes.

While an increasing number of these plant chemicals are being sold in supplement form, doctors maintain that the best thing to do is to eat a diversity of fresh produce, spanning a wide range of colours and sources.

# the big ten

All vegetables are good for you, but some are real superstars. The 10 given here feature in many recipes in the book. They all contain energy-giving macronutrients, micronutrients to keep your body working smoothly every day and phytochemicals to promote long-term health.

**broccoli** is a good source of the B vitamin folate and vitamin C and provides other nutrients such as calcium and potassium as well as beta carotene which the body converts to vitamin A.

**brussels sprouts** are part of the same family of cruciferous vegetables as broccoli, and contain many of the same vitamins and phytochemicals, including isothiocyanates, indoles and sulforaphane.

**cabbage** is a third member of the phytochemical-rich cruciferous vegetable family. Cabbage is thought to reduce hormone-related cancers as well as cancers of the colon and rectum. It is also a great source of vitamin C, carotenoids and folate.

**carrots** are super sources of beta carotene, an antioxidant and a precursor to vitamin A, which maintains healthy eyesight, cell growth, skin and hair.

**cauliflower** is another crucifer that is rich in vitamin C and folate and provides such phytochemicals as indoles and isothiocyanates. In a number of studies, indoles have been shown to interfere with hormones that fuel the growth of breast cancer tumours.

**dark leafy greens** such as kale, spinach and watercress contain disease-fighting phytochemicals as well as rich amounts of vitamin C, bone-building and anti-clotting vitamin K, beta-carotene and fibre. Chlorophyll in these greens may help block the changes that turn healthy cells into pre-cancerous ones. Kale is a rich source of lutein and zeaxanthin, both linked to the prevention of macular degeneration and some cancers.

**peppers** of all types contain good amounts of vitamin C. Red peppers contain lutein and zeaxanthin, carotenoids that may lower the risk of age-related blindness due to macular degeneration and cataracts, as well as forms of cancer. Chillies contain concentrated amounts of capsaicin, which is used topically to treat pain and can help to inhibit cholesterol formation.

**pumpkin & squash** are super-rich in beta carotene and also supply potassium, vitamin $B_6$, vitamin C and lutein. They contain large amounts of soluble fibre, which helps to lower cholesterol. They are also a source of brain-boosting thiamin.

**sweet potatoes** are extremely high in beta-carotene, which helps to prevent cancers such as those of the stomach, pancreas, mouth and gums; potassium, which is associated with lower blood pressure; vitamin $B_6$, which may help to prevent heart disease; vitamin C, which bolsters immunity; and, when eaten with the skin on, insoluble fibre, to prevent constipation and diverticulosis. Sweet potatoes also contain cancer-fighting chlorogenic acid; lutein and zeaxanthin to protect against cancer and eye diseases; and cholesterol-lowering plant sterols.

**tomatoes** and tomato products, such as sauce, paste, purée and juice, are rich sources of cancer-fighting beta-carotene and immunity-boosting vitamin C. Tomatoes contain lycopene, a carotenoid that suppresses damage caused by free radicals and is associated with the reduced risk of heart attack and prostate cancer; caffeic and ferulic acids, which enhance the body's production of cancer-fighting enzymes; and chlorogenic acid, which may help to guard against cancer by blocking the effects of toxins.

# top ten vitamins & minerals

| vitamin/mineral | may be helpful for | where to find it |
|---|---|---|
| calcium | anxiety and stress, high blood pressure, hyperthyroidism, osteoporosis, overweight, peri-menopause and menopause, PMS, pregnancy | broccoli, dairy products, salmon or sardines with bones, tofu |
| folate | anaemia, cancer, depression, heart disease, infertility and impotence, insomnia, osteoporosis, pregnancy, rheumatoid arthritis | asparagus, avocados, beans, beetroot, broccoli, cabbage family, citrus fruit, cooking greens, corn, lentils, peas, spinach |
| iron | anaemia, immune deficiency, memory loss, pregnancy | dried apricots, fatty fish, figs, lentils, meat, peas, poultry, shellfish |
| magnesium | allergies and asthma, anxiety and stress, chronic fatigue syndrome, constipation, diabetes, high blood pressure, kidney stones, migraine, PMS | avocados, grains, nuts, seeds, dark green leafy vegetables |
| selenium | allergies and asthma, cancer, hypothyroidism, infertility and impotence, macular degeneration, prostate problems | meat, mushrooms, nuts, poultry, rice, seeds, shellfish, whole grains |
| vitamin $B_6$ | acne, anaemia, anxiety and stress, depression, heart disease, hypothyroidism, insomnia, memory loss, PMS, pregnancy | asparagus, bananas, fatty fish, figs, mushrooms, peas, potatoes, poultry, pumpkin and squash, rice, sweet potatoes |
| vitamin $B_{12}$ | anaemia, depression, heart disease, infertility and impotence | dairy products, eggs, fatty fish, meat, poultry, shellfish |
| vitamin C | allergies and asthma, anaemia, bronchitis, cancer, cataracts, chronic fatigue syndrome, cold sores, colds and flu, diabetes, eczema, haemorrhoids, heart disease, infertility and impotence, high blood pressure, hyperthyroidism, immune deficiency, macular degeneration, osteoarthritis, osteoporosis, rheumatoid arthritis, sinusitis, sprains | berries, cabbage family, capsicums, citrus fruit, kiwifruit, melons, peas, pineapple, potatoes, pumpkins and squash, salad greens, spinach, sweet potatoes, tomatoes, turnips |
| vitamin E | bronchitis, cancer, cataracts, eczema, hyper-thyroidism, immune deficiency, infertility and impotence, macular degeneration, memory loss, osteoarthritis, prostate problems, rheumatoid arthritis | avocados, grains, nuts, olive oil, salad greens, seeds |
| zinc | acne, bronchitis, chronic fatigue syndrome, colds, eczema, haemorrhoids, hypothyroidism, immunity, infertility and impotence, macular degeneration, rosacea, sinusitis | beans, meat, poultry, seeds, shellfish, whole grains |

# your vegetable arsenal

Researchers are discovering that phytonutrients can help to heal many medical conditions. Here's a selection of vegetables that contain healing agents for 16 common health conditions or concerns.

| condition | vegetable | healing nutrient |
|---|---|---|
| allergies & asthma | red onions | quercetin |
| | broccoli | vitamin C |
| | peppers and chillies | vitamin C |
| cancer prevention | garlic | allium compounds |
| | onions | allium compounds |
| | carrots | beta carotene |
| | sweet potatoes | beta carotene |
| | broccoli | flavonoids, glucosinolates |
| | asparagus | folate |
| | beetroot | folate |
| | spinach | folate |
| | Brussels sprouts | glucosinolates |
| | cabbage | glucosinolates |
| | tomatoes | lycopene |
| | mushrooms | selenium |
| | peppers | vitamin C |
| diabetes | asparagus | fibre |
| | canola oil | monounsaturated fat |
| | olive oil | monounsaturated fat |
| | peppers | vitamin C |
| | broccoli | vitamin C |
| heart disease | asparagus | folate |
| | spinach | folate |
| | carrots | soluble fibre |
| high blood pressure | broccoli | calcium |
| | leafy greens | calcium |
| | asparagus | dietary fibre |
| | peppers | vitamin C |
| high cholesterol | onions | flavonoids |
| | tomatoes | lycopene |
| | carrots | soluble fibre |
| | garlic | sulphur compounds |
| immune deficiency | carrots | carotenoids |
| | sweet potatoes | carotenoids |
| | tomatoes | carotenoids |
| | onions | flavonoids |
| | peppers and chillies | vitamin C |

| condition | vegetable | healing nutrient |
|---|---|---|
| macular degeneration | carrots | beta carotene |
| | spinach | beta carotene |
| | pumpkins and squash | beta carotene |
| | spring greens | lutein and zeaxanthin |
| | peppers and chillies | lutein and zeaxanthin |
| | spinach | lutein and zeaxanthin |
| | sweet potatoes | lutein and zeaxanthin |
| | tomatoes | lycopene |
| | broccoli | vitamin C |
| osteoporosis | spring greens | calcium |
| | peppers and chillies | vitamin C |
| | kale | vitamin K |
| | spinach | vitamin K |
| skin problems | broccoli | antioxidants |
| | carrots | antioxidants |
| | tomatoes | antioxidants |
| | asparagus | beta carotene |
| | sweet potatoes | beta carotene |
| | pumpkins and squash | beta carotene |
| | potatoes | vitamin $B_6$ |
| stress | broccoli | calcium |
| | spring greens | calcium |
| | asparagus | folate |
| | peas | folate |
| | salad leaves | folate |
| | peas | tryptophan |
| | turnips | tryptophan |
| stroke | broccoli | calcium |
| | asparagus | dietary fibre |
| | beetroot | dietary fibre |
| | onions | flavonoids |
| tooth and mouth conditions | celery | insoluble fibre |
| | salad leaves | insoluble fibre |
| | peppers and chillies | vitamin C |
| yeast infections | garlic | allicin |
| | artichokes | fructo-oligosaccharides |
| | onions | fructo-oligosaccharides |

# ten ways to **eat more vegetables**

Your goal is to include more vegetables in your diet. Trying new recipes will help, of course, but there are many other simple ways to add vegetables to your meals. Here are ten to get you started that will be easy to adopt.

## 1 serve them straight up

Put a platter of sliced raw vegetables on the table each dinnertime. Particularly enjoyable for their crunchiness and fresh taste are carrots, celery, cucumbers and green peppers, and for sweetness, tomatoes. Serve them with a dip, salsa or vinaigrette.

## 2 have a nightly salad

A handful of salad greens either freshly assembled or from a convenient packet, a few cherry tomatoes, cucumber or apple and make a healthy salad in barely a minute. It's a great way to start a dinner.

## 3 roast them

Many vegetables develop a full-bodied, intense flavour when roasted in the oven. In winter, go for root vegetables such as parsnips, swede, beetroots and potatoes. In summertime, mushrooms, courgettes, tomatoes, peppers and onions work well. Cut the larger vegetables into chunks, toss them in oil, vinegar and seasonings and place in a roasting pan. Roast at a medium heat for about 30 minutes, depending on their thickness. To ensure even cooking, be sure to cook vegetables of similar textures and piece sizes in the one tin.

## 4 purée into soup

Potatoes, carrots, pumpkin, cauliflower and broccoli – just about any cooked (or leftover) vegetable can be made into a creamy, comforting soup.

## 5 do a fast sauté

Select two or three favourite vegetables and cut into bite-sized pieces. Heat a frying pan or small wok to a high temperature. Swirl a little groundnut oil in the pan until hot and add the vegetables. Toss until cooked through. Add salt, pepper and thyme or soy sauce and a little sesame oil, and toss to combine. Serve at once.

## 6 make into a sauce

Quick and easy cooked and uncooked sauces and salsas can be made with tomatoes, onions, peppers or mushrooms, on their own or in combination with other vegetables.

## 7 fill an omelette

There are few vegetables that aren't suitable to include in an omelette, especially when a little grated or crumbled cheese is added. Good ones to try are onions, peppers, tomatoes, mushrooms and potatoes.

## 8 grate into minced meat

To enhance the flavour and nutritional value of minced meat for burgers or bolognese, add up to 150g grated or finely chopped raw vegetables to the mixture before shaping and cooking. Carrots, courgettes, peppers, mushrooms, spinach and onions work well.

## 9 cook in the oven

Finely chopped peppers or onions will flavour the meat beautifully when placed inside rolled fillets of pork, beef or chicken.

## 10 try a recipe makeover

Add chopped cooked spinach or grated carrot to the sauce you use to make lasagne. Increase the amount of vegetables and decrease the amount of meat you use to make homemade soups, stews and casseroles.

# seasoning guide

Sometimes all you need is the right herb, spice, fruit or juice to turn a plain vegetable into a spectacular side dish. And sometimes the best way to season a vegetable is by cooking it with another vegetable.

| | |
|---|---|
| **artichokes globe** | lemon, butter, vinaigrette |
| **asparagus** | lemon, butter, mustard, dill, Parmesan cheese, capers |
| **aubergines** | basil, garlic, onion, tomato, chilli, toasted sesame oil |
| **avocados** | Worcestershire sauce, vinaigrette, cumin, lemon, lime, oregano |
| **beetroot** | balsamic vinegar, dill, lemon, rosemary, apple, pecan nuts |
| **broccoli** | orange, garlic, soy sauce, toasted sesame oil, pine nuts, onion, walnuts |
| **brussels sprouts** | chives, spring onions, mustard |
| **cabbage** | caraway seeds, garlic, sugar and vinegar (sweet and sour), soy sauce, toasted sesame oil, ginger, apple |
| **carrots** | citrus, parsley, honey, butter, lemon, dill, raspberry vinegar |
| **cauliflower** | thyme, almonds, curry powder, cheese and mustard |
| **celeriac** | lemon, mustard, capers, vinaigrette |
| **celery** | garlic, oregano, soy sauce, dark sesame oil |
| **cucumbers** | dill, sugar and vinegar (sweet and sour), sesame seeds, soy sauce |
| **fennel** | bay leaf, tomato, Parmesan cheese |

| | |
|---|---|
| **green beans** | garlic, soy sauce, sesame seeds |
| **leafy greens** | (such as chard and pak choi) garlic, pine nuts, sesame seeds, onion |
| **lettuce** | oil and vinegar, lemon juice, fresh coriander, garlic, mustard |
| **mushrooms** | balsamic vinegar, chives, spring onions, parsley, thyme |
| **okra** | lemon, marjoram, tomato, thyme |
| **parsnips** | Parmesan cheese, thyme |
| **peas** | mint, butter, chives |
| **peppers** | balsamic vinegar, tomato, garlic, olives, capers, thyme, oregano, soy sauce and ginger, cumin |
| **potatoes** | mint, chives, curry powder, garlic, yoghurt, roast peppers, rosemary |
| **pulses** | olive oil, parsley, garlic, onion, bay, fresh coriander, tomato |
| **pumpkin & squash** | nuts, citrus, garlic, ginger, rosemary, cinnamon, cranberries, dried fruit |
| **spinach** | nutmeg, garlic, black pepper, sea salt, pine nuts, soy sauce |
| **sweetcorn** | basil, butter, chilli powder |
| **sweet potatoes** | butter, ginger, cinnamon, black pepper |
| **tomatoes** | balsamic or white wine vinegar, basil, garlic, oregano, Parmesan or pecorino cheese |

# herbs & spices

One of the tastiest and healthiest ways to enhance the flavour of foods is to cook with a variety of herbs and spices.

**allspice** tastes like a mix of ginger, nutmeg, cinnamon and pepper.

**anise** has a strong liquorice flavour that works well in cakes and biscuits.

**basil** has a warm, aniseed flavour. It is a major ingredient in pesto and also boosts the flavour of tomato-based dishes.

**bay leaf**, with its woodsy flavour, is a staple in meat dishes and stews. Add the dry leaf at the start of cooking; remove just before serving.

**black pepper-corns** are sharp and aromatic. Grind black pepper as needed.

**caraway seeds** impart an aromatic, aniseed flavour to breads, cakes and cheese, vegetable and meat dishes. The seeds have a nutty texture.

**cardamom** is a relative of ginger. One of the main ingredients in curry powder, it is used in cakes, ice cream and mulled wine. Lightly crush whole pods to flavour slow-cooked dishes, as well as milk to be used in sauces.

**cayenne**, ground from dried red chillies and their seeds, adds a hot, peppery taste to sauces and stews. It is widely used in Mexican dishes.

**celery seeds** may be tiny but they pack a punch, adding a strong celery flavour to sauces, dips and soups.

**chervil** tastes of aniseed and parsley. It enhances chicken, egg, prawn, potato and salad dishes.

**chilli powder** varies in its degree of heat depending on what type of chilli it is made from. Taste a tiny bit before using to gauge how much to use.

**chives** add a sweet onion flavour to dips, salads and sauces. They're easy to grow yourself in a pot or they can be bought fresh, frozen or freeze-dried.

**cinnamon** in stick form can be used to flavour milk for sauce and custard recipes. Ground cinnamon is a popular flavouring in desserts and baking. It is also used in Moroccan and Greek cuisines. It is mixed with sugar to make cinnamon toast.

**cloves** have a very intense, musky taste that mellows during cooking. They can be used to stud hams before baking and to spike apples for cider punch or for pies. Use ground cloves in biscuits, cakes and sauces.

**coriander** is a herb (fresh green leaves) and a spice (seeds). In either form, it has a pungent taste that is popular in Mexican and Asian cuisines, and also tastes good with Mediterranean dishes. The lemony seeds are included in most curry powders and spice mixes.

---

**If you're not used to using a range of herbs and spices in your cooking it can seem intimidating. But the rules are easy.**

**choose fragrant**, fresh-looking herbs with no wilted, yellowing leaves or brown spots. Store loosely wrapped in damp kitchen paper and then in plastic, in the crisper drawer of the fridge. Most fresh herbs will last only a few days. Basil and mint do best standing upright in a jar of water in the fridge, loosely covered with a kitchen paper and then plastic.

**chop fresh herbs** just before using. Add herbs to cooked dishes during the last 30 minutes of cooking time or they will lose much of their pungency. Add herbs to uncooked dishes at least 1 hour before serving so that their flavours have plenty of time to marry with other ingredients.

**spices are sold dried**; you can grind them yourself for the freshest taste or buy them ready-ground, in which case replenish your stocks regularly.

**cumin** seeds and ground cumin both have an earthy flavour that adds richness to bean and shellfish recipes and Mexican cooking.

**dill** seeds and the feathery leaves (both fresh and dried) are used. Chopped leaves lift the flavour of eggs and seafood, as well as beetroot, cucumber and potatoes. Dill seeds are used in pickling.

**fennel seeds** have an aniseed taste that complements the rich flavour of pork.

**ginger** has a warm, slightly lemony flavour. Fresh ginger root is peeled and grated or diced and added to Asian dishes such as stir-fries and to spicy curries and stews. Store fresh ginger, well wrapped, in the freezer. Ground dried ginger is used in cake and biscuit making.

**mace** is the external covering of the nutmeg seed that is also ground as a spice. It is hotter than nutmeg and is used for sweet and savoury dishes.

**marjoram** has a spicy, cleansing taste that goes with most vegetables, especially those that are used in Mediterranean dishes and Mexican recipes.

**mint** is a refreshing, herb that enlivens salads, fruit salads and fruit drinks such as lemonade. As a jelly or sauce, it is a fresh-tasting accompaniment to roast lamb.

**mustard seeds** are used to make many popular commercial mustards ranging from fairly mild Dijon to fiery English mustard. Pungent ground mustard seed (powder) is used in homemade mayonnaise and many sauces that can be served with fish, poultry and meat.

**nutmeg** has a warm, nutty flavour that complements spinach, pumpkin and savoury dishes, as well as baked foods and custards.

**oregano** tastes like a stronger version of marjoram. A feature of Mediterranean cuisines, it enhances poultry, beef, veal and lamb dishes, tomatoes and cabbage.

**paprika**, like cayenne, is a product of ground dried red chillies, although sweeter and much milder than chilli powder. Hungarian paprika is among the best and is particularly aromatic. It is used in goulashes and other slow-cooked dishes.

**parsley** comes in curly leaf and flat-leaf varieties. They are interchangeable, both adding a fresh taste to potatoes, grains, mushrooms, salads, sauces and meat dishes. Chewing fresh parsley is said to freshen the breath.

**rosemary** has an intense, earthy taste. Use it in marinades and for flavouring barbecued, grilled and roast meat such as lamb. It also complements beans, peas, mushrooms and courgettes.

**saffron**, the most expensive of all spices, is obtained from the stamens of a single variety of crocus. Very fine strands of it are used to flavour and colour rice dishes, vegetable soups, seafood dishes and sweet breads.

**sage** has a woody, aromatic flavour that is popular in Italian cooking. It teams well with tomatoes and garlic and also complements onions, pulses, pork, poultry and stuffing.

**sea salt** comes in coarse granules. Depending on its source, it has subtle flavours from trace minerals. As well as its use as a food flavouring, it is a preserving medium in pickling and drying. It is used to make Asian soy and fish sauces and shrimp paste. Food without any salt added will taste bland.

**summer savory** is a peppery herb that spices up green beans, pulses, cabbages, potatoes and Brussels sprouts, as well as fish, poultry and pork.

**tarragon**, popular in French cuisine, has a mild aniseed flavour. Stir through scrambled eggs or sprinkle on salads, carrots, seafood and chicken.

**thyme** has a light, spicy flavour that complements salad leaves, carrots and mushrooms. It goes well with oily fish. It is a key ingredient, with parsley and bay, in a bouquet garni.

# a world of flavours

There are so many popular herbs and spices, you could spend a lifetime exploring them. But if you really want to add some flair and personality to your cooking, you need to explore the cuisines of the world.

each of the world's cuisines has its trademark fruit or vegetable and signature dishes that set it apart from the food of other countries. But it's the blend of seasonings and spices a cuisine utilises that most defines it. Here are some of the basic seasonings and condiments that help to give some of the world's best-known cuisines their distinct flavours.

## american

**tabasco sauce** A hot sauce from Louisiana made from chillies and vinegar, matured for three years to give it a fiery flavour. Use to spice up dressings, pizzas, sauces and stews.

## british

**english mustard** A fiery hot condiment made from the ground seeds to serve with beef or to add piquancy to cheese dishes.

**horseradish** A hot and peppery root, grated and added to dishes or made into a cream. Especially good with beef and oily fish.

**mint sauce** A fragrant sauce made with finely chopped mint leaves, vinegar and sugar to serve with lamb. Mint jelly is a sweeter alternative to serve with lamb or potatoes.

**worcestershire sauce** A strongly flavoured sauce made from molasses, anchovies, garlic and spices. Add to mushrooms, meat and eggs or to pep up pasta sauces.

**warm spices** include cloves, allspice berries, star anise, cumin (ground and seeds) and caraway seeds.

## chinese

**chilli bean paste** A peppery condiment that varies in intensity depending on the brand. Test before adding to food.

**five-spice powder** A blend of cinnamon, fennel, cloves, star anise and Szechuan peppercorns. Often used in marinades or as a seasoning for soups, stews and stir-fries.

**hoisin sauce** A dark, thick, sweet and salty sauce made from fermented soya beans. Use it in stir-fries and as a condiment served at the table.

**oyster sauce** A condiment with a strong shellfish flavour, made with soy sauce and dried oysters, to add to poultry, meat and seafood dishes.

**sesame oil** Toasted sesame oil has a richly nutty flavour that adds depth to stir-fries; add it sparingly at the end of cooking. Store in a cool place.

**soy sauce** The most important and commonly used seasoning in China and all of Asia, this salty sauce made from fermented soya beans comes in two main varieties. Light soy sauce is thinner and saltier. Dark soy sauce is thicker and less salty.

**star anise** This pretty star-shaped spice has a strong aniseed flavour. It comes from a Chinese evergreen tree. Use in soups and stews.

**yellow bean sauce** Made from fermented yellow soya beans and used in Szechuan dishes, with other flavourings such as soy sauce. Use in poultry, meat and fish dishes.

## french

**chestnut purée** Used to add a rich, nutty flavour to sauces, baked goods and vegetable side dishes.

**mustard** The most popular is from the Dijon region; it is sharp and of a medium intensity. Serve at the table or use to add piquancy to sauces and salad dressings.

**nut oils** These are richly flavoured oils made from hazelnuts, walnuts, almonds and pine nuts. Add a few drops to other milder oils such as groundnut oil to impart a little of their flavour. Also use in vinaigrettes or drizzle over cooked vegetables.

**peppercorns** Green and pink peppercorns feature in dishes where a milder pepper flavour is desired.

**tapenade** A rich purée of capers, anchovies and black olives with olive oil. Used as a dip or to spread on toast, or to accompany fish or eggs.

olive oil is richly endowed with phytochemicals, vitamin E and monounsaturated fat.

## greek

**extra virgin olive oil** This deep green, intensely flavoured, fragrant, high-grade olive oil is a basic condiment in Greek cuisine for roasting meats, cooking pulses and drizzling over salads and cooked vegetables. It is also widely used in Italian cuisine.

## indian

**curry paste** A mixture of cumin, coriander, chilli, turmeric and other herbs in an oily base to give a good rich flavour to curries. Available in different blends and strengths such as tikka masala, korma and Madras. Pastes must always be cooked.

**curry powder** An aromatic blend of seeds and spices used to flavour curries, lentils, meat, poultry, sauces and vegetable dishes. Some powders are much hotter than others.

**garam masala** A blend of cumin, cinnamon, black pepper, coriander, cloves and cardamom that is used to flavour curries, rice, beans, potatoes, aubergine and meat dishes. Usually added towards the end of cooking. Buy in small quantities and store in a sealed jar away from heat and light.

**mango chutney** A spicy, sweet, condiment used as a relish with rice dishes and curries. Makes a good foil for hot, spicy dishes.

## italian

**balsamic vinegar** The intense flavour of this vinegar comes from boiling down white grapes to about 50 per cent of their original volume and fermenting the resultant 'must'. Aged over as many as 25 years, the vinegar becomes sweet, viscous and very concentrated. Flavour depends on the type of wood used to make the casks. Use as a simple flavouring for fish, meats, green salads, vegetables and even berries.

**pesto** A purée of basil, pine nuts and Parmesan cheese mixed with olive oil. Toss with pasta or add to baked potatoes, pizza toppings, bruschetta and sauces.

## japanese

**miso** Fermented soya bean paste used in soups and marinades.

**tamari soy sauce** Darker and more intense than regular soy sauce.

**wasabi** A blast-furnace hot, slightly bitter powder or paste. Use sparingly in dips, dressings and sauces.

## latin american

**chilli powder** A blend that usually includes dried chillies, oregano, garlic and cumin. Chilli powders vary from brand to brand, depending on which chilli is used and its ratio to the other ingredients used. It's wise to add a little then taste before adding more.

## north african

**harissa** A hot paste of chillies, garlic, caraway, cumin, coriander and mint. The strengths of various brands vary, so use sparingly at first (about a teaspoon).

**preserved lemons** Just the finely sliced skin is used to add depth of flavour to tagines and salads.

## spanish

**sherry vinegar** Matured sherry vinegar has a sweet and nutty flavour that enhances sauces, salad dressings and steamed vegetables.

## thai

**chilli paste** Includes chillies and sweet basil. Use to flavour stir-fries, curries, sauces and marinades.

**fish sauce** A salty, fermented anchovy sauce that is used in small amounts to flavour soups, stir-fries and dipping sauces.

**lemongrass** Its sour lemon flavour works well in soups, stews, stir-fries, teas and curries.

**tamarind paste** Adds an intense sweet-and-sour flavour to stews and curried dishes.

## west indies

**hot pepper sauce** A blend of Scotch bonnet and habanero peppers with Caribbean spices to add to fish, meat and vegetables.

hot spices include chillies (fresh, dried and ground), peppercorns (black, white, green and pink) and mustard (seeds and ground).

# kitchen **essentials**

Life in the kitchen is made easier if you have a few small appliances and utensils to hand. To prepare vegetables, invest in some or all of the following items.

## blender
A good appliance for puréeing or liquefying. Although not as versatile as a food processor, a blender is preferable when only a small amount of food is involved. A hand-held blender is a narrow, appliance that is convenient for making sauces and purées. This type of blender can be immersed right into the cooking pan to purée a soup or a batch of tomato sauce. It can also be immersed into a liquid in a tall glass to blend a smoothie or shake.

## colander
Made of plastic or metal, with large holes to let liquids drain quickly. A metal colander can also be inserted into a large pan and used as a steamer.

## cutting board
Made of wood, acrylic or plastic. There is no evidence that one type is better, or safer, than another. The important thing is to use separate cutting boards for animal foods and plant foods to eliminate the risk of cross-contamination from raw meat, poultry or seafood to uncooked fruit or vegetables. Also, be sure to wash all types of boards thoroughly in very hot water.

## food processor
Handy when needing to chop, grate or purée large amounts. 'Mini' food processors are perfect for chopping or grinding smaller amounts of food or herbs. To chop or grate very small quantities, it is more efficient (and less messy) to use a knife or grater.

## grater
Comes in a variety of sizes and types. A four-sided box grater is good for grating, shredding and slicing vegetables and cheese. Extra-fine grating can be done with a small hand-held grater.

## kitchen scissors
Use for snipping fresh parsley and other herbs as well as trimming bacon and snipping it into small pieces for adding to recipes.

## mandolin
Ideal for slicing a variety of fruits and vegetables. The classic mandolin has interchangeable blades to slice, julienne, crinkle and waffle cut. Keep a mandolin's guard in place to prevent injury.

## potato masher
Not just useful for potatoes: works on cooked pumpkin, carrots, sweet potatoes and many other root vegetables.

## knives

**How many knives do you need? Start with these three (buy the best quality you can afford) and build up from there.**

**small paring knife**  Has a 9cm blade suitable for scraping carrots, paring asparagus stalks, peeling avocados and removing the strings from celery, among other jobs.

**medium-sized serrated knife** Slices tomatoes and other soft, juicy vegetables and fruits. It can also be used for slicing bread.

**large chef's knife**  Has a 20 to 25cm blade for precise, quick and easy slicing, dicing and chopping.

## salad spinner
Handy for drying salad leaves and herbs quickly and evenly.

## steamer
Consists of an upper section with a mesh or perforated base that fits into a larger pan, which holds water, stock or flavoured liquids. Stackable bamboo or metal steamers, which are designed to hold two or three layers of food can be placed over a large pan or wok. For small amounts of food, a metal, collapsible steamer that fits inside a large or medium-sized pan is useful and inexpensive. Collapsible steamers made of plastic are suitable for use in a microwave oven. If you don't have a steamer, improvise by standing a metal colander or a wire-mesh strainer in a large pan. Tightly cover the pan to retain the steaming heat. Steaming is an easy, quick cooking method that is ideal for retaining essential nutrients.

## strainers

Use over a bowl to drain liquids from solids. Strainers are also used to sift and separate out fine particles. They are available in a range of sizes and made of different gauges of wire or plastic mesh attached to a ring frame.

## vegetable peeler

Many people find these much easier to use than a knife to pare and peel vegetables. They are available in both horizontal and vertical forms. It is not worth spending a lot of money on one. Discard and replace once the blade becomes dull and hard to use.

# cooking to **preserve nutrients**

Cooking fresh vegetables helps to release certain nutrients and phytochemicals, making them more available to your body. But at the same time, improper handling and cooking can destroy essential nutrients, especially vitamin C and folate. Here's how to make sure you preserve these vital nutrients.

**store vegetables with care** The crisper section of the fridge, where many vegetables are stored, is designed to be several degrees cooler and more humid than the upper part of the fridge. (Refer to the storage instructions under the individual vegetable headings in the A–Z Guide to Vegetables, page 254.)

**leave skins on vegetables** such as carrots and potatoes when cooking. Vitamins and minerals are often concentrated in and near the skin. Clean vegetables very thoroughly when the skins are left on.

**chop and slice vegetables** into larger pieces to reduce the surface area exposed, thereby minimising nutrient loss. Cook vegetables whole whenever possible. For example, boil potatoes whole in their skins to retain nutrients, then slice or chop them after cooking.

**cook vegetables in the minimum amount of water** Water-soluble vitamins leach out into cooking water and vanish down the drain when the water is discarded. Steaming is a good method.

**cook vegetables only as long as necessary** Long cooking times destroy vitamins that are susceptible to heat.

**reheat leftover vegetables** as quickly as possible to avoid any further nutrient loss.

# cook smart

Stir-frying, blanching, steaming or microwaving are the cooking methods that best preserve the taste, texture and nutritional value of vegetables, but there are other cooking techniques that will also produce great results.

## barbecuing
Cooking vegetables over hot coals enhances their flavour. Allow the hot coals to die down for about 30 minutes, then brush the vegetables with oil or an oil-based marinade before placing on the grill rack. Use long-handled tongs to turn the vegetables once, halfway through cooking time, or when they are lightly charred and almost tender.

## blanching
Cooking vegetables in a large amount of boiling water for a brief period of time. The vegetables can then be immersed in cold water to arrest the cooking process and to retain their bright colour.

## boiling
Cooking vegetables in a pan of rapidly boiling water to cover. Use this method for hard vegetables such as green beans, broccoli spears and carrots. Cook the vegetable just long enough to freshen its colour and soften the texture. Bring water to the boil first, add the vegetable and cook uncovered or partially covered.

## braising
Sautéing vegetables briefly in fat before adding liquid to finish the cooking process. Braising works well with fibrous vegetables such as celery hearts, celeriac, leeks and fennel. Root vegetables and leafy greens also become very tender when they are braised.

## frying
Cooking vegetables in very hot fat. Pan-frying uses up to 2cm of fat in a pan to cook larger pieces of food such as breadcrumb-coated slices of aubergine. Deep-fat frying, where food is completely immersed in hot fat, is the method for cooking batter-coated vegetables, such as Japanese tempura.

## griddling
Cooking vegetables quickly in a ridged griddle. Preheat the griddle so that a drop of water splashed on to the surface instantly evaporates. Brush food with oil and griddle quickly on both sides.

## grilling
Browning the surface of vegetables with intense dry heat while cooking the inside. Marinate vegetables or brush with oil before grilling. Fibrous vegetables such as celery and leeks are best if they are first blanched. The grill should always be preheated before using.

## microwaving
Microwaving is a fast, clean and convenient method for cooking many vegetables and retains their nutrients, crispness and colour. Place vegetables in a microwave-safe dish with a vented cover and add a small amount of water. The greater the volume of vegetables, the longer it will take for them to be properly cooked.

## roasting
Cooking vegetables slowly in an oven with dry heat. When vegetables are roasted, they are usually tossed first in oil or melted butter. For well-browned, crisp food, roast between 200°C (180°C fan oven), gas 6 and 230°C (210°C fan oven), gas 8.

## sautéing
Cooking vegetables quickly in a small amount of fat over a relatively high heat. Shaking the pan frequently during cooking keeps the food from sticking. Tender vegetables such as onions, courgettes and mushrooms can be cut up and sautéed quickly. Hard ones such as carrots and broccoli may benefit from blanching to soften them slightly first.

## steaming
Cooking food on a rack above boiling or simmering liquid, usually water. Cooking vegetables in the oven wrapped in baking parchment or foil with a little liquid is also a form of steaming.

## stir-frying
Cooking small pieces of food fast in a wok or frying pan in a small amount of oil over high heat, stirring constantly. Stir-fry until just crisp-tender. Organised preparation is essential for successful stir-frying. Chop and slice vegetables ahead of time and measure out seasonings.

# roast vegetable broth

The flavour of vegetables is intensified by roasting, resulting in a full-bodied stock.

Makes about 1.5 litres

2 tablespoons olive oil
3 large carrots, peeled
2 medium parsnips, peeled
2 onions, cut into eighths
2 celery sticks, with leaves, halved
4 garlic cloves, unpeeled
3 medium tomatoes, halved
2 litres water
6 parsley sprigs
3 thin slices fresh root ginger, unpeeled
1 teaspoon salt
1 teaspoon dried rosemary

**1** Preheat oven to 200°C (180°C fan oven), gas 6. Pour oil into a large roasting tin. Add carrots, parsnips, onion, celery and garlic. Stir to coat vegetables well with oil. Roast until vegetables are lightly coloured, 30 minutes. Scrape up any browned bits from the bottom of the pan.

**2** Transfer vegetables to a large flameproof casserole or heavy-based pan. Add the tomatoes, water, parsley, ginger, salt and rosemary. Bring to the boil over high heat. Reduce heat to low. Partially cover dish. Simmer until vegetables are very tender and stock is richly flavoured, about 1 hour.

**3** Line a wire strainer with two layers of dampened cheese-cloth. Strain stock into a large bowl. Discard vegetables and herbs. Cool stock completely.

## tips for success

Be sure the vegetables are very clean before using, even if they are to be peeled. Simmer for just 1 hour or the stock may become bitter. For a richer taste, cook the strained stock for a further 30 minutes to reduce the liquid and concentrate the flavour.

# basic vegetable stock

For this essential staple, minimum effort is required to produce maximum results.

Makes about 500ml

2 large carrots, peeled and coarsely chopped
1 large onion, coarsely chopped
2 celery sticks, coarsely chopped
1 large tomato, cut into 2cm chunks
1 medium turnip, peeled and coarsely chopped
1 small parsnip, peeled and coarsely chopped
40g crisp lettuce, shredded
small handful of parsley
1 garlic clove, peeled
1 bay leaf
1 teaspoon dried thyme
1.75 litres water

**1** Put all the vegetables and herbs in a large pan. Add water. Bring to the boil over medium heat, skimming foam from the surface, as needed. Reduce the heat to low. Partially cover pan; simmer 1 hour.

**2** Line a wire strainer or metal colander with two layers of dampened muslin. Strain stock into a large bowl. Discard vegetables and herbs. Cool stock completely. Stocks can be frozen for up to six months.

# vegetable
## variations

The world of vegetables is flourishing. All year round, new flavours, colours, sizes and shapes are widely available.

anyone who cooks or shops for food will have noticed the quiet revolution that's taken place in the world of vegetables over the past 20 years. Today, there are an astonishing number of choices. Most supermarkets carry three or four kinds of cabbages, five different potatoes and six types of lettuce. Tomatoes, too, come in many shapes and sizes. There are red and yellow cherry tomatoes and plum varieties as well as vine-ripened and organic to choose from.

Other newcomers include pak choi and Chinese leaves; various salad leaves; Tenderstem broccoli; pea shoots, squashes; sprouted beans and baby vegetables. There are many new vegetables to experiment with.

One of the main forces behind this change is our expanding knowledge of the health benefits that come from eating vegetables. We know that nothing can beat a vegetable for providing rich amounts of fibre, nutrients, vitamins and fuel in a convenient, low-calorie form. Then there are the health benefits that go far beyond simply daily nutrition. Phytochemicals – the natural chemicals in vegetables that possess significant healing powers – are thought to bolster immunity, battle cancer, reduce stress, improve skin and hair … and much more.

Thanks to this new evidence, the medical world began campaigning in the 1980s to encourage people to eat at least five servings of fruits and vegetables a day. Add to that the fact that food distribution ensures there are plenty of choices available year-round, not to mention the ever-growing variety of vegetables on the market.

If you, like so many people, prefer not to buy produce that has travelled thousands of miles to get to you, there are excellent alternatives closer to home. As well as greengrocers, market stalls and organic Box Schemes, over the past few years, there's been a steady and welcome growth in farmers' markets around the country. Small growers bring their freshly picked and often organically grown produce to these markets, attracting customers who are happy to have the opportunity to buy from them direct.

# our sources
## for vegetables

Never before has there been so much debate about how vegetables are grown. Some farmers rely on cutting-edge science, while others try to use methods that they consider to be natural – and therefore healthier.

**m**ost vegetables produced in the United Kingdom are grown on farms specialising in one or two varieties of a particular plant. The varieties destined for the market or supermarkets have been bred to withstand travelling and to have a long shelf life.

The farms that grow these vegetables are remarkably efficient operations that skilfully use irrigation systems, chemical pesticides, herbicides and fertilisers to ensure bumper crops. The result can be good-looking, nutritious vegetables but with very little flavour.

## the organic alternative

Many people choose organic vegetables because they find the taste to be better, but there are other reasons too. Organic growing methods are environmentally friendly, with few chemicals used (just four are allowed by the Soil Association – the leading charity working for organic farming, with the highest organic standards of all the certifying oganisations). Natural ways are used to improve the soil, and control pests and weeds, such as adding manure, rotating the crops grown each year and using 'green fertilisers', such as clover, to nourish the soil.

Only foods that comply with strict regulations can be labelled as 'organic'; no genetically modified (GM) foods are approved. You can buy organic produce from your supermarket, and many greengrocers and farmers' markets also now sell it. You can also join a Box Scheme, where a weekly box of organic vegetables is delivered to your door. Note that during the 'hungry months' of April and May you may find more national or imported items in your box than the wider selection of locally grown vegetables the rest of the year. The Soil Association website lists all you need to know about organic produce and where you can buy it, including Box Schemes (**www.soilassociation.org**).

# to clean

**Vegetables should be cleaned before they're eaten, especially when the skin will be consumed. Some, such as mushrooms, leeks and spinach, hold on to the dirt they were grown in and require more careful cleaning than others.**

**leafy greens** Soak them in a sink filled with cold water, swirling the leaves around a few times to be sure all grit and soil is removed. Remove the greens from the water and inspect them for signs of soil or grit. If necessary wash them again in clean water. Greens that come straight from the farm may need washing several times.

**mushrooms** Wipe them with dry kitchen paper or use a soft-bristled brush designed for the purpose to remove surface dirt. Avoid cleaning mushrooms with water as they will become soggy.

**root vegetables** such as parsnips, carrots and sweet potatoes require a good scrubbing with a vegetable brush to remove all pockets of dirt.
Cut out any soft or damaged parts with a knife. You should not have to peel carrots unless the skin has dried out or is unusually dirty.

**leeks** need special care, as soil becomes caught in the layers. Cut off the root end. Trim the dark green tops, removing the outer layer. Cut lengthways through the green part and wash to remove the earth trapped between the leaves.

**smooth-skinned vegetables** such as courgettes, tomatoes, aubergines and peppers should be held under cool water and gently rubbed to remove residual dirt and chemicals.

## biotechnology and the food supply

When biology, biochemistry, chemical engineering, genetics and computer science merged to form the science of food biotechnology, new forms of plant and animal life were created, as well as a means of enhancing the quality and quantity of commercially produced agricultural products.

Genetically modified (GM) foods are a controversial result of this science. Genetic engineering is the transfer of genes among plants and animals, allowing scientists to copy a gene for a desirable trait in one organism and implant it into another. Because UK consumers are largely opposed to GM foods, there are no commercially grown GM crops in the UK, and some councils have designated their areas as GM-free so that GM crops cannot be grown there. However, in other countries, such as the US, GM crops such as soya beans are grown and exported in foods. Any foods using GM ingredients sold in the UK must be labelled.

The two major concerns are the possibility of allergic reactions in some people, and what is referred to as 'gene pollution', or the escape of genetically engineered genes into the wild through natural cross-pollination.

## food irradiation

Irradiation helps to preserve food using ionising radiation to destroy disease-causing and food-poisoning bacteria as well as other pathogens on food. It extends the shelf life of fresh vegetables by delaying the ripening and ageing process in some vegetables and by inhibiting sprouting in others, such as potatoes. It also kills some insects and parasites.

Strict regulations apply in the UK regarding irradiating food, and imported food must also adhere to them. Foods treated in this way must be clearly labelled. As many consumers are opposed to irradiated foods, hardly any UK companies hold the necessary licence to treat foods in this way and none of the major UK supermarkets have chosen to stock any irradiated foods so far.

## grow your own

If you have a garden, however small, you can enjoy eating wonderful, fresh home-grown vegetables. Choose some of the easily grown vegetables to start with and you can even mix them with flowers for a decorative effect.

Vegetables need a sunny spot and good, rich soil, so choose a site carefully and dig in lots of well-rotted manure and compost. Keep a compost bin where you can put raw kitchen vegetable and fruit waste, so that you have a ready supply of conditioner for your soil.

Good vegetables for beginners are sugar-snap peas, which have no waste and a long cropping season. Also try beetroot; their leaves make good cut-and-come-again vegetables for salads or steaming as a side vegetable. Swiss chard, spinach, parsnips, shallots, garlic and cherry tomatoes are all easy to grow. A double-layered black plastic bag of compost will be perfect for growing three potato plants; just make drainage holes in the bottom of the bags.

Make a wigwam of canes and grow runner beans or French beans to make a pretty focal point in a flowerbed, or grow rainbow chard among the flowers.

Create a pond where frogs can live – even a tiny pond makes a suitable home for them – then plant lettuces nearby so that the frogs eat the slugs rather than the slugs eating the lettuces.

## pick your own

Apart from growing your own, there's no better way to get fresh fruit and vegetables than by visiting a pick-your-own farm.

Each farm will have its own system, but in general you pay by weight or you buy a punnet or basket for a set price, which you fill as much as you like. To find a pick-your-own farm near you, check the *Yellow Pages* or search the Internet.

**tips to help you to get the most out of your visit:**
• **always contact growers** a day or two before going for up-to-date information on picking hours, to find out what's available, the field conditions and the current prices.
• **some pick-your-own farms** don't provide containers, so find out first and take your own if necessary.
• **it's a farm out there** Take a hat, sturdy shoes, protective clothing, insect repellent and sunblock.
• **remember to be respectful** and do not waste any of the produce. Don't litter and keep your children under control.
• **don't expect picture-perfect,** pristine produce. This is not a conglomerate farm that uses chemicals and genetic engineering to create perfectly round tomatoes. What the goods lack in appearance, they will make up for in flavour.
• **don't bring pets** – the farm animals will certainly appreciate that.

# buying vegetables locally

Not only has the way vegetables are grown undergone major changes; so has the way vegetables are sold. The supermarket is no longer your main option.

lthough supermarkets sell the majority of food eaten in the UK today, consumers are increasingly becoming attracted to other ways to buy fresh produce, and when it comes to vegetables they have plenty of choices. In cities and towns all over the UK there have always been busy street markets selling fresh produce at competitive prices. Some markets sell specialist foods such as Asian vegetables, herbs and spices or Afro-Caribbean fruit and vegetables, and there are often bulk buys or special offers to be had, as well as opportunities for a bit of haggling to get even better value.

For some people it's the lively atmosphere of the market that holds the attraction. For many, market shopping means buying food that is more likely to be grown locally, or at least grown in the UK, avoiding the thousands of air miles that supermarket produce often travels before it is set out on the brightly lit shelves.

## a new wave of market

More recently, there has been a growth of a different kind of market: farmers' markets. Here, fresh, local produce and

ethical rearing is paramount, and of the 500 farmers' markets in the UK today over half are certified by FARMA (the National Farmers' Retail and Markets Association), ensuring that those markets really do offer quality produce grown by the stallholders. As well as the chance to buy organic fruit and vegetables, you will find a wonderful choice of seasonal foods grown for taste rather than size or appearance. So, as well as flavoursome tomatoes and cucumbers, and unusual varieties of potatoes or apples, you can expect to find deliciously sweet carrots that are knobbly and all different sizes – so different from the carrots you buy in a supermarket. Now that growers can also use polytunnels, the growing season is extended so that many frost-tender vegetables are available in winter as well as summer.

Farmers' markets give stallholders the opportunity to tempt shoppers to buy their foods by offering samples to taste or advice on cooking and preparation. The whole atmosphere is enticing for people who love their food and appreciate quality.

## your nearest shops

Farmers' markets are growing in number, but if you live in a large town or city you may find that there is not one close enough to where you live for regular shopping. If you're looking for choice and locally grown vegetables, your greengrocer should be able to supply a good variety and may also stock organic produce. A good greengrocer will buy the freshest produce daily from local suppliers, a wholesaler or market and, depending on where you live, you may find a variety of ethnic foods and flavourings as well. Look out for labels indicating locally grown food.

If you live outside a town or city you also have a wide choice of farm shops. There are over 1,000 of these in the UK and they all sell produce that has been grown in their own fields. If you're buying from a farm shop you should expect the freshest seasonal produce you could ever ask for, as well as knowing that it has travelled the shortest possible distance from field to shop.

## websites

Find your nearest farmers' market or farm shop by looking at the websites below, which give a map showing all the markets and shops in your area.

- **Farmers' markets: www.farmersmarkets.net**
- **Farm shops: www.farmshopping.net**

## how to shop at a market

**Go early in the day** The market is likely to be less crowded, nothing will have run out and you will have the pick of the crop.

**Browse before you buy** Wander around the market to see everything that is offered and to compare quality and prices.

**Talk to the vendors** Farmers' market stalls are set up by the farmers or producers themselves. They can provide ideas, tips and sometimes even recipes for using their products.

**Plan your meals around what is available,** especially if you're shopping at a farmers' market, as they sell seasonal, locally grown vegetables and fruits. Whatever is there is at its peak, so it's best to see what's available rather than shop with a set menu in mind.

**Taste the samples** Many farmers' market stalls will offer a taste tester or sample of their products for you to try before you buy.

**Bring a large shopping bag or trolley,** although you may find that there are environmentally friendly bags on sale at the market.

# eggs & breakfast

# spinach omelette with tomato-mushroom sauce

Lutein, a phytochemical found in spinach helps to keep eyes bright and healthy.

**SERVES** 2   **PREPARATION** 10 minutes   **COOKING** 25 minutes

1½ teaspoons olive oil
125g mushrooms, sliced
250ml tomato pasta sauce
4 large egg whites
1 large egg
ground black pepper, to taste
1 small onion, chopped
125g spinach, cooked and chopped
pinch of salt
non-stick cooking spray
2 teaspoons grated Parmesan cheese

**1** Heat ½ tsp oil in a small non-stick pan over medium-high heat. Add the mushrooms; cook until softened, 4 minutes, stirring once. Add pasta sauce; simmer until thickened, about 5 minutes. Remove from heat. Cover to keep warm.

**2** Beat egg whites, egg and pepper in a small bowl.

**3** Heat the remaining oil in a large non-stick frying pan over medium heat. Add onion; sauté until softened, 4 minutes. Stir in spinach and salt; cook until heated through. Stir half of the spinach mixture into the egg mixture.

**4** Coat the same frying pan with non-stick cooking spray. Heat over medium heat. Pour in spinach-egg mixture; spread evenly. Cook, without stirring, until the eggs begin to thicken slightly around the edge, about 1 minute. Run a thin spatula around the edge of the pan, lifting omelette so the uncooked portion flows underneath the cooked one. Cook until centre is still moist but not runny, about 3 minutes.

**5** Spread remaining spinach mixture over one half of the omelette; sprinkle with Parmesan cheese. Fold omelette over to cover filling. Reduce heat to low. Cover; cook until egg is set but still soft, 3 to 4 minutes. Slide omelette on to serving plate. Top with mushroom sauce.

**PER SERVING** 203Kcals, 17g protein, 10g fat, 2.5g saturated fat, 12g carbohydrate, 2.5g fibre, 2g salt

**3** of your **5 a day**

• QUICK RECIPE

# broccoli, tomato & cheese omelette

Just a few broccoli florets – provided in this omelette – contain more vitamin C than a fresh orange.

**SERVES** 2   **PREPARATION** 10 minutes   **COOKING** 8 minutes

non-stick cooking spray
3 large eggs
1 large egg white
1 tablespoon milk
pinch of salt
165g broccoli florets, cooked
1 large plum or round tomato, sliced
55g coarsely grated Emmental cheese

**1** Coat a 25cm non-stick frying pan with non-stick cooking spray. Heat over medium heat. Beat eggs, egg white, milk and salt in a medium bowl until combined. Add broccoli. Pour into pan, spreading evenly. Cook, without stirring, until the mixture starts to thicken slightly around the edge, about 1 minute. Run a thin spatula around the edge of the pan, lifting mixture so the uncooked portion flows underneath the cooked one. Cook until centre is still moist but not runny, about 3 minutes.

**2** Arrange tomato slices over one half of omelette. Top with cheese. Fold omelette over to cover filling. Reduce heat to low. Cover; cook until the egg is set but still soft, 3 to 4 minutes. Slide omelette on to serving plate.

**PER SERVING** 294Kcals, 26g protein, 20g fat, 8g saturated fat, 3g carbohydrate, 2.5g fibre, 0.8g salt

**1** of your **5 a day**

# pepper & ham quiche

• MAKE AHEAD

All peppers are rich in vitamin C, but red ones are an especially good source.

**SERVES** 6   **PREPARATION** 10 minutes   **COOKING** 1 hour 5 minutes

375g shortcrust pastry, thawed if frozen
flour, for dusting
1 tablespoon vegetable oil
1 medium onion, finely chopped
1 medium red pepper, seeded and finely chopped
55g lean ham, finely chopped
260g ricotta cheese
225g low-fat plain yoghurt
3 large eggs
¼ teaspoon salt
ground black pepper, to taste

**1** Preheat oven to 200°C (180°C fan oven), gas 6. Roll out pastry on a floured surface and use to line a 24cm flan tin. Prick the base with a fork. Bake 8 minutes. Remove from oven. Reduce temperature to 170°C (150°C fan oven), gas 3.

**2** Heat oil in a large non-stick frying pan over medium heat. Add onion; sauté until softened, 5 minutes. Add pepper; sauté 2 minutes. Stir in ham. Spoon mixture into pastry case.

**3** Process the ricotta, yoghurt, eggs and seasoning in a blender or food processor until very smooth, about 2 minutes. Pour over mixture in pastry case; stir gently.

**4** Bake until mixture is set but still slightly wobbly in the centre, 45 to 55 minutes. Remove to a wire rack; cool slightly. Serve warm or at room temperature.

**PER SERVING**  327Kcals, 14g protein, 21g fat, 8g saturated fat, 23g carbohydrate, 1g fibre, 1g salt

½ of your 5 a day

# spanish omelette

A scrumptious mix of potatoes, tomato and peppers adds plenty of vitamin C to a healthy tortilla.

**SERVES** 4   **PREPARATION** 10 minutes   **COOKING** 22 minutes

1 tablespoon olive oil
1 medium onion, coarsely chopped
2 garlic cloves, chopped
1 small green pepper, seeded and coarsely chopped
1 small tomato, seeded and coarsely chopped
1 medium roasted red pepper from a jar,
   coarsely chopped
2 small cooked potatoes, cut into 15mm dice
½ teaspoon salt
non-stick cooking spray
4 large eggs, lightly beaten

**1** Heat 2 tsp oil in a large non-stick frying pan over medium heat. Add the onion and garlic; sauté 5 minutes. Add green pepper and tomato; sauté 3 minutes. Add roasted pepper, potatoes and salt. Cover and cook, stirring frequently, until the vegetables are tender, about 10 minutes. Add a little water if the vegetables begin to stick.

**2** Coat a large non-stick frying pan with non-stick cooking spray. Heat over medium heat. Swirl in remaining oil. Add the eggs; cook, without stirring, until they begin to thicken slightly around the edge of the pan, about 1 minute. Run a thin spatula around the edge of the pan, lifting mixture so uncooked egg flows under the cooked portion. Cook until centre is still moist but no longer runny, about 3 minutes. Slide the omelette on to a plate. Top with vegetable mixture.

**PER SERVING**  182Kcals, 12g protein, 12g fat, 2.5g saturated fat, 9g carbohydrate, 2g fibre, 0.8g salt

1 of your 5 a day

# helpful hint

To make a crustless quiche that's much lower in fat and calories, coat the base and side of a 23cm pie dish with non-stick cooking spray. Combine the sautéed vegetables and the ricotta mixture; pour into the pie dish. Bake as for the main recipe, but start checking how well the quiche is cooked after 30 minutes.

A traditional Spanish omelette, also known as a tortilla, is made with a combination of potatoes and onions. Add tomatoes and peppers to enliven the mix. A flat omelette is a versatile dish and you can try many variations including courgette and diced ham; marinated artichokes and pitted olives; cooked chicken and grated cheese. Serve with a green salad to make a complete, balanced meal.

## helpful hint

Look out for omega-3 enriched eggs. Laid by hens fed a diet high in rapeseed, the yolks contain omega-3 fats, which are the polyunsaturated fats associated with lower risk of heart disease and stroke. These eggs are also low in saturated fat and are a better source of vitamin E than regular eggs.

# summer spinach scramble

• QUICK RECIPE

Leafy green vegetables such as kale and spinach contain calcium, folic acid and fibre, all of them essential nutrients for a healthy heart.

**SERVES** 4   **PREPARATION** 10 minutes   **COOKING** 10 minutes

275g fresh spinach or kale, stems removed, shredded
5 large eggs
5 large egg whites
¼ teaspoon ground cumin
¼ teaspoon salt
non-stick cooking spray
35g lean ham, chopped
2 spring onions, trimmed and thinly sliced

**1** Cook spinach or kale in a large pan of boiling water until tender, 3 to 5 minutes. Drain. Rinse under cold water. Leave to drain well.

**2** Whisk eggs, egg whites, cumin and salt in a large bowl.

**3** Coat a large non-stick frying pan with non-stick cooking spray. Heat over medium heat. Add egg mixture; stir until eggs start to thicken slightly, 2 to 3 minutes. Stir in spinach, ham and spring onion. Cook, stirring occasionally, until eggs are soft-scrambled, 2 to 3 minutes.

**PER SERVING** 167Kcals, 18g protein, 10g fat, 3g saturated fat, 2g carbohydrate, 1.5g fibre, 1.2g salt

½ of your 5 a day

**fresh ideas**
Spinach can be served raw or cooked. Stir-frying or steaming helps to retain its flavour and texture.

# mushroom & pepper frittata

• MAKE AHEAD

Mushrooms contain niacin, a B vitamin that helps your body to generate more energy.

**SERVES** 4   **PREPARATION** 10 minutes   **COOKING** 26 minutes

2 tablespoons olive oil
1 medium red or orange pepper, seeded and cut into 5mm slices
1 medium yellow pepper, seeded and cut into 5mm slices
150g mushrooms, sliced
8 large eggs
¼ teaspoon salt
ground black pepper, to taste
30g grated Parmesan cheese
10 basil leaves, torn into small pieces

**1** Heat oil in a large non-stick frying pan over medium-high heat. Add the red and yellow peppers; sauté until softened, about 4 minutes. Add mushrooms; sauté until vegetables are lightly browned, about 5 minutes. Reduce heat to medium.

**2** Whisk eggs, salt and pepper in a bowl. Pour into pan; cook, stirring frequently, until soft-scrambled, 3 to 4 minutes. Reduce heat to medium-low. Stir in the Parmesan and basil; smooth top. Cook 5 minutes. Cover and cook until eggs are firm and underneath is browned, about 8 minutes.

**3** To serve, loosen frittata around the edge with a spatula. Invert on to a large plate and cut into 4 equal wedges. Serve warm or at room temperature.

**PER SERVING** 307Kcals, 21g protein, 23g fat, 6g saturated fat, 4.5g carbohydrate, 1.5g fibre, 0.9g salt

1 of your 5 a day

## on the **menu**

A hearty strata is an ideal and easy centrepiece for a brunch menu. Serve it with orange juice and plenty of strong fresh coffee. Fresh fruit such as strawberries or slices of melon makes a good, light accompaniment.

# tomato & bacon strata

• MAKE AHEAD

Try to use a bread made with oats for this recipe as they help to lower cholesterol and make a tasty layer.

**SERVES** 8   **PREPARATION** 10 minutes **CHILL** 1 to 8 hours
**COOKING** 45 minutes   **REST** 5 to 10 minutes

4 large eggs
4 large egg whites
375ml semi-skimmed milk
1½ teaspoons curry powder
¼ teaspoon salt
ground black pepper, to taste
2 teaspoons vegetable oil
10 slices seed and oat bread
2 medium tomatoes, thinly sliced
120g mature Cheddar cheese, coarsely grated
4 slices rindless unsmoked back bacon

**1** Whisk eggs, egg whites, milk, curry powder, salt and pepper in a large bowl.

**2** Grease a 30 x 23 x 5cm baking dish with oil. Place 5 slices of bread in a single layer in the bottom, cutting 1 slice to fit, if necessary. Layer on tomato slices; scatter half the cheese on top. Repeat layering. Pour egg mixture over the top, pushing bread down into the liquid – it should come almost to the top of the bread. Cover. Leave for 1 hour or chill overnight.

**3** Preheat oven to 180°C (160°C fan oven), gas 4. Bake uncovered strata until puffed and golden, about 45 minutes. For the final 10 minutes, place bacon on top. Allow to rest for 5 to 10 minutes before serving.

**PER SERVING** 277Kcals, 18g protein, 13.5g fat, 6g saturated fat, 23g carbohydrate, 2.5g fibre, 1.7g salt

**½** of your **5 a day**

## helpful hint

If you're planning a breakfast party for a large crowd, Eggs in Tomato Cups (right) is an easy option for the busy cook. The filling and tomatoes can be prepared several hours in advance. Fill tomatoes and top with the eggs just before guests arrive. While the tomatoes are baking, grill bacon and sausages and sauté some potatoes to complete the menu. Alternatively you can serve with bread.

# eggs in tomato cups

• MAKE AHEAD

Cooked tomatoes are particularly rich in cancer-fighting lycopene and vitamin C.

**SERVES** 6   **PREPARATION** 35 minutes   **COOKING** 30 minutes

6 large beef tomatoes
1½ teaspoons salt
350g spinach, stems removed
non-stick cooking spray
1 tablespoon olive oil
½ onion, finely chopped
300g mushrooms, finely chopped
20g fresh breadcrumbs
2 tablespoons grated Parmesan cheese
ground black pepper, to taste
6 large eggs

**1** Cut a 3mm thick slice off the top of each tomato. Core and seed. Sprinkle inside of tomatoes evenly with 1 tsp salt. Place tomatoes upside down on kitchen paper to drain.

**2** Wash spinach, letting water cling to the leaves. Place in a very large pan. Cover and cook over medium heat until leaves are wilted, 1 to 2 minutes. Drain.

**3** Preheat oven to 180°C (160°C fan oven), gas 4. Lightly coat 30 x 23 x 5cm baking dish with non-stick cooking spray. Heat oil in a large frying pan over medium heat. Add onion; sauté until softened, about 3 minutes. Add mushrooms; sauté until moisture evaporates, 5 minutes. Stir in spinach, breadcrumbs, Parmesan cheese, remaining salt and the pepper.

**4** Pat insides of tomatoes dry with kitchen paper. Stuff each tomato with spinach mixture. Arrange in baking dish. Crack an egg on top of each tomato cup. Cover loosely with foil and bake until eggs are set, 20 to 25 minutes.

**PER SERVING** 193Kcals, 14g protein, 12g fat, 3.5g saturated fat, 8g carbohydrate, 3g fibre, 1.8g salt

**2** of your **5 a day**

# huevos rancheros

• QUICK RECIPE

Peppers, chillies, tomatoes and avocado give a spicy hothouse of vitamins in this Mexican-inspired dish.

**SERVES** 6   **PREPARATION** 15 minutes   **COOKING** 15 minutes

1 tablespoon olive oil
1 medium red or yellow pepper seeded
  and cut into 5mm pieces
2 medium tomatoes, seeded
  and cut into 1.25cm pieces
250ml ready-made salsa
100g green chillies in vinegar, drained
½ teaspoon ground cumin
6 large eggs
30g Cheddar cheese, grated
6 large soft flour tortillas, warmed (see Hint)
2 tablespoons fresh coriander leaves
1 avocado, stoned, peeled and chopped

**1** Heat oil in a medium frying pan over medium heat. Add pepper; sauté until slightly softened, about 3 minutes. Add tomatoes, salsa, chillies and cumin. Simmer gently for 7 to 10 minutes, until thickened.

**2** Crack eggs on to sauce without breaking yolks; top with cheese. Cook, covered, until whites are set, 3 to 5 minutes.

**3** To serve, place an egg with sauce on top of each tortilla. Sprinkle with coriander and avocado.

**PER SERVING** 410Kcals, 17g protein, 18g fat, 4.5g saturated fat, 48g carbohydrate, 4g fibre, 1.1g salt

# egg burritos with roasted pepper

• QUICK RECIPE

The vitamin C in peppers and the protein in eggs are essential nutrients for supple, healthy skin.

**SERVES** 4   **PREPARATION** 5 minutes   **COOKING** 5 minutes

1 tablespoon vegetable oil
8 large eggs, lightly beaten
¼ teaspoon salt
ground black pepper, to taste
1 large roasted red pepper from a jar,
  coarsely chopped
2 tablespoons chopped fresh coriander,
  plus leaves to garnish
4 large soft flour tortillas, warmed (see Hint)
60ml ready-made salsa, at room temperature

**1** Heat oil in a medium non-stick frying pan over medium heat. Whisk eggs with salt and pepper and add to pan. Stir until eggs start to thicken slightly, 1 to 2 minutes. Stir in the pepper and coriander; cook, stirring occasionally, until the eggs are soft-scrambled, 2 to 3 minutes.

**2** Spoon a quarter of the egg mixture in the middle of each tortilla; top each one with 1 tbsp salsa. Fold the edges of each tortilla over, then roll to enclose filling. Garnish and serve.

**PER SERVING** 438Kcals, 23g protein, 21g fat, 4.5g saturated fat, 44g carbohydrate, 3g fibre, 1.3g salt

# helpful hint

To warm tortillas, preheat oven to 180°C (160°C fan oven), gas 4. Stack tortillas (up to 6 at a time) and wrap loosely in foil. Warm for 8 to 10 minutes. Leave wrapped until ready to serve.

# asparagus & eggs on toast with tomatoes & ham

Folic acid, vitamin C and beta carotene in asparagus can help to protect against heart disease.

**SERVES** 4  **PREPARATION** 15 minutes  **COOKING** 6 minutes

24 thin stalks asparagus
  or 12 thick stalks, trimmed
4 slices grainy wholemeal bread
4 teaspoons Dijon mustard
8 slices lean ham
2 hard-boiled eggs, peeled and sliced
8 thin slices of tomato
55g Cheddar cheese, cut into thin strips

**1** Preheat the grill. Place the asparagus in a pan of simmering water; cook until crisp-tender, 3 to 4 minutes. Leave to drain well.

**2** Place sliced bread on baking sheet. Grill until toasted, about 1 minute each side.

**3** Spread 1 tsp mustard on each slice. Place 2 slices of ham, 6 thin or 3 thick asparagus spears, half a sliced hard-boiled egg, 2 tomato slices and a quarter of the cheese on top.

**4** Grill the open sandwiches until heated through and cheese is melted and golden brown, 1 to 2 minutes.

**PER SERVING**  223Kcals, 16g protein, 10g fat, 4g saturated fat, 18g carbohydrate, 3g fibre, 1.4g salt

**½** of your **5 a day**

## helpful hint

Choose spears of asparagus that are a bright, clear colour. Whether buying thin or thick asparagus, the stalks should be firm, full and round, with compact tips and tight scales. If the stalks are limp or bend easily, or the colour is dull, the asparagus is well past its best. Snap off the tough ends of the stalks before cooking, keeping these trimmings to flavour a homemade vegetable stock.

# potato pancakes with apple rings

Carrot shavings give a big beta carotene boost to these sweet and savoury cakes, while the potatoes and apples supply plenty of vitamins C and $B_6$ – both useful for fighting arthritis.

**MAKES** 12 (7cm) pancakes   **PREPARATION** 20 minutes
**COOKING** 45 minutes

2 teaspoons unsalted butter
2 medium apples, cored and sliced
　 into 5mm thick rings
500g Desirée potatoes, grated and blotted dry
1 medium carrot, peeled, grated, and blotted dry
1 medium onion, grated
2 large eggs, lightly beaten
2 tablespoons plain flour
¾ teaspoon salt
60ml vegetable oil

**1** Preheat oven to 130°C (110°C fan oven), gas 1/2. Melt the butter in a large non-stick frying pan over medium heat. Add apple rings; cook, turning occasionally, until tender, 10 to 12 minutes. Place in oven to keep warm.

**2** Combine potato, carrot, onion and eggs in a large bowl. Stir in flour and salt until well combined.

**3** Heat 2 tbsp oil in a large non-stick frying pan over medium heat. Use about 4 tbsp mixture for each pancake and cook, 4 pancakes at a time, until well browned and crisp underneath, about 4 minutes. Turn over; flatten slightly with a spatula. Cook until browned, crisp and cooked through, a further 4 minutes. Drain on kitchen paper. Place on a baking sheet and keep warm in the oven. Make another 8 pancakes, using remaining oil as needed. Serve topped with apple rings.

**PER PANCAKE**  105Kcals, 3g protein, 6g fat,
1g saturated fat, 11g carbohydrate, 1g fibre, 0.4g salt

½ of your 5 a day

**fresh ideas** Apples are a good source of vitamin C as well as potassium. Eating the peel ensures that you get the full measure of fibre. There are many apple varieties to try, including Fuji, Pink Lady, Royal Gala, Granny Smith and Braeburn.

# drinks,
# snacks & starters

# raspberry -beet smoothie

The vibrant colour and luxurious texture of this vitamin C-packed beetroot-and-berry mix has appeal for both the eye and the tastebuds.

**SERVES** 4    **PREPARATION** 10 minutes

150g cooked beetroots, coarsely chopped
60g fresh or frozen raspberries
250ml cranberry juice, chilled
225g low-fat plain yoghurt
chilled raspberries, to garnish (optional)

**1** In a food processor or blender, purée beetroot, raspberries and cranberry juice until smooth.

**2** Pour purée through a strainer into a large jug. Whisk in most of the yoghurt.

**3** Pour into four glasses and top with remaining yoghurt. Garnish with extra raspberries, if you like. Serve immediately.

**PER SERVING**  94Kcals, 4g protein, 0.7g fat, 0g saturated fat, 18g carbohydrate, 1g fibre, 0.2g salt

½ of your 5 a day

**fresh ideas** For extra flavour and vitamins, try adding a sprinkling of fresh herbs to your smoothie, such as chopped parsley or crushed mint, or a few feathery fronds of dill or fennel.

# spicy vegetable cocktail

The cancer-fighting phytochemical lycopene is found in highly concentrated form in commercial tomato products such as tomato juice and canned tomatoes.

**SERVES** 4    **PREPARATION** 8 minutes

750ml tomato juice
30g coarsely chopped, seeded green pepper
1 spring onion, trimmed to 10cm, thinly sliced
1 tablespoon coarsely chopped parsley
1 tablespoon horseradish sauce
1 teaspoon Worcestershire sauce
½ teaspoon sugar
½ teaspoon Tabasco sauce, or to taste
celery stalks and lemon slices, to garnish (optional)
ice, to serve

**1** In a blender, process the tomato juice, pepper, spring onion, parsley, horseradish sauce, Worcestershire sauce, sugar and Tabasco until smooth, 2 to 3 minutes.

**2** Serve over ice. Garnish with celery and lemon, if you like.

**PER SERVING**  36Kcals, 2g protein, 0.5g fat, 0.3g saturated fat, 7g carbohydrate, 1g fibre, 1.2g salt

1 of your 5 a day

# tomato
## smoothie

• QUICK RECIPE
• HEART HEALTHY

The yoghurt in this tasty smoothie is an excellent source of bone-building calcium.

**SERVES** 2  **PREPARATION** 5 minutes

225g low-fat plain yoghurt
2 large ripe plum or round tomatoes,
    peeled, seeded and chopped
½ teaspoon dried basil
½ teaspoon salt
cherry tomatoes and ice, to serve (optional)

In a blender, whiz yoghurt, tomatoes, basil and salt until very smooth, 2 minutes. Serve over ice and garnish with cherry tomatoes, if you like.

**PER SERVING** 88Kcals, 7g protein, 1.6g fat, 0.9g saturated fat, 12g carbohydrate, 1g fibre, 1.2g salt

**1** of your **5 a day**

# carrot-orange
## juice

• QUICK RECIPE
• MAKE AHEAD
• HEART HEALTHY

An immune-boosting antioxidant cocktail that supplies all your daily vitamin A and more than half of the vitamin C that you need.

**SERVES** 2  **PREPARATION** 5 minutes

375ml fresh or bottled carrot juice, chilled
170ml freshly squeezed orange juice (2 oranges)
2cm thick slice fresh root ginger, peeled
orange slices, to decorate (optional)

Combine carrot juice and orange juice in a bowl. Crush ginger in garlic press to make ½ tsp. Stir into juice mixture and serve decorated with orange slices, if you like. (If making ahead, stir just before serving.)

**PER SERVING** 76Kcals, 1.4g protein, 0.3g fat, 0g saturated fat, 18g carbohydrate, 0.5g fibre, 0.2g salt

**1** of your **5 a day**

## did you **know...**

...that you need a special appliance to make your own vegetable juices? Food processors and blenders purée vegetables to a suitable consistency for soup, but a juice extractor is needed to separate out a vegetable's liquid. Some extractors can press juice out of citrus fruits, but that's a separate process.

Many different vegetables can be used to
scoop up dips. Try sticks of fennel or celery,
whole endive leaves, the firm ribs of
pak choi, slices of cucumber or small
radicchio leaves.

# steamed vegetables with peanut dip

• MAKE AHEAD

This easy-to-make favourite is rich in fibre, bursting with flavour and superb for parties.

**SERVES** 8 **PREPARATION** 20 minutes **COOKING** 20 minutes

170ml water
100g smooth peanut butter
1 garlic clove, crushed
2 teaspoons grated fresh root ginger
2 spring onions, chopped
2 tablespoons soft light brown sugar
2 tablespoons salt-reduced soy sauce
pinch of chilli powder
1 tablespoon freshly squeezed lemon juice
6 large carrots, peeled, halved lengthways,
    cut into 3 x 5mm sticks, or 16 baby carrots
    with tops, scraped
2 large red or yellow peppers, halved
    and seeded, sliced 5mm thick
250g mange-touts or green beans, trimmed
8 radishes, thinly sliced

**1** To make the peanut dip, bring the water to the boil in a small pan. Stir in the peanut butter, garlic, ginger, spring onions, sugar, soy sauce and chilli powder. Simmer 2 minutes. Remove from heat. Stir in lemon juice. Set aside to cool slightly or chill until ready to serve.

**2** In a large pan with a steamer basket, bring water to the boil. Fill a bowl with iced water. Steam carrots for 3 minutes, lift out and plunge into iced water to cool. Steam peppers for 1 minute, lift out and plunge into iced water to cool. Steam mange-touts or beans for 2 minutes, lift out and plunge into iced water to cool. Drain vegetables well and dry with kitchen paper.

**3** Spoon peanut dip into a small bowl and place on a serving platter. Arrange the carrot sticks, pepper, mange-touts or green beans around the bowl. Add the radish as a garnish.

**PER SERVING** 140Kcals, 4.5g protein, 7g fat, 2g saturated fat, 15g carbohydrate, 4g fibre, 0.8g salt

**1** of your **5 a day**

# creamy spinach dip

• QUICK RECIPE
• MAKE AHEAD

Many leafy green vegetables – of which spinach is a prime example – are rich in folate, which helps to protect against heart disease and birth defects.

**SERVES** 6 **PREPARATION** 10 minutes **CHILL** 1 hour

250g frozen chopped spinach,
    thawed and squeezed dry
225g low-fat plain yoghurt
125g reduced-fat mayonnaise
2 teaspoons dried dill
½ teaspoon celery seeds
pinch of salt
1 garlic clove, crushed

Whiz spinach, yoghurt, mayonnaise, dill, celery seeds, salt and garlic in a food processor or blender until smooth and creamy. Chill for 1 hour before serving.

**PER SERVING** 94Kcals, 3g protein, 6.5g fat, 1g saturated fat, 6g carbohydrate, 1g fibre, 0.9g salt

**½** of your **5 a day**

## helpful hint

Make dips well ahead of serving time. Leaving them in the refrigerator for an hour or more allows the mixture to become thoroughly chilled. It also allows the flavours to develop fully so that they better complement one another.

# chillies con queso with vegetables

Antioxidant-rich fresh vegetables are ideal scoops for this creamy yet spicy starter.

**SERVES** 8  **PREPARATION** 20 minutes  **COOKING** 12 minutes

2 teaspoons olive oil
1 medium green pepper, seeded and chopped
1 medium onion, chopped
100g chillies in vinegar, chopped
200g tomatoes, chopped
1½ teaspoons ground cumin
½ teaspoon salt
225g low-fat cream cheese
3 tablespoons chopped fresh coriander
2 teaspoons Tabasco sauce
1 medium red pepper, seeded and sliced
2 small carrots, peeled and cut into sticks
1 medium celery stick, cut into sticks

**1** Heat oil in a large non-stick frying pan over medium heat. Add green pepper and onion; sauté until softened, about 5 minutes. Add chillies, tomatoes, cumin and salt; cook for about 3 minutes.

**2** Add cheese, coriander and Tabasco. Reduce heat to low. Cook, stirring, until cheese melts and the mixture is creamy, about 3 minutes. Serve warm with red pepper, carrots and celery.

**PER SERVING**  77Kcals, 4g protein, 4.5g fat, 2g saturated fat, 6g carbohydrate, 2g fibre, 0.3g salt

**1**
of your
**5 a day**

# vegetable-stuffed mushrooms

A fun, attractive first course that's packed with fibre.

**SERVES** 4  **PREPARATION** 20 minutes  **COOKING** 20 minutes

24 large or 12 extra-large mushrooms,
  stems removed
2 teaspoons vegetable oil
1 medium onion, finely chopped
3 garlic cloves, crushed
1 medium carrot, finely chopped
1 medium red pepper, finely chopped
125ml vegetable or chicken stock
½ teaspoon dried oregano
3 tablespoons grated Parmesan cheese
2 tablespoons chopped fresh parsley

**1** Preheat oven to 200°C (180°C fan oven), gas 6. Blanch mushroom caps in a pan of boiling water for 2 minutes. Drain on kitchen paper.

**2** Heat oil in a large frying pan over medium heat. Add onion and garlic; sauté for 5 minutes. Add carrot and pepper; cook for 4 minutes. Add the stock and oregano; cook for 4 minutes or until the vegetables are very soft. Remove from heat; stir in Parmesan and parsley.

**3** Spoon mixture into the mushroom caps and place on a baking tray. Bake for 10 minutes or until piping hot.

**PER SERVING**  104Kcals, 7g protein, 6g fat, 2.5g saturated fat, 7g carbohydrate, 2.5g fibre, 0.5g salt

**2**
of your
**5 a day**

## did you know...

...that cooking mushrooms breaks down their fibrous cell walls, which makes some of their nutrients more easily available to the body?

# grilled **tomato & pepper** salsa

• MAKE AHEAD

Red and yellow peppers each contain about
2 teaspoons of natural sugar, which gives a slightly
sweet taste to this chunky salsa.

**SERVES** 6 **PREPARATION** 20 minutes
**COOKING** 12 minutes, plus chilling

2 medium firm, ripe tomatoes
1 small onion, cut into 2cm thick slices
2 teaspoons olive oil
1 corn on the cob, inner layer of husk intact
1 small red pepper, seeded and finely chopped
1 small yellow pepper, seeded and finely chopped
2 garlic cloves, finely chopped
½ teaspoon ground cumin
½ teaspoon dried oregano
½ teaspoon salt
¼ teaspoon chilli powder
2 tablespoons fresh coriander leaves

**1** Preheat grill to medium-high. Brush tomatoes and onion with oil and place, with the corn, on the grill.

**2** Grill, turning frequently, until lightly browned all over, 10 to 12 minutes.

**3** When cool enough to handle, finely chop tomatoes and onion. Remove husk from corn and cut kernels from cob.

**4** Combine all the ingredients in a serving bowl. Chill until ready to serve.

**PER SERVING** 45Kcals, 1g protein, 1.5g fat, 0.2g saturated fat, 7g carbohydrate, 1.5g fibre, 0.4g salt

**1** of your **5 a day**

## helpful **hint**

Coriander's distinctive flavour does not please every palate. If it is too intrusive for you, try dill, chervil or flat-leaf parsley in your salsa.

## on the **menu**

Thin slices of ham could be used in place of the beef.
Sprinkle the finished dish with chopped fresh flat-leaf
parsley instead of coriander for a milder flavour.

# beef, spring onion & asparagus roll-ups

• QUICK RECIPE

The green tops of spring onions are a good source of vitamin C and beta carotene, both antioxidants that offer protection against all kinds of chronic disease.

**SERVES** 4 (2 roll-ups per serving)  **PREPARATION** 15 minutes  **COOKING** 6 minutes

8 asparagus stalks, trimmed to 15cm lengths
4 spring onions, trimmed to 15cm lengths
8 thin slices sirloin steak, about 125g total weight
2 teaspoons vegetable oil
3 tablespoons teriyaki sauce
1 tablespoon sesame seeds
2 tablespoons fresh coriander leaves

**1** Bring a pan of water to the boil. Cut asparagus and spring onions in half. Blanch in boiling water 1 minute; drain. Pound sirloin slices with a rolling pin until very thin.

**2** Place 2 pieces of asparagus and 1 piece of spring onion near one end of each beef strip. Roll beef around middle of vegetables to form 8 bundles.

**3** Heat oil in a large non-stick frying pan over medium-high heat. Add rolls. Brown 2 minutes, turning rolls frequently. Add teriyaki sauce. Lower heat to medium; boil 3 minutes.

**4** Transfer rolls to serving platter. Sprinkle with sesame seeds and coriander.

**PER SERVING** 94Kcals, 9g protein, 5g fat, 1g saturated fat, 3g carbohydrate, 2.5g fibre, 1.2g salt

½ of your 5 a day

## did you know...

...that when you see the word 'negamaki' on a Japanese menu, the term refers to beef roll-ups, such as Beef, Spring Onion & Asparagus Roll-Ups, as in the recipe above?

## pitta pizzas

• QUICK RECIPE
• HEART HEALTHY

Eating peppers, which are packed with vitamin C, may help to reduce the risk of stroke.

**SERVES** 4  **PREPARATION** 10 minutes  **COOKING** 3 minutes

1 small roasted red pepper from a jar, coarsely chopped
¼ teaspoon fennel seeds, crushed, or dried oregano
salt and ground black pepper, to taste
30g hard mozzarella cheese, coarsely grated
20g Emmental cheese, coarsely grated
2 wholewheat pitta breads
8 teaspoons tomato sauce or pizza sauce
½ small red onion, thinly sliced
2 tablespoons roughly chopped flat-leaf parsley

**1** Preheat grill to high. Combine pepper, fennel seeds or oregano, salt and pepper in a small bowl. Combine the mozzarella and Emmental in another bowl.

**2** Split each pitta bread horizontally. Place on a baking tray, insides facing up. Grill until golden brown around edges, about 1 minute.

**3** Spread 2 tsp tomato or pizza sauce up to the edges of each pitta slice. Spoon 2 tbsp pepper mixture over the top. Sprinkle evenly with cheese; top with onion.

**4** Grill until cheese is melted and pizzas are hot, about 2 minutes. Scatter with parsley.

**PER SERVING** 164Kcals, 7g protein, 5g fat, 2g saturated fat, 23g carbohydrate, 2g fibre, 0.9g salt

½ of your 5 a day

# spinach-stuffed clams

• HEART HEALTHY

Clams are packed with iron to boost the blood and zinc which strengthens the immune system.

**SERVES** 4 **PREPARATION** 15 minutes **COOKING** 20 minutes

1kg fresh clams, scrubbed
3 teaspoons olive oil
½ onion, finely chopped
2 garlic cloves, crushed
4 teaspoons flour
170ml semi-skimmed milk
pinch of cayenne pepper
100g frozen chopped spinach, thawed and squeezed dry
20g fresh breadcrumbs
4 teaspoons grated Parmesan cheese

**1** Place clams in a large frying pan with water up to 1.25cm. Bring to the boil and cover. Cook 4 minutes or until clams open. Start checking after 2 minutes. Remove clams as they open; discard any that do not. Transfer clams to a bowl; when cool enough to handle, discard top shell halves. Place shell halves with clams attached on a baking tray.

**2** Preheat oven to 220°C (200°C fan oven), gas 7. In a small pan, heat 2 tsp oil over low heat. Add the onion and garlic; sauté for 5 minutes or until soft. Whisk in flour and cook for 1 minute. Whisk in milk and cayenne; cook for 3 minutes or until lightly thickened. Stir in spinach. Spoon over clams.

**3** Combine breadcrumbs and Parmesan in a small bowl. Top clams with breadcrumb mixture and drizzle with remaining oil. Bake just until clams are bubbly and hot, about 5 minutes.

**PER SERVING** 181Kcals, 16g protein, 7g fat, 2g saturated fat, 13g carbohydrate, 1g fibre, 0.9g salt

½ of your 5 a day

• QUICK RECIPE

# grilled aubergine & tomato sandwiches

You'll get heart-protective nutrients in every bite of these unusual vegetable sandwiches.

**SERVES** 6 **PREPARATION** 15 minutes **COOKING** 12 minutes

50g goat's cheese, crumbled
1 tablespoon snipped fresh chives,
   plus extra chives to garnish
30g dry breadcrumbs
2 tablespoons grated Parmesan cheese
½ teaspoon dried basil
1 large egg
1 large egg white
¼ teaspoon salt
2 large aubergines, peeled, cut into
   12 horizontal slices 6mm thick
6 thin slices tomato, blotted dry
2 tablespoons olive oil

**1** Combine goat's cheese and chives in a small bowl. Combine breadcrumbs, Parmesan and basil in a shallow dish. Beat egg, egg white and salt in a second shallow dish.

**2** Spread about 2 tsp goat's cheese mixture on to a slice of aubergine. Top with a tomato slice and an aubergine slice. Make 5 more sandwiches the same way.

**3** Dip each sandwich in egg mixture, then breadcrumb mixture to coat both sides. Place on baking parchment.

**4** In large non-stick frying pan over medium-low heat, heat about 1½ tbsp oil. Add sandwiches in a single layer, working in batches, if necessary. Cook until fork-tender and golden brown, 10 to 12 minutes, turning over halfway through cooking. Add more oil as needed if pan becomes dry. Garnish with chives and serve warm.

**PER SERVING** 124Kcals, 6g protein, 9g fat, 3g saturated fat, 6g carbohydrate, 0.8g fibre, 0.6g salt

½ of your 5 a day

For a sharper taste, substitute feta cheese or a more aged goat's or sheep's cheese for the mild goat's cheese suggested in the recipes. Goat's milk and sheep's milk are higher in fat than whole cow's milk, but lower in cholesterol. The longer these cheeses are aged, the more tart their flavour becomes. Feta, made from sheep's or goat's milk, is brined and should be rinsed in cold water to reduce the salt content.

## on the **menu**

These Tex-Mex snacks are delicious eaten as they are, but for added taste, top with a spoon of salsa and a dollop of yoghurt or soured cream. To fill out a lunch, add a mixed green salad and serve fresh fruit for dessert.

# chilli-cheese quesadillas with tomato

• QUICK RECIPE

Chillies contain phytonutrients that offer protection against cancer and other chronic diseases.

Serves 4 (3 wedges per serving)  **PREPARATION** 15 minutes  **COOKING** 12 minutes

6 large soft flour tortillas
1 large tomato, seeded and finely chopped
120g Cheddar cheese, coarsely grated
100g chillies in vinegar, drained and chopped
1 tablespoon chopped fresh coriander
¼ teaspoon salt
ground black pepper, to taste
non-stick cooking spray

**1** Preheat oven to 130°C (110°C fan oven), gas 1–2. Place 3 tortillas on a work surface. Sprinkle equally with tomato, cheese, chillies, coriander, salt and pepper. Place the remaining tortillas on top. Gently press the quesadillas to flatten.

**2** Coat a large non-stick frying pan with non-stick cooking spray. Heat over medium-high heat. Place one quesadilla at a time in the pan; cook until lightly browned on both sides and cheese is melted, 2 minutes per side. Transfer to a baking tray; place in the oven to keep warm. Repeat with the remaining quesadillas. To serve, cut each quesadilla into 4 wedges.

**PER SERVING**  410Kcals, 16g protein, 12g fat, 7g saturated fat, 63g carbohydrate, 3g fibre, 1.5g salt

½ of your 5 a day

## did you know...

...that pan-grilled sandwiches in Italy are called panini? While their close relation, the classic grilled cheese sandwich, uses Cheddar and butter, panini use mozzarella and olive oil. Italian sandwiches are versatile and can be filled with herbs, mushrooms, olives and other fresh and pickled ingredients.

# pan-grilled tomato, mozzarella & basil sandwich

• QUICK RECIPE

Fresh green herbs such as basil contain small quantities of protective antioxidant nutrients including vitamin C and beta carotene.

**MAKES** 4 sandwiches  **PREPARATION** 10 minutes  **COOKING** 4 minutes

8 small slices ciabatta bread
125g mozzarella cheese, cut into 4 thin slices
2 tomatoes, seeded and each cut into 4 thin slices
1 medium red onion, cut into 8 thin slices
8 basil leaves, shredded
¼ teaspoon salt
ground black pepper, to taste
4 teaspoons olive oil

**1** Pat dry mozzarella and tomato with kitchen paper.

**2** On each of 4 slices of bread, put 1 mozzarella slice, 2 tomato slices, 2 onion slices and 2 shredded basil leaves. Sprinkle with salt and pepper. Top with remaining bread.

**3** Heat oil in a large non-stick frying pan over medium heat. Add sandwiches; cook, firmly pressing down with a spatula, until lightly browned, about 2 minutes. Turn sandwiches over. Cook, pressing down, until sandwiches are browned and the cheese is melted, about 2 minutes.

**PER SANDWICH**  253Kcals, 11g protein, 12g fat, 5g saturated fat, 28g carbohydrate, 2g fibre, 1.2g salt

½ of your 5 a day

# bean & vegetable
## tostadas

• QUICK RECIPE
• HEART HEALTHY

Fibre from pulses and vegetables helps to keep the digestive system healthy and can lower cholesterol.

**MAKES** 6 tostadas   **PREPARATION** 15 minutes   **COOKING** 10 minutes

6 soft flour tortillas
non-stick cooking spray
400g can black beans or red kidney beans,
    drained and rinsed
400g can sweetcorn, drained and rinsed
1 small tomato, cored and chopped
1 small red onion, finely chopped
1 small jalapeño or other hot chilli,
    seeded and finely chopped
2 tablespoons fresh coriander leaves
1 tablespoon freshly squeezed lime juice
½ teaspoon salt
dash of Tabasco sauce
1 small ripe avocado, stoned,
    peeled and chopped

**1** Preheat oven to 220°C (200°C fan oven), gas 7. Place tortillas in a single layer on a baking sheet; coat both sides of each one with non-stick cooking spray. Bake until lightly browned and crisp, about 10 minutes; turn them over halfway through. Transfer to wire racks to cool.

**2** In a large bowl combine beans, corn, tomato, onion, chilli, coriander, lime juice, salt and Tabasco sauce. Gently fold in avocado. Top each tortilla evenly with bean mixture.

**PER TOSTADA**   313Kcals, 11g protein, 4g fat,
0.7g saturated fat, 61g carbohydrate, 7g fibre, 1.7g salt

**1** of your **5 a day**

# japanese-style
## steak & broccoli
## tartlets

• MAKE AHEAD

Attractive filo tartlets are packed with glazed steak, and the goodness of leek, broccoli and white radish.

**SERVES** 6   **PREPARATION** 35 minutes   **COOKING** 11 minutes

3 tablespoons sunflower or groundnut oil
6 sheets filo pastry, about 30 x 17.5cm each, thawed if frozen
½ small leek, rinsed, quartered lengthways and thinly sliced
150g broccoli floret tops, chopped
1 small red pepper, seeded and chopped
200g lean frying steak, trimmed and very thinly shaved
1 tablespoon salt-reduced soy sauce
½ teaspoon sugar
1 tablespoon dry sherry
150g white radish or mooli, finely grated
2 teaspoons wasabi paste (optional)
2 limes, cut into wedges, to garnish

**1** Preheat oven to 190°C (170°C fan oven), gas 5. Pour 1 tbsp oil into a cup. Lightly grease a 12 hole patty tin. Lightly brush the lengthways half of a pastry sheet with oil. Fold in half (30 x 8.5cm) and brush top with oil. Cut into quarters (7.5 x 8.5cm). Lay a piece over one patty cup and top with a second piece, offsetting the corners. Press pastry into cup, with edges outwards. Make 12 pastry cups. Brush pastry corners with oil, if dry.

**2** Bake tartlets until pale golden and crisp, about 5 minutes. Remove from tin and cool.

**3** Heat 1 tbsp oil in a frying pan over high heat and stir-fry the leek, broccoli and pepper, until slightly softened, about 3 minutes. Transfer to a bowl.

**4** Heat remaining oil over high heat. Add steak slices and cook 1 minute without stirring. Stir-fry until lightly browned, about 1 minute. Stir in soy sauce, sugar and sherry. Bubble briefly, stirring to glaze the meat. Remove from heat to prevent burning.

**5** Squeeze juice from radish. Divide broccoli mixture among tartlets. Top with beef, mounding to one side. Put a small mound of radish beside the beef. Add a dot of wasabi, if using, on the radish. Serve two tartlets each and garnish with lime wedges if liked. Serve hot or warm.

**PER TARTLET**   146Kcals, 10g protein, 7g fat,
1.5g saturated fat, 10g carbohydrate, 1g fibre, 0.4g salt

**1** of your **5 a day**

# on the **menu**

For a light summer lunch, serve two tartlets per person with a crisp green salad on the side with ice cream or a fruit sorbet for dessert.

# avocado-turkey
## wraps

Rich, buttery-tasting avocados are rich in heart-protective monounsaturated fats and vitamin E.

**MAKES** 12 mini-wraps   **PREPARATION** 10 minutes

3 tablespoons reduced-fat mayonnaise
1 tablespoon Dijon mustard
2 large soft flour tortillas
1 medium ripe avocado, stoned, peeled
   and cut lengthways into thin slices
250g thinly sliced cooked turkey breast
280g jar roasted red peppers,
   drained and cut into strips

**1** Combine mayonnaise and mustard in a small bowl. Lay tortillas on a work surface. Spread mayonnaise mixture evenly over each one.

**2** Place the avocado slices on top, leaving a small border around the edge. Top with turkey and pepper strips.

**3** Roll up each tortilla tightly and place, seam side down, on a cutting board. Trim the ends of the wraps evenly with a serrated knife. Cut each wrap into six equal pieces and place, cut side down, on a serving platter.

**PER MINI-WRAP**   120Kcals, 7g protein, 6g fat, 1g saturated fat, 8g carbohydrate, 1.5g fibre, 0.2g salt

½ of your 5 a day

## on the **menu**

To make four servings for lunch, cut each wrap in half. And serve as finger food at a party or for a snack, cut each wrap into six equal pieces.

## helpful **hint**

Pitta breads, lavash and other thin flatbreads are all good for wraps. Although it may look better to layer the ingredients separately, it is often more practical to mix some together so that the filling is firmer and stays intact, making the wrap easier to eat. For example, instead of slicing the avocado for Avocado-Turkey Wraps, mash it with mayonnaise and mustard to make a spread that keeps all the ingredients in place.

# peachy brie & pea shoot rolls

• QUICK RECIPE

These filling, summery rolls are overflowing with fruit and vegetable goodness and fresh flavour.

**SERVES** 4   **PREPARATION** 20 minutes

8 ready-to-eat dried peaches, thinly sliced
2 tablespoons raspberry vinegar
1 red pepper, seeded and cut into thin strips
4 large mixed-grain baps, such as giant Granary
  or Harvest Grain baps
250g Brie, cut into eight thin wedges
35g pea shoots
35g rocket
8 fresh coriander sprigs
16 large fresh basil leaves

**1** Put peaches in a bowl and pour over the vinegar. Add the pepper strips. Set aside.

**2** Slice the baps in half and add two wedges of Brie to each. Arrange half the peach and pepper mixture on top.

**3** Divide the pea shoots and rocket between the rolls, then add the coriander and basil. Top with the remaining slices of peaches and peppers, drizzling over any remaining vinegar. Put the tops on the rolls.

**PER ROLL**  518Kcals, 22g protein, 21g fat, 12g saturated fat, 65g carbohydrate, 2g fibre, 1.9g salt

½ of your 5 a day

fresh ideas

Watercress can be used instead of pea shoots, and ready-to-eat dried apricots instead of the peaches. Blueberry or balsamic vinegar can be used instead of the raspberry vinegar – good with Stilton, Roquefort or Gorgonzola instead of Brie.

# smoked salmon & celeriac salad baguette

• QUICK RECIPE
• MAKE AHEAD

Celeriac adds crunch and flavour as well as valuable potassium, vitamin C and soluble fibre.

**SERVES** 4   **PREPARATION** 25 minutes

200g celeriac, peeled and coarsely grated
175g carrots, peeled and coarsely grated
100g bean sprouts
2 spring onions, thinly sliced
1 lemon, zest grated and fruit reserved
1 tablespoon olive oil
1 large baguette
200g low-fat soft cheese
50g watercress
300g smoked salmon slices
ground black pepper to serve

**1** In a large bowl, mix the celeriac and carrots, bean sprouts, spring onions, lemon zest and olive oil.

**2** Cut the baguette into quarters, then slice each piece horizontally in half. Flatten the bottom halves slightly to spread them out and spread top and bottom halves with soft cheese.

**3** Put the bottom halves on plates and top with watercress. Divide the smoked salmon among the bottom halves, folding the slices at an angle on top of the salad. Add the celeriac salad evenly, pressing it in place with a spoon. Cut the lemon into wedges and squeeze the juice on top of the salmon and salad. Season lightly with pepper.

**4** Lay the baguette tops beside the bases. Serve immediately.

**PER BAGUETTE** 372Kcals, 29g protein, 13g fat, 5g saturated fat, 36g carbohydrate, 3g fibre, 1.5g salt

**1** of your **5 a day**

**fresh ideas**
Spread the bread with 4 tbsp creamed horseradish before spreading with soft cheese. Add 300g thinly sliced lean roast beef instead of the smoked salmon.

## helpful hint

Baguettes, loved for their wonderful crusts and chewy texture, don't keep well because they are made without fat. Buy them fresh on your way home to accompany dinner and use them right away. Fresh baguettes can be frozen for later use.

# taco with homemade salsa & guacamole

• QUICK RECIPE

A terrific taco packed with goodness that will tempt even the most ardent of meat lovers.

**SERVES** 4    **PREPARATION** 10 minutes    **COOKING** 20 minutes

2 tablespoons extra virgin olive oil
1 medium onion, finely chopped
300g aubergine, cubed
750g butternut squash, peeled, seeded and cubed
1 large courgette, cubed
¼ teaspoon chilli powder
½ teaspoon ground cumin
1 garlic clove, crushed
400g can tomatoes
salt and ground black pepper, to taste
1 large ripe avocado
juice of ½ lime
3 medium ripe tomatoes, diced
½ medium red onion, finely chopped
4 tablespoons chopped fresh coriander
8 taco shells
225g low-fat plain yoghurt
lime wedges and coriander sprigs, to garnish

**1** Heat oil in a large pan over medium-high heat. Add onion and aubergine; sauté, stirring frequently, until vegetables are lightly browned.

**2** Add squash and courgette. Stir in chilli powder, cumin and garlic. Pour in canned tomatoes with their juice. Add salt and pepper, to taste. Heat to boiling, breaking up tomatoes with a wooden spoon. Cover and simmer 15 minutes, stirring occasionally, until squash is just tender. Check occasionally, adding water, if needed, to prevent vegetables from sticking.

**3** Preheat oven to 180°C (160°C fan oven), gas 4. To make the guacamole, halve and stone the avocado, scoop flesh into a bowl and mash with lime juice. To make salsa, combine tomatoes, red onion and coriander in a small bowl. Set guacamole and salsa aside.

**4** Put taco shells on a baking tray; warm 3 to 4 minutes in the oven. Transfer shells to serving plates. Fill with aubergine mixture and top with guacamole, yoghurt and salsa. Garnish with lime wedges and coriander.

**PER SERVING** 424Kcals, 11g protein, 25g fat, 4g saturated fat, 40g carbohydrate, 7.5g fibre, 0.2g salt

**6** of your **5 a day**

## did you know...

...that when tomatoes were introduced into Europe, they were regarded with suspicion and thought to have aphrodisiac properties? Nutritionists now know that 'love apples', as these fruits were called, do have benefits for the heart, but not in the romantic sense.

# vegetable **tart**

• MAKE AHEAD

Every slice of this flavoursome tart is rich in fibre and vital nutrients such as vitamin C and beta carotene.

**SERVES** 6   **PREPARATION** 30 minutes   **COOKING** 45 minutes

375g shortcrust pastry, thawed if frozen
flour, for dusting
350g butternut squash, peeled
1 medium red onion, cut into 5mm slices
1 tablespoon plus 1 teaspoon olive oil
½ teaspoon salt
1 large courgette, cut into 5mm slices
20g grated Parmesan cheese
3 tablespoons chopped fresh basil
280g roasted red peppers from a jar,
    cut into strips

**1** Preheat oven to 200°C (180°C fan oven), gas 6. Roll out pastry on a floured surface and use to line a 20cm tart tin. Fold edges of pastry over and crimp to make a decorative edge. Prick base with a fork. Line pastry case with foil; fill with uncooked rice or dried beans. Bake 15 minutes. Remove foil and rice or beans and bake until golden, 5 to 10 minutes.

**2** Slice squash into 6mm thick rounds up to the seeded part. Scoop out seeds. Slice remaining squash into rings.

**3** Place squash and onion in a single layer on a baking tray; drizzle with ½ tbsp oil and sprinkle with salt. Put into oven. Place courgette on a second tray; drizzle with ½ tbsp oil and sprinkle with salt. Roast until courgette is tender, 10 to 12 minutes. Remove from baking tray. Continue roasting squash and onion just until tender, about 5 minutes. Reduce oven temperature to 130°C (110°C fan oven), gas 1–2.

**4** Assemble tart just before serving. Sprinkle base of tart shell with 1 tbsp Parmesan. Top with an even layer of courgette, half the onion, 1 tbsp Parmesan and 1 tbsp basil. Add a layer of squash, the remaining onion, 1 tbsp Parmesan and 1 tbsp basil. Arrange roasted pepper on top. Brush with remaining oil; sprinkle with the remaining Parmesan. Heat tart in oven for 10 minutes. Sprinkle with remaining basil and serve.

**PER SERVING**  384Kcals, 6.5g protein, 24g fat, 6.5g saturated fat, 38g carbohydrate, 4g fibre, 1g salt

**1** of your **5 a day**

# cheese & spinach terrine with leeks

• MAKE AHEAD

Vitamin C from the red peppers helps your body to absorb more iron from the spinach.

**SERVES** 12   **PREPARATION** 30 minutes   **COOKING** 1 hour 10 minutes

non-stick cooking spray
1 tablespoon olive oil
2 medium leeks cut in 15mm pieces
    and rinsed
2 garlic cloves, crushed
700g spinach, stems removed
250ml semi-skimmed milk
2 medium red peppers, seeded and
    cut in 5mm pieces
1½ teaspoons salt
1 teaspoon curry powder
ground black pepper, to taste
120g hard mozzarella cheese,
    coarsely grated
5 large eggs

**1** Preheat oven to 180°C (160°C fan oven), gas 4. Lightly coat a 23 x 13cm loaf tin with non-stick cooking spray. Line base of tin with baking parchment. Coat paper with cooking spray.

**2** Heat oil in a large non-stick frying pan over medium heat. Add leeks and garlic; sauté until softened, 7 minutes. Remove to large bowl.

**3** Wash spinach, leaving some water clinging to leaves. Place in the frying pan over medium-low heat. Cook, covered, until spinach wilts, 2 minutes. Add to leeks.

**4** Place vegetable mixture in food processor or blender with 50ml milk and whiz until smooth. Return mixture to bowl. Add peppers, salt, curry powder, black pepper and cheese.

**5** Beat eggs lightly with remaining milk. Stir into the vegetable mixture. Pour into prepared loaf tin. Place tin in a roasting tin half-filled with hot water.

**6** Bake 1 hour. Remove loaf from roasting tin. Leave terrine to cool completely. Chill until ready to serve.

**7** To serve, press out on to a platter and remove paper.

**PER SERVING** 111Kcals, 8g protein, 7g fat, 3g saturated fat, 4g carbohydrate, 2g fibre, 0.9g salt

**1** of your **5 a day**

## on the menu

Spinach terrine is suitable either as a first course or as part of a party buffet, where it can be served with crackers or slices of French bread.

# italian spinach pie

• MAKE AHEAD

Vitamins A and C and folate in spinach boost the heart. Cheese, rice and leeks add flavour and texture.

**SERVES** 6   **PREPARATION** 10 minutes   **COOKING** 40 minutes

1 tablespoon olive oil
2 medium leeks, white part only, halved
    lengthways, thinly sliced and rinsed
non-stick cooking spray
250g frozen chopped spinach, thawed
    and squeezed dry
100g long-grain white rice, cooked
3 large eggs
85g grated Parmesan cheese
½ teaspoon dried marjoram
½ teaspoon salt
ground black pepper, to taste

**1** Preheat oven to 190°C (170°C fan oven), gas 5. Heat oil in a medium non-stick frying pan. Add the leeks; sauté until softened, about 8 minutes. Set aside.

**2** Lightly coat a 23cm pie plate with non-stick cooking spray. Combine the leeks, spinach, rice, eggs, 65g Parmesan, marjoram, salt and pepper in a medium bowl. Spoon mixture into the prepared pie plate, smooth the top and sprinkle with remaining Parmesan.

**3** Bake until firm and browned, about 30 minutes. Serve warm or at room temperature, cut into wedges.

**PER SERVING**   257Kcals, 14g protein, 11g fat,
4g saturated fat, 27g carbohydrate, 2g fibre, 0.9g salt

# crustless quiche vegetable squares

• MAKE AHEAD

Carrots, the key ingredient in an unusual quiche, are super-rich in the disease-fighting antioxidant beta carotene, which your body uses to make vitamin A.

**MAKES** 16 small squares   **PREPARATION** 15 minutes
**COOKING** 1 hour   **COOL** 10 minutes

non-stick cooking spray
1 teaspoon olive oil
1 large onion, finely chopped
1 large courgette, cut into small cubes
½ teaspoon salt
2 large eggs
60ml semi-skimmed milk
3 medium carrots, peeled, grated and blotted dry
120g Cheddar cheese, coarsely grated
1 tablespoon chopped fresh dill

**1** Preheat oven to 190°C (170°C fan oven), gas 5. Lightly coat a 20cm square or round baking tin or tart tin with non-stick cooking spray. Heat oil in a large non-stick frying pan over medium heat. Add onion; sauté until softened, 3 minutes. Stir in courgette. Increase heat to medium-high; sauté until courgette is soft and the liquid has evaporated, 7 to 10 minutes. Stir in ¼ tsp salt. Remove from heat.

**2** In a large bowl, beat eggs, milk and remaining salt. Add carrots, courgette, cheese and dill. Spread in prepared tin.

**3** Bake until quiche is just set in the centre, about 45 minutes. Transfer to a wire rack and cool for at least 10 minutes before cutting. Serve warm or at room temperature.

**PER SQUARE**   57Kcals, 3g protein, 4g fat, 2g saturated
fat, 2g carbohydrate, 0.6g fibre, 0.4g salt

## on the **menu**

Cut the Crustless Quiche Vegetable Squares into four portions instead of 16 to make a main course for lunch that is both nutritious and low in calories. Complete the meal with a crisp baguette, a salad and a healthy dessert, such as Sweet & Spicy Carrot Pie with Nut Crust (page 248).

# savoury
## soups

# gazpacho

• MAKE AHEAD
• HEART HEALTHY

Tomatoes give plenty of the cancer-fighting phytochemical lycopene to a delightful summer soup.

SERVES 4    PREPARATION 25 minutes    CHILL 1 hour

1 litre tomato juice
4 plum or ripe tomatoes, seeded and coarsely chopped
1 cucumber, peeled, seeded and coarsely chopped
1 small yellow pepper, seeded and coarsely chopped
3 spring onions, finely chopped
60ml freshly squeezed lemon juice
4 tablespoons coarsely chopped basil,
   plus shredded basil to garnish
1 garlic clove, crushed
¼ teaspoon salt
ground black pepper, to taste
¼ teaspoon Tabasco sauce

Combine all the ingredients in a large jug. Chill for at least 1 hour before serving. Garnish and serve cold.

PER SERVING  74Kcals, 4g protein, 0g fat, 0g saturated fat, 15g carbohydrate, 4g fibre, 1.7g salt

## helpful hint

Make a quick version of borscht using 2 litres shop-bought vegetable stock, canned beetroot and packaged shredded cabbage. Serve chilled.

# summer borscht

• MAKE AHEAD

Beetroots provide the B vitamin folate while cabbage and onions boost the vitamin C content of this vividly coloured classic chilled soup.

SERVES 6    PREPARATION 25 minutes    COOKING 50 minutes

2 litres water
2 medium celery sticks, chopped
1 medium carrot, peeled and chopped
2 medium onions, 1 quartered and
   1 very finely chopped
3 garlic cloves, crushed
4 parsley sprigs
2 bay leaves
½ teaspoon salt
4 medium beetroots
1 small turnip
2 teaspoons olive oil
175g green cabbage, thinly sliced
2 tablespoons finely chopped dill,
   plus dill sprigs to garnish
1½ tablespoons freshly squeezed lemon juice
65g light soured cream

**1** Put water in a large pan, with celery, carrot, quartered onion, garlic, parsley, bay leaves and salt; bring to the boil. Reduce heat. Simmer, covered, for about 25 minutes, to make a stock. Meanwhile, peel the beetroots and turnip, adding all the peel to the pan. Chop beetroots and turnip into small pieces.

**2** Heat oil in a large pan over medium heat. Add the chopped onion. Sauté until softened, about 5 minutes. Add the beetroot, turnip and cabbage. Strain the stock, discarding the vegetables. Add the stock to the beetroot mixture. Simmer, uncovered, until root vegetables are tender, about 20 minutes.

**3** Remove from heat. Stir in dill and lemon juice. Cool to room temperature. Cover; chill until cold. Whisk in soured cream just before serving. Garnish with dill.

PER SERVING  87Kcals, 3g protein, 4g fat, 1.5g saturated fat, 11g carbohydrate, 4g fibre, 0.4g salt

## on the **menu**

Traditionally, warm boiled potatoes are eaten as an accompaniment to the borscht. They are served on a separate plate, sprinkled with chopped chives. Instead of mixing the soured cream into the soup, it is served in a bowl so that people can add it to both the soup and the potatoes, as they like.

## did you **know...**

...that carrots are one of the sweetest vegetables? That may explain why so many children who don't like other vegetables enjoy eating them. People who are watching their intake of carbohydrates should eat carrots in moderation.

# carrot soup with dill

• MAKE AHEAD
• HEART HEALTHY

One bowl of this superb soup provides four times the daily requirement of vitamin A. It's also rich in vitamin C, potassium and fibre.

**SERVES** 4 **PREPARATION** 10 minutes **COOKING** 45 minutes

1 tablespoon vegetable oil
1 medium onion, coarsely chopped
1 garlic clove, crushed
850ml vegetable or chicken stock
600g carrots peeled and coarsely chopped
½ teaspoon dried thyme
¼ teaspoon salt
ground white pepper, to taste
50g low-fat plain yoghurt
1 tablespoon finely chopped dill,
   plus dill sprigs, to garnish

**1** Heat oil in a medium pan over medium heat. Add onion and garlic; sauté until softened, 5 minutes. Add stock, carrots and thyme. Simmer, uncovered, until vegetables are very tender, about 40 minutes.

**2** Purée soup in batches in a blender or food processor. Add salt and pepper. To serve hot, ladle into bowls and garnish with yoghurt and dill. To serve cold, cool to room temperature. Cover and chill until cold. Garnish just before serving.

**PER SERVING** 107Kcals, 3g protein, 4g fat, 0.6g saturated fat, 17g carbohydrate, 5g fibre, 1.5g salt

## helpful hint

The delicious flavour of pumpkins of all varieties is complemented by seasonings such as grated nutmeg, the juice and zest of citrus fruits, fresh herbs or a hit of Tabasco sauce or chopped chilli.

# pumpkin soup

• MAKE AHEAD

As well as being full of flavour, pumpkin is a useful source of fibre and vitamins A and C.

**SERVES** 4 **PREPARATION** 10 minutes **COOKING** 45 minutes

1 tablespoon vegetable oil
1 small onion, finely chopped
2 medium carrots, peeled and finely chopped
2 medium celery sticks, finely chopped
4 tablespoons tomato purée
850ml vegetable or chicken stock
1 bay leaf
½ teaspoon dried thyme
450g pumpkin, cooked and puréed
65g light soured cream
¼ teaspoon salt
ground white pepper, to taste
lime slices and fresh coriander leaves,
   to garnish (optional)

**1** Heat oil in a large pan over medium heat. Add onion, carrots and celery; sauté until softened, about 5 minutes. Stir in the tomato purée. Cook 1 minute. Add the stock, bay leaf and thyme; simmer, uncovered, until all the vegetables are tender, about 30 minutes.

**2** Stir in pumpkin. Cook for 5 minutes. Remove bay leaf.

**3** Purée soup in batches in a blender or food processor. Pour soup back into pan. Add soured cream. Bring to a simmer. Add salt and pepper. Add a little water if mixture is too thick. Garnish with lime and coriander just before serving.

**PER SERVING** 155Kcals, 11g protein, 8g fat, 3g saturated fat, 16g carbohydrate, 4g fibre, 1.7g salt

# asparagus soup

The B vitamin, folate, found abundantly in asparagus, helps to prevent heart disease and birth defects.

**SERVES** 6   **PREPARATION** 20 minutes   **COOKING** 50 minutes

1kg asparagus, trimmed
1 tablespoon vegetable oil
1 teaspoon butter
2 medium leeks, pale green and white parts only,
   rinsed and finely chopped
1 small onion, finely chopped
2 garlic cloves, crushed
3 tablespoons long-grain white rice
grated zest of 1 lemon
1.25 litres vegetable or chicken stock
½ teaspoon salt
ground black pepper, to taste
1 tablespoon fresh tarragon or ½ teaspoon dried,
   plus extra fresh leaves to garnish
3 tablespoons plain yoghurt
cooked asparagus tips, to garnish (optional)

**1** Cut off the tips from the asparagus; blanch in boiling water for 1 minute. Drain. Coarsely chop remaining asparagus.

**2** Heat oil and butter in a large pan over medium heat. Add leeks, onion and garlic; sauté until softened, 5 minutes. Add chopped asparagus. Cook, covered, 10 minutes. Add rice, lemon zest, stock, salt and pepper. Partially cover; simmer for 30 minutes.

**3** Purée soup in batches in a blender or food processor. Return to pan. Stir in tarragon and asparagus tips. Simmer 3 minutes. Remove from heat. Stir in yoghurt, garnish, if using, and serve.

**PER SERVING**  150Kcals, 14g protein, 5g fat, 1.5g saturated fat, 13g carbohydrate, 4g fibre, 1.4g salt   **2** of your **5 a day**

## on the menu

Both asparagus and cauliflower go well with mustard, so if you want to serve either soup with a sandwich, ham on granary bread with Dijon mustard would be a perfect companion.

# cauliflower soup with gruyère

• MAKE AHEAD

You can satisfy your daily vitamin C requirement with just a single serving of this soup.

**SERVES** 4   **PREPARATION** 15 minutes   **COOKING** 35 minutes

1 tablespoon vegetable oil
1 small leek, white part only, rinsed and coarsely chopped
1 medium onion, finely chopped
850ml vegetable or chicken stock
½ large head of cauliflower, coarsely chopped
½ teaspoon dried thyme
½ teaspoon ground cumin
ground white pepper, to taste
75g gruyère cheese, coarsely grated

**1** Heat oil in a large pan over medium-high heat. Add leek and onion. Sauté until softened, about 5 minutes. Add the stock, cauliflower, thyme and cumin. Simmer, uncovered, until cauliflower is tender, about 30 minutes.

**2** Add pepper. Ladle soup into individual bowls and sprinkle cheese over each serving.

**PER SERVING**  192Kcals, 17g protein, 12g fat, 5g saturated fat, 7g carbohydrate, 3g fibre, 1.4g salt   **1** of your **5 a day**

# sweetcorn
## chowder with chillies

Pepper and chillies pump up the flavour and the vitamin C content of a traditional comfort soup.

**SERVES** 6   **PREPARATION** 15 minutes   **COOKING** 50 minutes

3 slices rindless unsmoked back bacon
1 tablespoon olive oil
1 large onion, finely chopped
250g potatoes, unpeeled and
    cut into small cubes
850ml chicken stock
400g can sweetcorn, drained
1 medium red pepper, seeded
    and finely chopped
500ml semi-skimmed milk
¼ teaspoon salt
ground black pepper, to taste
3 mild green chillies, finely chopped

**1** Cook bacon in a large pan until crisp, about 6 minutes. Drain on kitchen paper.

**2** Heat oil in same pan over medium heat. Add onion; sauté until softened, 5 minutes. Add the potatoes and stock; simmer, partially covered, until potato is tender, about 20 minutes. Stir in sweetcorn. Simmer 5 minutes.

**3** Place half the potato and sweetcorn with a little liquid in a food processor or blender. Purée. Return to pan. Add red pepper, milk and season. Cover and simmer for 10 minutes.

**4** Finely chop the bacon. Stir into the chowder with the chillies. Heat through and serve.

**PER SERVING** 200Kcals, 13g protein, 7g fat, 2g saturated fat, 24g carbohydrate, 3g fibre, 1.8g salt

**1** of your **5 a day**

• MAKE AHEAD
• HEART HEALTHY

# creamy
## greens soup

Spinach and Swiss chard provide plenty of beta carotene in every sip of this smooth, creamy soup.

**SERVES** 8   **PREPARATION** 25 minutes   **COOKING** 1 hour

2 teaspoons olive oil
2 medium leeks, pale green and white parts only,
    rinsed and coarsely chopped
1 medium onion, coarsely chopped
2 garlic cloves, crushed
350g spinach, stems removed,
    coarsely chopped
1kg Swiss chard, stems removed,
    coarsely chopped
2 medium potatoes, unpeeled,
    coarsely chopped
1 medium carrot, peeled and
    coarsely chopped
850ml vegetable or chicken stock
1 litre water
½ teaspoon salt
125g light soured cream
toast fingers, to serve

**1** Heat oil in a large pan over medium heat. Add leeks and onion; sauté until softened, about 5 minutes. Add garlic; sauté 2 minutes. Add spinach, Swiss chard, potatoes and carrot. Stir in stock, water and salt. Partially cover, simmer for 50 minutes.

**2** Purée soup in batches in a blender or food processor. Return to pan. Stir in soured cream. Heat until just warmed. Serve with fingers of toast.

**PER SERVING** 171Kcals, 11g protein, 8g fat, 3g saturated fat, 15g carbohydrate, 5g fibre, 1.4g salt

**2** of your **5 a day**

**fresh ideas**
To make the sweetcorn chowder suitable for vegetarians, use vegetable stock and serve topped with a dollop of half-fat crème fraîche instead of bacon.

## on the **menu**

Kick-start a Tex-Mex-style meal with a bowl of this satisfying sweetcorn chowder. For added flavour, top it with sprigs of coriander.

**fresh ideas** To turn Summer Garden Soup into a main dish for lunch or a light supper, add protein by stirring in small pieces of ham, cooked chicken, turkey or lamb just before serving.

# summer garden soup

• MAKE AHEAD
• HEART HEALTHY

A mixture of vegetables ensures a variety of vitamins and minerals as well as fresh flavours and textures.

**SERVES** 6  **PREPARATION** 25 minutes  **COOKING** 45 minutes

2 teaspoons olive oil
1 medium onion, finely chopped
1 large celery stick, finely chopped
2 teaspoons peeled, finely chopped fresh ginger
125g green beans, cut into short pieces
2 medium potatoes, unpeeled,
 cut into small cubes
1 large carrot, peeled and cut into small cubes
1 medium yellow squash or courgette, cubed
1 bay leaf
salt and ground black pepper, to taste
100g fresh or frozen peas
2 plum or ripe tomatoes,
 seeded and coarsely chopped
2 tablespoons finely chopped fresh basil leaves
1½ teaspoons finely chopped fresh thyme leaves,
 plus thyme sprigs to garnish

**1** Heat oil in a large pan over medium heat. Add onion, celery and ginger. Sauté until very tender, 10 minutes. Add green beans, potatoes, carrot, squash or courgette, 2 litres water, bay leaf, and seasoning. Simmer, covered, 20 minutes.

**2** Uncover soup. Simmer 15 minutes. For the last 5 minutes, add peas, tomatoes, basil and thyme. Remove bay leaf and garnish with thyme. Serve.

**PER SERVING** 120Kcals, 4g protein, 4g fat, 0.5g saturated fat, 18g carbohydrate, 3.5g fibre, 0.3g salt

**1** of your **5 a day**

## helpful **hint**

The vegetables used in Sweet Vegetable Soup can be cooked alongside a meat main dish. Meat needs a longer oven time, so the soup can be prepared while the meat finishes. Leave the meat to rest on top of the oven while you serve the soup.

# sweet vegetable soup

• MAKE AHEAD
• HEART HEALTHY

Using carrot juice instead of stock gives a sweeter flavour and boosts the soup's beta carotene content.

**SERVES** 4  **PREPARATION** 10 minutes  **COOKING** 40 minutes

1 tablespoon olive oil
5 garlic cloves, peeled
375g potatoes, unpeeled, cut into small cubes
2 medium green peppers, seeded and cut
 into small squares
2 tablespoons fresh rosemary
1 medium yellow or green courgette,
 halved lengthways
 and cut into small cubes
1 large red onion, cut into small dice
375ml carrot juice or vegetable stock
375g tomatoes, diced
1 teaspoon dried tarragon
salt and ground black pepper, to taste

**1** Preheat oven to 220°C (200°C fan oven), gas 7. Combine oil and garlic in a large roasting pan; roast 5 minutes.
Add potatoes, peppers and 1 tbsp rosemary. Toss to coat. Roast until potato begins to soften, about 15 minutes.

**2** Stir in courgette and onion. Roast a further 15 minutes.

**3** Put the juice or stock, tomatoes, tarragon and seasoning into a large pan. Bring to the boil. Add vegetables.

**4** Pour 250ml water into roasting pan; scrape up any sediment from base of pan. Pour the juices into the pan; simmer for 2 minutes and serve garnished with rosemary.

**PER SERVING** 160Kcals, 5g protein, 4g fat, 0.5g saturated fat, 29g carbohydrate, 4g fibre, 0.5g salt

**3** of your **5 a day**

# celery, mushroom & cashew soup

Delicious creamy cashew nuts enrich this soup and provide vitamin E and protein.

**SERVES** 6   **PREPARATION** 10 minutes   **COOKING** 21 minutes

2 tablespoons olive oil
1 large onion, chopped
1 head of celery, sliced, including the leafy top
2 potatoes, about 300g, peeled and diced
400ml boiling water
350g small closed-cap or button mushrooms, sliced
salt and ground black pepper
1 tablespoon freshly squeezed lemon juice
4 tablespoons snipped fresh chives, plus extra to garnish
small pinch of freshly grated nutmeg
120g plain unsalted cashew nuts
500ml apple juice

**1** Heat 1 tbsp oil in a large pan over medium-high heat. Add onion, stir and cook 3 minutes, stirring once. Stir in celery, cover and cook 2 minutes. Stir in potatoes and water. Reduce the heat so that soup does not boil over. Cover and boil 10 minutes.

**2** Heat remaining oil in a frying pan over medium-high heat. Add mushrooms and a pinch of salt. Cook 3 minutes, turning frequently until mushrooms reduced and liquor has evaporated. Add lemon juice; cook until beginning to brown, 2 minutes. Remove from heat; add chives and nutmeg.

**3** Stir in cashew nuts; remove pan from heat. Purée soup in a blender. Return to pan. Gradually stir in apple juice and heat gently for 1 minute. Ladle into bowls; divide mushrooms among them, and garnish with chives.

**PER SERVING** 231Kcals, 6g protein, 14g fat, 2.5g saturated fat 22g carbohydrate, 3g fibre, 0.1g salt

**2** of your **5 a day**

---

• QUICK RECIPE

# tomato egg drop soup

Lots of garlic adds rich flavour and extra cancer-fighting power to this Cuban-inspired soup.

**SERVES** 6   **PREPARATION** 10 minutes   **COOKING** 16 minutes

1 tablespoon olive oil
1 small onion, finely chopped
6 garlic cloves, crushed
4 medium ripe tomatoes, seeded
    and finely chopped
850ml vegetable or chicken stock
1 bay leaf
½ teaspoon salt
2 large eggs, lightly beaten
6 slices (about 2cm thick) Italian bread
    such as ciabatta, toasted
3 tablespoons coarsely chopped flat-leaf parsley
    and small sprigs, to garnish

**1** Heat oil in a large pan over medium heat. Add onion; sauté until softened, 5 minutes. Add garlic; sauté 30 seconds. Stir in tomatoes; sauté 1 minute.

**2** Add stock, bay leaf and salt. Reduce heat to low. Simmer, uncovered, 10 minutes. Remove from heat. Discard bay leaf. Stir in eggs. Place a slice of bread in each serving bowl and ladle in hot soup. Sprinkle with parsley; serve immediately.

**PER SERVING** 173Kcals, 12g protein, 7g fat, 1.5g saturated fat, 19g carbohydrate, 1.5g fibre, 1.2g salt

**1** of your **5 a day**

## helpful hint

Egg yolks enrich and thicken soups, but they do add fat and cholesterol. If this is a problem for you, substitute 2 egg whites for every whole egg used in a soup recipe. Or, use 1 whole egg and substitute egg whites for a second or third egg.

## on the **menu**

Tomato Egg Drop Soup is a perfect light start to a meal featuring roast meat and a starchy vegetable such as potatoes as the main dish. Finish with a simple, palate-cleansing dessert of fruit sorbet or slices of fresh pineapple wedges.

## on the **menu**

This soup serves six as a first course or four as a light main dish. If you are serving it as a main course, round out the meal with a salad of crisp lettuce leaves dressed with a herb-flavoured vinaigrette. Finish with fruit for dessert.

# chicken-tomato soup with tortillas

A light but chunky soup packed with vitamin C gets extra flavour punch from lime juice and coriander.

**SERVES** 6  **PREPARATION** 20 minutes  **COOKING** 50 minutes

1 chicken breast on the bone, skin removed
1.5 litres chicken stock
3 garlic cloves
ground black pepper, to taste
1 teaspoon dried oregano
1 tablespoon olive oil
5 spring onions, coarsely chopped
100g green chillies in vinegar, drained
4 medium tomatoes, coarsely chopped
125ml freshly squeezed lime juice
4 soft corn or flour tortillas,
   sliced into 3 even strips, toasted
3 tablespoons chopped fresh coriander
   and small sprigs, to garnish

**1** Place chicken, stock, 500ml water, 2 garlic cloves, pepper and oregano in a medium pan. Simmer, uncovered, 25 minutes.

**2** Remove chicken from pan. Discard bones. Cut chicken into large chunks. Strain and reserve stock.

**3** Heat oil in a large pan over medium heat. Crush remaining garlic and add to pan with the spring onions. Sauté until softened, 5 minutes. Add chillies, tomatoes and strained stock. Simmer, partially covered, 15 minutes. (Recipe can be made ahead up to this point.)

**4** Add chicken and lime juice. Simmer 5 minutes. Garnish with toasted tortilla strips and coriander.

**PER SERVING**  238Kcals, 20g protein, 6g fat, 1g saturated fat, 32g carbohydrate, 2g fibre, 1.6g salt

**1** of your **5 a day**

## did you know...

...that laboratory studies show that chicken soup slows the migration of neutrophils, which cause inflammation at the site of an infection, thereby relieving sore throats and runny noses?

# country-style chicken soup with noodles

• HEART HEALTHY

A good helping of root vegetables adds earthy flavours and a mix of the antioxidant nutrients that protect against chronic disease.

**SERVES** 4  **PREPARATION** 15 minutes  **COOKING** 40 minutes

1 tablespoon vegetable oil
1 medium onion, coarsely chopped
3 medium carrots, peeled and diced
1 medium celery stick, diced
850ml chicken stock
400g can chopped tomatoes
250g bone-in chicken breast, skin removed
1 small turnip or parsnip, peeled and diced
1 teaspoon dried basil
100g fine egg noodles
ground black pepper, to taste

**1** Heat oil in a large pan over medium heat. Add onion, carrots and celery. Sauté until softened, 5 minutes. Add stock, tomatoes, chicken breast, turnip or parsnip and basil. Simmer, uncovered, until chicken is cooked through, 30 minutes.

**2** Remove chicken from pan. Discard bones. Coarsely chop chicken. Return to soup with the noodles. Cook until noodles are tender, 3 minutes. Add pepper.

**PER SERVING**  274Kcals, 24g protein, 9g fat, 2g saturated fat, 26g carbohydrate, 3g fibre, 1.4g salt

**2** of your **5 a day**

# turkey, spinach & rice in roasted garlic broth

• MAKE AHEAD
• HEART HEALTHY

A combination of rice, fresh spinach and lean turkey makes this hearty broth a healthy source of the B vitamins needed to produce energy.

**SERVES** 4  **PREPARATION** 15 minutes  **COOKING** 1 hour

2 medium whole heads of garlic, unpeeled
2 tablespoons tomato purée
850ml chicken stock
150g cooked turkey, cubed
100g long-grain rice, cooked
350g spinach, stems removed, coarsely chopped
ground black pepper, to taste
¼ teaspoon crushed chilli flakes, or to taste
1 tablespoon freshly squeezed lemon juice

**1** Preheat oven to 200°C (180°C fan oven), gas 6.

**2** Cut top third off garlic heads and discard. Wrap each head in foil. Bake until very soft, about 50 minutes. Leave to cool. Remove foil. Squeeze out pulp into a small bowl.

**3** Combine garlic pulp and tomato purée in a large pan. Stir in stock. Bring to the boil. Add the turkey, rice, spinach, pepper and chilli flakes. Simmer, uncovered, 8 minutes. Just before serving, stir in lemon juice.

**PER SERVING** 300Kcals, 26g protein, 5g fat, 1.5g saturated fat, 40g carbohydrate, 3g fibre, 1.5g salt

**1** of your **5 a day**

• HEART HEALTHY

# summer chicken & chickpea soup

A satisfying soup, with goodness from summer vegetables and protein-packed pulses.

**SERVES** 6  **PREPARATION** 20 minutes  **COOKING** 15 minutes

1 tablespoon sunflower or groundnut oil
350g skinless chicken breast fillets, diced
1 large leek, rinsed and finely chopped
3 celery sticks, finely diced
1 fresh bay leaf and 1 fresh rosemary sprig
   tied in a bouquet garni
1 chicken bouillon cube
1.2 litres boiling water
200g green beans, thinly sliced
1 large red pepper, seeded and finely diced
400g can chickpeas, drained and rinsed
¼ teaspoon salt
4 spring onions, thinly sliced
4 tablespoons low-fat soft cheese
6 thin, small baguette slices (baguettine),
   preferably from a day-old loaf
6 basil leaves
6 pitted black olives

**1** Heat oil in a large pan over medium-high heat. Add chicken and cook for 2 minutes. Stir in leek and celery; cook 1 minute. Add bouquet garni, bouillon cube and water. Stir well and bring to the boil. Reduce heat to medium-low, cover pan and simmer for 5 minutes.

**2** Add the beans, pepper and chickpeas; bring back to the boil. Reduce heat, cover and simmer until vegetables are tender, 5 to 7 minutes. Taste and stir in salt and spring onions.

**3** Spread soft cheese on the baguette slices. Top each with a basil leaf and olive. Discard the bouquet garni and ladle soup into large bowls, Float a baguette slice in each.

**PER SERVING** 238Kcals, 20g protein, 7g fat, 2g saturated fat, 24g carbohydrate, 2.5g fibre, 1.3g salt

**2** of your **5 a day**

## helpful hint

Most soups will thicken if they are made ahead, chilled and reheated before serving. Should a soup become too thick, stir in enough extra stock or water to achieve the desired consistency.

**fresh ideas**

Instead of chicken and chickpeas, use the vegetable soup as a delicious base for smoked haddock and cannellini beans. At step 2 add 500g skinless boneless smoked haddock fillet, cut into chunks, with cannellini beans.

# quick fish chowder with tomato & fennel

Aromatic fennel seeds and a splash of wine give a refreshing flavour to a light fish soup.

**SERVES** 4  **PREPARATION** 8 minutes  **COOKING** 25 minutes

1 tablespoon olive oil
1 medium onion, coarsely chopped
2 garlic cloves, crushed
1 teaspoon fennel seeds
500ml fish stock
400g can tomatoes, drained and
    roughly chopped
125ml dry white wine
250g Desirée or other red potatoes,
    unpeeled, cut into small dice
salt and ground black pepper, to taste
500g firm fish fillets, such as cod,
    cut into 8 even pieces
4 tablespoons chopped fresh flat-leaf parsley,
    plus leaves to garnish

**1** Heat oil in a large pan over medium-high heat. Add onion and garlic; sauté until softened, 5 minutes. Add fennel seeds; sauté 30 seconds. Add stock, tomatoes, wine, potatoes and seasoning. Simmer, uncovered, until potato is tender, about 15 minutes.

**2** Add fish and parsley. Bring to a gentle boil. Remove from heat and serve immediately, garnished with parsley.

**PER SERVING** 224Kcals, 26g protein, 4g fat, 0.5g saturated fat, 17g carbohydrate, 2.5g fibre, 0.5g salt

**1** of your **5 a day**

# root vegetable chowder with bacon

A filling soup that is a nutritious blend of sweet potatoes, carrots, onions, potatoes and other vitamin and mineral-rich vegetables.

**SERVES** 4  **PREPARATION** 25 minutes  **COOKING** 40 minutes

2 teaspoons olive oil
1 large onion, finely chopped
2 medium celery sticks,
    coarsely chopped
1¼ teaspoons dried thyme
2 medium carrots, peeled and
    coarsely chopped
1 large sweet potato, peeled and
    coarsely chopped
1 medium parsnip, peeled and
    coarsely chopped
1 large red potato, peeled and
    coarsely chopped
½ medium green pepper, seeded and
    coarsely chopped
420ml chicken or vegetable stock
salt and ground black pepper, to taste
420ml semi-skimmed milk
1 tablespoon balsamic vinegar
3 slices rindless unsmoked back bacon,
    cooked and coarsely chopped

**1** Heat oil in a large pan over medium heat. Add the onion, celery and thyme; sauté until softened, 5 minutes. Add carrots, sweet potato, parsnip, potato, green pepper, stock and seasoning. Add just enough water to cover the ingredients. Simmer, covered, until vegetables are tender, 30 minutes.

**2** Purée half the soup in a blender until smooth. Return the purée to the pan. Stir in milk and heat gently. Stir in vinegar. Sprinkle with bacon just before serving.

**PER SERVING** 277Kcals, 14g protein, 8g fat, 3g saturated fat, 41g carbohydrate, 6g fibre, 1.5g salt

**2** of your **5 a day**

**fresh ideas**
Two or three slices of coarsely chopped hot salami or a little pancetta or prosciutto can be sprinkled on the soup in place of bacon.

# chicken & turkey

A chef's salad can include any combination of meat, vegetables and cheese. You can substitute lean roast beef or turkey for some or all of the chicken and ham and include more salad vegetables, such as sliced cucumber and radishes, in the mix. In place of goat's cheese, try crumbled feta or cubes of Emmental cheese.

# chef's salad

• QUICK RECIPE

A nutritional makeover updates this classic main-dish salad to include dark leafy greens, roasted peppers, lean chicken breast and creamy goat's cheese.

**SERVES** 6   **PREPARATION** 15 minutes   **COOKING** 15 minutes

2 skinless chicken breast fillets,
   about 400g total weight
salt and ground black pepper, to taste
1 medium cos lettuce or other dark
   green lettuce
125g baby spinach leaves
175g thinly sliced smoked lean ham,
   cut into strips
1 medium roasted yellow pepper from a jar,
   cut lengthways into thin strips
1 medium roasted orange pepper from a jar,
   cut lengthways into thin strips
18 baby plum or cherry tomatoes, halved
100g goat's cheese, crumbled
125ml extra virgin olive oil
60ml balsamic vinegar
1 teaspoon Dijon mustard
1 garlic clove, crushed
¾ teaspoon dried tarragon

**1** In a medium pan, gently simmer chicken in lightly salted water, uncovered, until cooked, 10 minutes. Drain well.

**2** Divide lettuce leaves evenly among serving plates. Top each serving with a portion of spinach, mounding it in the centre. Cut chicken lengthways into thin strips. Place chicken, ham, peppers, tomatoes and goat's cheese on each salad plate.

**3** Whisk together oil, vinegar, mustard, garlic, tarragon and seasoning. Serve the dressing with the salad.

**PER SERVING** 331Kcals, 24g protein, 22g fat, 6g saturated fat, 8g carbohydrate, 2g fibre, 1.5g salt

**1** of your **5 a day**

# grilled chicken
## salad

This tangy mix of sweet mango, lean chicken and salad vegetables is rich in antioxidants.

**SERVES** 4   **PREPARATION** 15 minutes   **CHILL** 30 minutes
**COOKING** 6 minutes

60ml freshly squeezed orange juice
3 tablespoons freshly squeezed lime juice
2 tablespoons olive oil
1 tablespoon white wine vinegar
½ teaspoon Dijon mustard
¾ teaspoon salt
ground black pepper, to taste
375g skinless chicken breast fillets
1 medium mango, peeled and cut into thin wedges
1 medium tomato, cored and cut into thin wedges
½ medium cucumber, seeded and thinly sliced
1 medium red onion, thinly sliced
150g mixed salad leaves

**1** Whisk orange juice, lime juice, oil, vinegar, mustard, salt and pepper in a small bowl. Transfer 50ml dressing to another small bowl; add chicken breasts and turn to coat. Chill, covered, 1 hour. Reserve remaining dressing.

**2** Preheat grill to medium-hot. Grill chicken until browned on one side, 3 minutes. Baste with marinade from the bowl that held the chicken. Turn chicken and grill until cooked through, 3 minutes. Transfer to a cutting board for 5 minutes. Cut into thick slices.

**3** Combine remaining dressing, mango, tomato, cucumber and onion in a large bowl. Add the grilled chicken. Serve over salad leaves.

**PER SERVING** 222Kcals, 22g protein, 10g fat, 2g saturated fat, 11g carbohydrate, 2g fibre, 0.9g salt

**2** of your **5 a day**

# teriyaki **chicken &**
# **vegetable** kebabs

Kebabs are a fun, easy way to include a variety of healthy vegetables in one meal.

**SERVES** 4   **PREPARATION** 20 minutes   **CHILL** 30 minutes
**COOKING** 14 minutes

500g skinless chicken thigh fillets,
    cut into 2.5cm chunks
125ml teriyaki marinade
1 medium courgette, quartered lengthways
    and cut crossways into 5mm thick pieces
1 large red pepper, cut into 2.5cm squares
4 spring onions, trimmed and halved
8 canned whole water chestnuts, drained and rinsed

**1** In a small bowl, combine chicken and half the teriyaki marinade. Chill, covered, 30 minutes.

**2** Preheat grill to medium-hot. Thread chicken, courgette, pepper, spring onions and water chestnuts on eight 30cm metal skewers, finishing with a water chestnut. Brush with a little of the remaining teriyaki marinade.

**3** Grill kebabs, turning often and brushing with marinade, until vegetables are crisp-tender and chicken is cooked through, 12 to 14 minutes.

**PER SERVING**  186Kcals, 28g protein, 4g fat,
1g saturated fat, 10g carbohydrate, 1g fibre, 3g salt

**1** of your **5 a day**

---

• QUICK RECIPE
• HEART HEALTHY

# griddled
# chicken breasts
# with sweetcorn relish

Beans add heart-healthy soluble fibre and a rich flavour to the Mexican-style relish.

**SERVES** 4   **PREPARATION** 20 minutes   **COOKING** 8 minutes

2 garlic cloves, crushed
2 teaspoons chilli powder
¼ teaspoon salt
3 tablespoons freshly squeezed lime juice
2 tablespoons vegetable oil
750g skinless chicken breast fillets,
    pounded 10mm thick
185ml chicken stock
230g fresh, drained canned,
    or thawed frozen sweetcorn
1 large roasted red pepper from a jar, diced
115g canned black beans or red kidney beans,
    drained and rinsed
1 small red onion, coarsely chopped
1 jalapeño chilli, seeded and finely chopped
¼ teaspoon salt
3 tablespoons fresh coriander leaves

**1** Combine garlic, chilli powder, salt, 2 tbsp lime juice and the oil in a medium bowl. Add chicken and rub with marinade. Leave at room temperature for up to 15 minutes.

**2** Preheat a ridged griddle. Griddle chicken breasts until just cooked through, 3 to 4 minutes each side.

**3** To make relish, heat stock in a large frying pan. Add sweetcorn, pepper, beans, onion, chilli and salt. Heat through. Just before serving, stir in coriander and remaining lime juice. Serve chicken topped with relish.

**PER SERVING**  356Kcals, 51g protein, 9g fat,
1g saturated fat, 18g carbohydrate, 4g fibre, 1.3g salt

**1** of your **5 a day**

## on the menu

To follow a main course of grilled or griddled chicken, sliced fresh strawberries topped with a purée of frozen raspberries make a refreshing, palate cleanser.

# pan-fried chicken with **carrots** in orange sauce

Each healthy serving includes a day's requirement of vitamin A, in the form of disease-fighting beta carotene.

**SERVES** 4  **PREPARATION** 10 minutes  **COOKING** 25 minutes

250ml freshly squeezed orange juice
3 tablespoons balsamic vinegar
   or red wine vinegar
4 chicken breast fillets, with skin,
   about 125g each
¼ teaspoon salt
ground black pepper, to taste
35g plain flour
2 tablespoons vegetable oil
4 spring onions, thinly sliced
½ teaspoon ground coriander
4 medium carrots, peeled and cut into
   5mm thick slices
2 tablespoons chopped fresh parsley

**1** Combine orange juice and vinegar in a small bowl.

**2** Season chicken with salt and pepper; coat with flour. Heat oil in a large non-stick frying pan over medium heat. Add the chicken and cook until browned, 3 minutes each side. Transfer to a plate.

**3** Add spring onions, coriander and 50ml orange juice mixture to the frying pan, scraping up any sediment from the base of the pan. Cook 30 seconds. Add the remaining juice mixture, the carrots and chicken. Bring to the boil. Tightly cover frying pan, lower heat and simmer until chicken is cooked through and carrot tender, about 20 minutes. Add parsley. Place a chicken breast on each of four plates. Spoon carrot mixture and sauce over the top.

**PER SERVING**  336Kcals, 28g protein, 15g fat, 3.5g saturated fat, 23g carbohydrate, 3g fibre, 0.6g salt

**1** of your **5 a day**

**fresh ideas**  For the Chicken Stir-fry, many other fresh vegetables can be used, such as broccoli and green beans.

# chicken **stir-fry**

Easily prepared peppers, tomatoes and courgettes, and flash-cooked chicken make for a quick dish.

**SERVES** 4  **PREPARATION** 10 minutes  **COOKING** 12 minutes

2 tablespoons olive oil
500g skinless chicken breast fillets,
   cut into 1.25cm wide strips
½ teaspoon salt
ground black pepper, to taste
1 red, green or yellow pepper,
   seeded and sliced
1 medium courgette sliced
2 garlic cloves, crushed
150g cherry tomatoes, halved
1 tablespoon fresh oregano leaves
   or ½ teaspoon dried
2 teaspoons balsamic vinegar

**1** Heat oil in a large non-stick frying pan over medium-high heat. Add chicken. Sauté until barely cooked through, about 4 minutes. Sprinkle on half the salt and the pepper. Remove chicken from pan.

**2** In the same pan, sauté pepper and courgette until just tender, 4 minutes. Sprinkle with remaining salt. Add garlic; sauté 30 seconds. Add tomatoes and dried oregano, if using. Cook 1 minute. Return chicken to pan. Sprinkle with vinegar; heat through, add fresh oregano. Serve.

**PER SERVING**  239Kcals, 28g protein, 12g fat, 3g saturated fat, 5g carbohydrate, 1g fibre, 0.8g salt

**½** of your **5 a day**

# mediterranean chicken

Fennel and white beans add folate, calcium and plenty of extra fibre to this earthy chicken dish.

**SERVES** 4   **PREPARATION** 20 minutes   **COOKING** 1 hour

2 tablespoons olive oil
1 whole chicken, about 1.75kg, cut into
  8 serving pieces, skin removed
35g plain flour
1 large fennel bulb, trimmed and sliced
4 garlic cloves, cut into slivers
250ml chicken stock
2 tablespoons freshly squeezed lemon juice
½ teaspoon salt
ground black pepper, to taste
¼ teaspoon each dried rosemary and thyme
2 x 400g cans cannellini or butter beans, drained and rinsed
250g green beans, cut into short pieces

**1** Preheat oven to 180°C (160°C fan oven), gas 4. In a flameproof casserole with a tight-fitting lid, heat oil over medium-high heat. Dredge the chicken with flour. Sauté until golden, about 4 minutes each side. Transfer to a plate.

**2** Add fennel to pan. Reduce heat to medium. Cook, stirring frequently, until fennel is golden, 7 minutes. Add garlic; cook 1 minute. Add stock, lemon juice, seasoning, rosemary and thyme. Bring to the boil. Add chicken, cover, put in oven.

**3** Cook until chicken is done, about 35 minutes. Stir in the beans and green beans. Cook a further 5 minutes.

**PER SERVING**  588Kcals, 69g protein, 20g fat,
5g saturated fat, 35g carbohydrate, 10g fibre, 1.4g salt

**4**
of your
**5 a day**

# chicken baked with 40 cloves of garlic

Garlic is believed to fight cancer, cholesterol and heart disease. Given the amount of garlic included here, this dish is a recipe for good health.

**SERVES** 8   **PREPARATION** 25 minutes   **COOKING** 1 hour 15 minutes

6 tablespoons olive oil
2 whole chickens, about 1.75kg each, each cut
  into 8 serving pieces, skin removed
45g plain flour
40 garlic cloves, unpeeled
3 medium celery sticks, halved lengthways and
  cut crossways into 2.5cm lengths
4 fresh rosemary sprigs or 1 teaspoon dried
3 fresh thyme sprigs or ½ teaspoon dried thyme
250ml dry vermouth or white wine
250ml chicken stock
1½ teaspoons salt
ground black pepper, to taste

**1** Preheat oven to 180°C (160°C fan oven), gas 4. Heat 2 tbsp oil in a large frying pan over medium heat. Dredge chicken with flour, shaking off excess. Add a third of the chicken to the pan; sauté until golden brown, about 4 minutes each side. Transfer to a large roasting pan. Sauté remaining chicken in two more batches, using 2 tbsp oil each batch. Transfer to roasting pan.

**2** Add garlic, celery, rosemary and thyme to the frying pan; cook 1 minute. Add vermouth or wine. Increase heat to high, bring to the boil and cook 2 minutes so the alcohol evaporates. Add the stock and seasoning to the pan; bring to the boil. Remove from heat. Pour vegetables and cooking liquid over chicken in roasting pan. Cover pan with foil.

**3** Bake until chicken is cooked and garlic is meltingly tender, about 45 minutes. Serve chicken with a little of the garlic.

**PER SERVING**  463Kcals, 56g protein, 21g fat,
5g saturated fat, 7g carbohydrate, 0.5g fibre, 1.5g salt

**½**
of your
**5 a day**

## did you **know...**

...that when garlic is cooked in the oven for 45 minutes or more, it loses its characteristic bite and strong odour and adds a very mellow flavour to whatever it has been cooked with?

## helpful **hint**

To cut the amount of saturated fat in these dishes by half, remove the skin from the chicken pieces after cooking and discard. To remove even more fat from the stew, chill it overnight and then scoop off all the solidified fat the next day. Reheat the stew and serve.

# chicken stew with butternut squash & beans

• MAKE AHEAD

A satisfying and delicious cold-weather comforter that is rich in folate and fibre.

**SERVES** 6  **PREPARATION** 15 minutes  **COOKING** 1 hour

1 tablespoon olive oil
1.5kg chicken pieces
½ teaspoon salt
ground black pepper, to taste
1 medium onion, coarsely chopped
4 garlic cloves, peeled and halved
250ml white wine
2 tablespoons tomato purée
2 bay leaves
2 fresh thyme sprigs or ½ teaspoon
    dried thyme
400g can cannellini or butter beans,
    drained and rinsed
750g butternut squash, peeled,
    seeded and cut into 5cm pieces

**1** Preheat oven to 180°C (160°C fan oven), gas 4. Heat the oil in a large flameproof casserole over medium-high heat. Season chicken with half the salt and the pepper. Brown chicken in batches in casserole, about 6 minutes. Transfer to a plate.

**2** Lower heat to medium. Add onion and garlic. Sauté until slightly softened, about 3 minutes. Add wine and scrape up any sediment from the base of the dish. Stir in tomato purée, bay leaves, thyme and remaining salt. Add chicken. Bring to the boil. Cover.

**3** Cook in the oven for 20 minutes. Stir in the beans and squash. Cover. Bake until chicken and squash are tender, 20 to 30 minutes. Discard bay leaves and serve.

**PER SERVING** 377Kcals, 65g protein, 5g fat, 1g saturated fat, 19g carbohydrate, 4g fibre, 1.3g salt

2 of your 5 a day

# poussins with honeyed vegetables

Cook tender poussins with fibre-rich sweet potatoes, parsnips and celeriac that protect the digestive tract.

**SERVES** 4  **PREPARATION** 15 minutes  **COOKING** 1 hour

2 large sweet potatoes, peeled and cut
    into 2.5cm chunks
2 large parsnips, peeled and cut into 2.5cm chunks
1 large celeriac, peeled and cut into 2.5cm chunks
1 medium red onion, quartered
2 teaspoons fresh thyme or 1 teaspoon dried thyme
½ teaspoon salt
ground black pepper, to taste
2 tablespoons olive oil
4 poussins (about 400g each)
½ teaspoon paprika
2 tablespoons honey
fresh thyme sprigs, to garnish (optional)

**1** Preheat oven to 180°C (160°C fan oven), gas 4. Place oven rack in lowest position. In large roasting pan or two smaller pans, combine potatoes, parsnips, celeriac, onion, thyme, salt, pepper and oil. Place poussins, breast side up, in among the vegetables; sprinkle with paprika.

**2** Bake for 50 minutes, stirring vegetables occasionally. Stir honey into vegetables. Bake until poussins are cooked through and vegetables are fork-tender, 10 to 15 minutes. Cut each poussin in half to serve. Garnish with thyme, if you like.

**PER SERVING** 434Kcals, 52g protein, 9g fat, 1.5g saturated fat, 38g carbohydrate, 10g fibre, 1.2g salt

3 of your 5 a day

• HEART HEALTHY

# poached chicken with seasonal vegetables

Try different combinations of seasonal vegetables as they are available in this simple all-in-one supper dish.

**SERVES** 4   **PREPARATION** 10 minutes   **COOKING** 30 minutes

4 skinless chicken breast fillets,
    about 150g each
750ml chicken stock
3 tablespoons dry sherry or dry white wine
1 bouquet garni (parsley, thyme and bay leaf)
750g mixed vegetables, such as carrots,
    corn on the cob, broccoli, cauliflower, leeks,
    savoy cabbage, asparagus spears,
2 tablespoons chopped fresh parsley

**1** Put the chicken breasts, stock, sherry or wine, and the bouquet garni in a large flameproof casserole or deep frying pan. Bring to the boil. Lower heat, cover; poach chicken for about 20 minutes, skimming off foam that forms, as necessary.

**2** Meanwhile, cut all the vegetables into bite-sized pieces, reserve the asparagus tips, if using.

**3** Add all the vegetables except the asparagus tips to pan. Cover; cook until vegetables are tender and chicken juices run clear when breasts are pierced with the tip of a knife, about 5 minutes. Add asparagus tips. Cook for 2 minutes until just tender. Discard bouquet garni. Add parsley.

**4** Spoon the pan juices and vegetables into large, shallow serving bowls. Top with chicken, whole or sliced, as you prefer, and serve.

**PER SERVING**  271Kcals, 52g protein, 5g fat,
1g saturated fat, 5g carbohydrate, 5g fibre, 1.2g salt

**2** of your **5 a day**

# thai green turkey curry with vegetables

Crunchy water chestnuts contrast with a mix of tender vegetables in this creamy curry.

**SERVES** 4   **PREPARATION** 10 minutes   **COOKING** 15 minutes

2 tablespoons sunflower or groundnut oil
450g skinless turkey breast fillets,
    cut into 3cm wide strips
50g fresh root ginger, peeled and finely chopped
4 teaspoons Thai green curry paste
120g fresh shiitake mushrooms, sliced
100g baby corn
227g can pineapple pieces in juice,
    drained and juice reserved
400ml can coconut milk
300g bean sprouts
250g Chinese leaves, sliced
220g can water chestnuts, drained and sliced
8 spring onions, thinly sliced at an angle
salt, to taste
4 tablespoons chopped fresh mint, plus
    mint leaves to garnish
plain boiled rice, to serve

**1** Heat the oil in a large skillet, sauté pan or flameproof casserole over high heat. Add turkey and sprinkle ginger over the top. Cook 3 minutes, turning the pieces occasionally after the first minute. Reduce heat to medium-high.

**2** Stir in green curry paste to coat all the turkey pieces. Then stir in shiitake mushrooms and corn. Pour in pineapple juice and allow it to bubble quite hard for 2 minutes, stirring frequently. Reduce heat to medium and pour in the coconut milk. Stir until the coconut milk is boiling.

**3** Stir in bean sprouts, Chinese leaves and water chestnuts; bring back to the boil. Reduce the heat to medium and simmer, uncovered, for 3 minutes until corn is tender and all the vegetables are hot and lightly cooked.

**4** Stir in spring onions and pineapple. Remove pan from heat and season lightly with salt to taste. Stir in chopped mint, garnish and serve with rice.

**PER SERVING** 450Kcals, 35g protein, 25g fat, 16g saturated fat, 20g carbohydrate, 3g fibre, 1g salt

**3** of your **5 a day**

**fresh ideas**
For a hotter curry, increase the amount of green curry paste, adding up to 8 teaspoons.

# chicken **breasts** stuffed with **spinach & cheese**

• MAKE AHEAD

The phytochemical-packed spinach and pepper filling fights chronic disease and helps to protect your eyes.

**SERVES** 6   **PREPARATION** 20 minutes   **COOKING** 35 minutes

non-stick cooking spray
6 skinless chicken breast fillets,
   about 125g each
¾ teaspoon salt
ground black pepper, to taste
½ teaspoon dried basil
250g frozen spinach, thawed and squeezed dry
3 medium roasted red peppers from a jar, halved
6 thin slices Emmental cheese,
   about 115g total weight
125ml buttermilk
120g fresh wholemeal breadcrumbs

**1** Preheat oven to 220°C (200°C fan oven), gas 7. Coat baking dish with non-stick cooking spray.

**2** Place each chicken breast between two sheets cling film; pound to 3mm thickness. Season one side with salt, pepper and basil. Top each breast evenly with spinach, pepper and cheese, leaving a 5mm border around the edge. Roll up the chicken breasts to encase filling; secure with cocktail sticks.

**3** Dip chicken in buttermilk; coat evenly with breadcrumbs. Place, seam side down, on the baking dish.

**4** Bake until chicken is cooked through and crumb coating is browned, about 35 minutes. Remove cocktail sticks; serve.

**PER SERVING**  320Kcals, 40g protein, 8g fat, 4g saturated fat, 22g carbohydrate, 2.5g fibre, 1.4g salt

# chicken and chunky vegetable pie

Classic comfort food with a healthy, new-age twist: the pie contains a higher ratio of vegetables to poultry.

**SERVES** 6   **PREPARATION** 25 minutes   **COOKING** 45 minutes

2 tablespoons olive oil
3 medium leeks, rinsed, white and pale
   green parts coarsely chopped
2 medium celery sticks, coarsely chopped
2 large carrots, peeled and thickly sliced
1 large red potato, unpeeled,
   cut into bite-sized chunks
75g mushrooms, thickly sliced
3 tablespoons plain flour
½ teaspoon dried thyme
¼ teaspoon salt
ground black pepper, to taste
425ml chicken stock
250g cooked chicken, cut into bite-sized pieces
150g fresh or frozen peas
375g puff pastry, thawed if frozen
flour, for dusting
1 large egg beaten with 1 tablespoon milk,
   for glazing

**1** Heat oil in a large pan over medium heat. Add leeks, celery, carrots and potato. Cook, 5 minutes, stirring occasionally. Add mushrooms. Cook, stirring occasionally, 5 minutes. Stir in flour, thyme, salt and pepper until blended. Stir in stock. Increase heat to medium-high. Cook, stirring, until thickened, 2 minutes. Stir in chicken and peas. Transfer to 23cm deep pie plate. Leave to cool to room temperature.

**2** Preheat oven to 200°C (180°C fan oven), gas 6. Roll out pastry on a floured surface to cover pie. Brush underside of pastry with glaze; place over filling. Trim edge of pastry; crimp with a fork, if you like. Brush top with glaze. Cut four 2.5cm slits in the centre to allow steam to escape.

**3** Bake until filling is bubbling and pastry is golden brown, 25 to 30 minutes. Allow to stand for 10 minutes before serving.

**PER SERVING**  450Kcals, 23g protein, 25g fat, 7g saturated fat, 46g carbohydrate, 5g fibre, 1.2g salt

1 of your 5 a day

# on the **menu**

Start an autumn dinner with a creamy tomato soup. Follow with this hearty pie accompanied by a crisp green salad. Then end the meal on a light note with a fresh lemon mousse.

# asian-style
## vegetable and
## turkey burgers

• QUICK RECIPE

Grated carrot is the secret ingredient that boosts both the flavour and the antioxidant power of these low-fat, low-calorie burgers with a hint of oriental taste.

**MAKES** 6 burgers  **PREPARATION** 10 minutes  **COOKING** 10 minutes

750g lean turkey mince
2 medium carrots, peeled and finely grated
3 spring onions, finely chopped
2 tablespoons salt-reduced soy sauce
2 teaspoons finely chopped fresh root ginger
¼ teaspoon salt
ground black pepper, to taste

**1** Preheat grill to medium-high. Combine turkey, carrots, spring onions, soy sauce, ginger, salt and pepper in a medium bowl. Shape into six equal patties.

**2** Grill burgers for 5 minutes. Turn over and grill until no longer pink in the centre, 4 to 5 minutes.

**PER BURGER**  146Kcals, 26g protein, 3g fat, 1g saturated fat, 4g carbohydrate, 1g fibre, 1g salt

½ of your 5 a day

## on the menu

Place the burgers on bread rolls with lettuce and tomato, or serve on a bed of thin noodles with finely sliced pepper and spring onions, tossed with a few drops of toasted sesame oil. Cucumber slices in rice vinegar make a refreshing side dish.

# tex-mex turkey casserole

- MAKE AHEAD
- HEART HEALTHY

Spicy and hearty, this family dish is rich in vitamins C, $B_6$, E and folate and can be prepared in advance.

**SERVES** 6 **PREPARATION** 15 minutes **COOKING** 55 minutes

1 tablespoon vegetable oil
1 medium onion, coarsely chopped
1 tablespoon chilli powder
½ teaspoon cinnamon
¼ teaspoon salt
3 tablespoons plain flour
400g can chopped tomatoes
1 mild green chilli, finely chopped
420ml chicken stock
250g oven-roasted turkey
   (available from delicatessens and supermarkets),
   sliced thinly and cut into cubes
2 medium courgettes, cut into small cubes
150g frozen sweetcorn
150g long-grain rice, cooked
120g Cheddar cheese, coarsely grated

**1** Preheat oven to 180°C (160°C fan oven), gas 4. Heat oil in a large pan over medium heat. Add onion; sauté until softened, 5 minutes. Stir in the chilli powder, cinnamon, salt and flour. Cook, stirring, 2 minutes. Stir in the tomatoes, chilli and stock. Cook, stirring, until slightly thickened, about 2 minutes. Off the heat, stir in the turkey, courgettes, sweetcorn and rice. Pour the mixture into a 23 x 23 x 5cm baking dish. (This recipe can be prepared ahead to this point.)

**2** Bake until mixture is bubbling, about 40 minutes. Sprinkle with cheese. Bake until cheese has melted, about 5 minutes. Allow to stand 5 minutes before serving.

**PER SERVING** 324Kcals, 24g protein, 13g fat, 6g saturated fat, 29g carbohydrate, 1.5g fibre, 1g salt

**1** of your **5 a day**

## did you know...

...cooking sweetcorn releases beneficial nutrients that can substantially reduce the risk of heart disease and cancer? Research indicates that the longer the corn is cooked, the higher the level of antioxidants produced.

# beef,
## lamb & pork

fresh ideas

Try this recipe using duck breasts, pork or lamb fillet or grilled lamb cutlets instead of steak. For a vegetarian alternative, serve with pieces of pan-fried halloumi cheese instead of the steak.

# steak pasta salad

Bright soya beans add vitamin C, fibre, protein and folic acid to an exciting main course salad.

**SERVES** 4    **PREPARATION** 15 minutes    **COOKING** 18 minutes

200g frozen fresh soya beans
200g fusillini soup pasta
3 tablespoons olive oil
15g fresh parsley, chopped
grated zest of 1 lime, fruit reserved
85g watercress
400g can artichoke hearts, well drained,
    patted dry and quartered
400g lean frying steak, about 2cm thick
1 red onion, halved and thinly sliced
400g radishes, halved
2 tablespoons honey
4 tablespoons cider vinegar
salt and ground black pepper, to taste

**1** Put soya beans in a large pan with boiling water to cover; bring to the boil. Boil for 3 minutes; drain and set aside. Bring fresh water to the boil in the same pan; add the soup pasta. Bring back to the boil and cook until tender, about 5 minutes. Drain and return to the pan. Add 1 tbsp oil, the parsley and lime zest; mix well.

**2** Divide the pasta among four large plates. Arrange watercress around the pasta and top with artichoke hearts and soya beans. If liked, cut the lime into 8 wedges; arrange on the sides of the plates.

**3** Heat 1 tbsp oil in a frying pan over high heat. Add steak and cook for 2 minutes on each side, pressing it flat occasionally, until very well browned. The steak will be medium-rare: well-cooked outside and at any thin edges but still slightly bloody in the middle. For medium to well-done steak, reduce heat to low and continue to cook for 1 to 2 minutes on each side. Transfer steak to a warm plate, cover loosely with foil. Leave to rest.

**4** Heat remaining oil in the pan over medium heat. Add the onion. Cook, stirring, 1 minute. Use a fish slice or tongs to remove the onion and sprinkle it over the salads. Add radishes to pan and stir over medium heat for 1 minute. Remove the pan from the heat and stir in the honey and vinegar.

**5** Drain any juices from the meat over the radishes and stir in salt to taste. Thinly slice the beef and arrange on the salads. Season with pepper. Add the radishes. Drizzle over the honey and vinegar dressing from the pan and serve. If liked, the juice from the lime wedges can be squeezed over, to taste.

**PER SERVING** 468Kcals, 34g protein, 14g fat, 3g saturated fat, 54g carbohydrate, 8g fibre, 0.3g salt

**3** of your **5 a day**

• QUICK RECIPE

# beef & green salad

Deeply coloured salad greens are a fresh base for beef strips and contain a host of vitamins and minerals.

**SERVES** 4    **PREPARATION** 20 minutes    **COOKING** 2 minutes

25g fresh parsley, roughly chopped
1 tablespoon capers, drained
1 tablespoon Dijon mustard
1 tablespoon white wine vinegar
1 garlic clove, peeled
3 tablespoons olive oil
2 tablespoons chicken stock
1 tablespoon vegetable oil
500g lean rump steak, cut into wide,
    thin strips
1 medium cos lettuce or other dark green lettuce,
    torn into bite-sized pieces
1 large red pepper, seeded and cut into strips
½ medium red onion, thinly sliced

**1** Put parsley, capers, mustard, vinegar, garlic, olive oil and stock in a food processor or blender. Whiz together until smooth to make a dressing.

**2** Heat oil in a medium non-stick frying pan over high heat. Add steak; sauté until just pink, about 2 minutes. Transfer to a plate. Leave to cool.

**3** Combine lettuce, pepper and onion on a serving platter. Top with beef strips. Serve with dressing.

**PER SERVING** 285Kcals, 28g protein, 17g fat, 4g saturated fat, 5g carbohydrate, 1g fibre, 0.8g salt

**1** of your **5 a day**

# stir-fried beef

Along with broccoli, peppers and mange-touts, mushrooms supply selenium and potassium – useful minerals that can help to reduce the risk of stroke.

**SERVES** 4  **PREPARATION** 20 minutes
**MARINATING** 20 minutes  **COOKING** 13 minutes

3 tablespoons salt-reduced soy sauce
2 teaspoons soft dark brown sugar
500g lean rump steak, cut across the grain
    into 3mm thick strips
200g broccoli, cut into 10cm long florets
2 tablespoons vegetable oil
150g sliced shiitake mushroom caps
1 medium red pepper, seeded and thinly sliced
150g mange-touts
4 spring onions, finely sliced diagonally
3 garlic cloves, crushed
2.5cm piece fresh root ginger, peeled
    and finely chopped
pinch of crushed chilli flakes
85ml chicken stock
1 tablespoon balsamic vinegar
2 teaspoons cornflour
orange for dressing if liked

**1** Mix 1 tbsp soy sauce and all the brown sugar in a medium bowl. Add steak; toss to coat. Marinate at room temperature for 20 minutes. Steam broccoli until crisp-tender, 3 to 4 minutes. Cool under cold running water. Drain.

**2** Heat oil in a large non-stick frying pan over a high heat. Add meat. Stir-fry until just pink, 2 minutes. Remove from pan.

**3** Add mushrooms, pepper, mange-touts, spring onions, garlic, ginger and crushed chilli flakes to pan. Stir-fry until mange-touts are crisp-tender, 3 to 4 minutes.

**4** Combine the stock, remaining soy sauce, the vinegar and cornflour in a small bowl until smooth. Add to pan. Bring to the boil (mixture will be thick). Add broccoli. Cook until just heated through, about 2 minutes.

**5** Drain beef. Add to pan. Heat through, about 30 seconds. Serve immediately with orange to use as dressing if liked.

**PER SERVING**  286Kcals, 34g protein, 12g fat,
3g saturated fat, 14g carbohydrate, 3g fibre, 1.5g salt

**fresh ideas**

A beef stir-fry is an adaptable dish that is easily varied to make use of seasonal vegetables and a range of seasonings. Try a combination of mange-touts, asparagus spears and radishes with onions and lemon zest. Go for a mix of red, yellow and green peppers with fresh basil and garlic. Green or butter beans, baby corn and courgettes with spring onions and dill taste good, too.

# thai-style
## beef sandwich

• HEART HEALTHY

A light, freshly made, vitamin-packed coleslaw enriches a simple beef sandwich.

**SERVES** 4  **PREPARATION** 10 minutes  **MARINATING** 30 minutes
**COOKING** 10 minutes  **REST** 10 minutes

2 tablespoons tomato purée
125ml freshly squeezed lime juice (about 3 limes)
1½ teaspoons ground coriander
500g well-trimmed sirloin steak
1 teaspoon sugar
1 teaspoon salt
1 teaspoon crushed chilli flakes
250g green cabbage, shredded
2 medium carrots, coarsely grated
1 large red pepper, cut into matchsticks
25g fresh coriander, chopped
3 tablespoons fresh chopped mint
4 crusty rolls, halved

**1** Mix tomato purée, half the lime juice and all the ground coriander in a shallow dish. Add the steak, turning to coat. Chill for 30 minutes.

**2** Whisk the remaining lime juice, the sugar, salt and crushed chilli flakes in a large bowl. Add the cabbage, carrots, pepper, coriander and mint; toss thoroughly to combine. Chill coleslaw until ready to serve.

**3** Preheat grill to medium-high. Remove steak from marinade. Grill for 4 minutes each side for medium-rare, brushing any remaining marinade over steak halfway through the cooking time. Allow to rest for 10 minutes. Cut steak diagonally across the grain into thin slices.

**4** To serve, fill rolls with coleslaw and top with steak.

**PER SERVING**  366Kcals, 37g protein, 8g fat,
3g saturated fat, 38g carbohydrate, 7g fibre, 2g salt

2 of your 5 a day

# moroccan beef stew with chickpeas

• MAKE AHEAD

Chickpeas add low-fat protein to this dish while dried apricots and raisins give it a sweetness that complements the warmth of the spices.

**SERVES** 6   **PREPARATION** 15 minutes
**COOKING** 1 hour 50 minutes

1 tablespoon vegetable oil
500g beef topside, cut into 2.5cm cubes
1 medium onion, finely chopped
4 garlic cloves, crushed
½ teaspoon each freshly grated nutmeg,
    ground ginger, cinnamon and turmeric
½ teaspoon salt
ground black pepper, to taste
70g chopped ready-to-eat dried apricots
40g sultanas or raisins
2 medium sweet potatoes, peeled and cut
    into 2.5cm chunks
750ml chicken stock
400g can chickpeas, drained and rinsed
thinly sliced strips of spring onion and thin strips
    of orange peel, to garnish

**1** Heat oil in a large non-stick pan over medium-high heat. Cook beef in batches, browning meat on all sides, 3 to 4 minutes each batch. Transfer the meat to a plate as it browns. Add onion to pan. Cook until softened, about 5 minutes. Add a spoonful of water, if necessary, to prevent onions from sticking.

**2** Add garlic, nutmeg, ginger, cinnamon, turmeric, salt and pepper. Cook 1 minute. Add the apricots, sultanas or raisins, sweet potatoes, beef and the stock. Cover and simmer until meat is very tender, about 1 hour 30 minutes.

**3** Stir in chickpeas. Heat through. Garnish with spring onion strips and orange peel.

**PER SERVING** 320Kcals, 29g protein, 9g fat,
3g saturated fat, 34g carbohydrate, 5g fibre, 1.4g salt

# veal stew with beer

• MAKE AHEAD
• HEART HEALTHY

A rich but heart-healthy main dish that is low in saturated fat and high in fibre.

**SERVES** 4   **PREPARATION** 15 minutes   **COOKING** 1 hour 30 minutes

500g stewing veal, cut into 2.5cm cubes
¾ teaspoon salt
ground black pepper, to taste
2 tablespoons vegetable oil
2 large, flat mushrooms, stems removed and
    caps cut into 2.5cm slices
8 large shallots, or 1 medium onion,
    finely chopped
2 tablespoons plain flour
375ml dark beer, such as Guinness
1 tablespoon white wine vinegar
½ teaspoon dried thyme
500g large carrots, peeled and cut into 5cm lengths

**1** Pat veal pieces dry with kitchen paper. Season with ¼ tsp salt and the pepper. Heat oil in a large flameproof casserole over high heat. Working in batches, add veal and brown on all sides, about 4 minutes each batch. Transfer veal to a plate.

**2** Lower heat to medium. Add mushrooms and shallots or onion to casserole. Sauté until shallots are just golden, about 5 minutes. Stir in flour. Add veal, beer, vinegar, thyme and the remaining salt. Bring to the boil. Add carrots; cover. Lower the heat and simmer until veal is tender, about 1 hour 15 minutes.

**3** Transfer veal, carrot and mushrooms to serving dish. Boil sauce until reduced slightly. Pour over veal.

**PER SERVING** 300Kcals, 29g protein, 10g fat,
2g saturated fat, 22g carbohydrate, 4g fibre, 1.2g salt

# griddled **steak** • QUICK RECIPE
# with **mushrooms**

Give extra nutritional value to an iron-rich steak with
a range of vitamin-packed vegetables.

**SERVES** 4   **PREPARATION** 15 minutes   **COOKING** 15 minutes

2 teaspoons olive oil
2 garlic cloves, crushed
4 thin slices red onion
4 large, flat mushrooms, stems removed
non-stick cooking spray
2 boneless rib-eye steaks, about 350g each
½ teaspoon salt
ground black pepper, to taste
3 small ripe tomatoes
flat-leaf parsley, roughly chopped, to garnish

**1** Preheat a ridged griddle to hot. Heat oil in a small pan over medium heat. Add garlic; sauté 2 minutes. Transfer oil and garlic to a large bowl.

**2** Coat onion slices and mushroom caps thoroughly with cooking spray.

**3** Griddle onion and mushrooms just until browned, about 2 minutes each side. Cut mushrooms into thick slices. Add mushrooms and onion to garlic oil. Toss to coat.

**4** Cut steaks crossways into two equal pieces. Pat meat dry with kitchen paper. Season with salt and pepper. Coat lightly with cooking spray.

**5** Griddle steaks until seared with browned griddle marks, about 4 minutes. Turn steaks over. Griddle 2 to 3 minutes for medium-rare, or until cooked as you like.

**6** To serve, cut each tomato into 4 slices. Place 3 slices on top of each cooked steak. Top with the mushroom mixture. Sprinkle with parsley.

**PER SERVING** 265Kcals, 40g protein, 10g fat, 3.5g saturated fat, 3g carbohydrate, 1.5g fibre, 0.8g salt

**1** of your **5 a day**

## did you **know...**

...that cooked fresh mushrooms have almost three times the niacin and potassium, twice the iron and 15 times the riboflavin of a comparable amount of canned mushrooms?

# beef, onion & pepper fajitas

A fajita is a tortilla wrapped around meat and an assortment of vegetables, which means it's naturally loaded with vitamins, minerals and phytochemicals.

**MAKES** 8 fajitas   **PREPARATION** 15 minutes
**MARINATING** 1 to 2 hours   **COOKING** 12 minutes   **REST** 5 minutes

500g sirloin steak, in one piece
1 medium red onion, sliced
1 small red pepper, seeded and cut into thin strips
1 small green pepper, seeded and cut into thin strips
1 small yellow pepper, seeded and cut into thin strips
4 garlic cloves, crushed
125ml freshly squeezed lime juice
2 tablespoons olive oil
2 tablespoons balsamic vinegar
1 teaspoon ground cumin
½ teaspoon salt
ground black pepper, to taste
1 serrano or jalapeño chilli, seeded and finely chopped
8 medium soft flour tortillas, warmed according to the
   pack instructions
125g Cheddar cheese, coarsely grated

**1** Combine steak, onion and peppers in a shallow baking dish. In a small bowl whisk together garlic, lime juice, oil, vinegar, cumin, salt, pepper and chilli. Pour over steak mixture; toss to coat. Chill, covered, for 1 to 2 hours.

**2** Preheat the grill to medium-high. Put steak in the grill pan and cook 2 minutes each side. Add the onion and peppers. Spoon any remaining marinade over steak and vegetables. Grill, turning meat and vegetables occasionally, until the meat is cooked as you like it and vegetables are crisp-tender, about a further 7 minutes. Leave meat to rest 5 minutes.

**3** Cut meat diagonally across grain into thin slices. Divide meat, onion and pepper evenly among warmed tortillas. Top with cheese. Place under grill until the cheese just melts, about 30 seconds. Fold tortillas over filling and serve.

**PER FAJITA** 354Kcals, 23g protein, 11g fat, 5g saturated fat, 40g carbohydrate, 2g fibre, 1g salt

2 of your 5 a day

## on the menu

Other flatbreads such as lavash and pitta bread can be used for this recipe. Warm them lightly in the oven, under the grill or in the microwave. You can vary the cut of beef used depending on your taste and budget.

• MAKE AHEAD

# peppers stuffed with sausages & rice

Load peppers with rice, pork, cheese and carrots for a tasty way to get more than half your daily vegetables.

**SERVES** 4　**PREPARATION** 15 minutes　**COOKING** 40 minutes

4 large peppers (any colours)
300g pork and herb sausages
1 teaspoon dried oregano
150g long-grain rice, cooked
1 medium carrot, peeled and grated
60g Cheddar cheese, coarsely grated
375ml tomato pasta sauce,
　warmed, to serve (optional)

**1** Preheat oven to 190°C (170°C fan oven), gas 5. Cut peppers in half through the stem end. Scrape out membranes and seeds. Steam peppers for 5 minutes to soften them slightly.

**2** Heat a large non-stick frying pan over medium heat. Take sausage meat out of casings; crumble into pan. Add oregano. Cook sausage, breaking it up with a wooden spoon, until it is browned and cooked through, about 3 minutes. Remove pan from heat. Add rice, carrot and cheese.

**3** Put peppers in a baking dish. Using a small spoon, fill each pepper with rice mixture. Cover with foil.

**4** Bake until peppers are tender, 25 to 30 minutes. Serve with tomato pasta sauce, if you like.

**PER SERVING** 480Kcals, 17g protein, 25g fat, 11g saturated fat, 47g carbohydrates, 3.5g fibre, 3g salt

**3** of your **5 a day**

---

• HEART HEALTHY

# cider-braised ham with sweet potato

High-fibre sweet potatoes combine with apples and lean pork in a low-fat, low-calorie sweet 'n' sour dish.

**SERVES** 4　**PREPARATION** 15 minutes　**COOKING** 30 minutes

250ml plus 1 tablespoon apple cider
1 tablespoon Dijon mustard
2.5cm piece fresh root ginger,
　peeled and finely chopped
½ teaspoon ground cloves
1 medium sweet potato, peeled and thinly sliced
500g extra-lean gammon steak
1 green dessert apple, peeled,
　cored and cut into 12 wedges
1 tablespoon cornflour
ground black pepper, to taste
4 spring onions, green part diagonally sliced

**1** Combine 2ml cider, the mustard, ginger and cloves in a large frying pan. Bring to a simmer. Add the sweet potato. Cover tightly and simmer until partially tender, 15 minutes.

**2** Add gammon steak; cover with sweet potato slices. Arrange apple wedges over the top. Cover and simmer until apples and potato are tender and ham is heated through, 10 to 15 minutes.

**3** Using a draining spoon, transfer ham, sweet potato and apple to a plate. Cover with foil to keep warm.

**4** Blend cornflour and 1 tbsp cider in a small bowl. Stir a little of the hot pan liquid into the mixture until smooth. Add cornflour mixture into pan. Cook over medium heat, stirring, until slightly thickened, about 1 minute. Add pepper.

**5** Divide gammon, sweet potato and apple among four plates. Spoon on sauce from the pan. Garnish with spring onion strips.

**PER SERVING** 287Kcals, 23g protein, 10g fat, 3g saturated fat, 22g carbohydrates, 2g fibre, 3.1g salt

**1** of your **5 a day**

Adding fresh fruit to a meat dish is an easy way to include more vitamins and fibre. Sliced pears, halved kumquats, orange segments or pineapple chunks could be used in this recipe in place of the apple.

# did you know...

...that pak choi leaves can be braised or stir-fried just like other greens? Or that pak choi stems can be cut up and used for seasoning stews just like stalks of celery?

# stir-fried pork with pak choi

Pak choi, like other cabbages has plenty of disease-fighting antioxidants, as well as considerably higher amounts of calcium and beta carotene.

**SERVES** 4 **PREPARATION** 15 minutes
**MARINATING** 15 minutes **COOKING** 10 minutes

3 tablespoons dry sherry or rice wine
2 tablespoons soy sauce
1 tablespoon cornflour
1 teaspoon toasted sesame oil
1 teaspoon brown sugar
ground black pepper, to taste
500g pork tenderloin, cut into 3mm thick slices
2 tablespoons vegetable oil
450g pak choi, coarsely chopped
2 garlic cloves, crushed
orange wedges, to serve (optional)

**1** Stir together half the sherry and all the soy sauce, cornflour, sesame oil, sugar and pepper in a small bowl. Add pork. Toss to coat. Marinate at room temperature for 15 minutes.

**2** Heat 1 tbsp oil in large non-stick frying pan or wok over high heat. Add pak choi. Stir-fry 2 minutes. Cover. Cook until wilted, about 2 minutes. Transfer pak choi to a plate. Discard liquid left in frying pan.

**3** Add remaining oil to pan. Add garlic. Sauté 15 seconds. Add the pork mixture and stir-fry until the meat is just cooked through, 3 to 4 minutes. Add pak choi and remaining sherry. Cook until heated through. Serve immediately, with orange wedges, if you like.

**PER SERVING** 272Kcals, 30g protein, 12g fat, 3g saturated fat, 7g carbohydrates, 2.5g fibre, 1.7g salt

**1** of your **5 a day**

• MAKE AHEAD

# pork & bean chilli

Tender pork chunks, tomato, peppers and cannellini beans create a richly spiced healthy chilli.

**SERVES** 6 **PREPARATION** 20 minutes **COOKING** 2 hours

750g pork shoulder, cut into 1cm cubes
70g plain flour
2 tablespoons vegetable oil
1 large onion, finely chopped
1 medium green pepper, seeded
    and coarsely chopped
1 jalapeño or other hot chilli, seeded
    and finely chopped
3 garlic cloves, crushed
2 x 400g cans tomatoes with juice,
    coarsely chopped
250ml chicken stock
3 tablespoons chilli powder
¼ teaspoon salt
2 x 400g cans cannellini or butter beans,
    drained and rinsed
2 tablespoons fresh coriander leaves, to garnish

**1** Coat pork with flour; shake off any excess. Heat oil in a large non-stick pan over medium-high heat. Working in batches, add pork and brown on all sides, about 5 minutes each batch. Transfer pork to a plate as it browns.

**2** Lower heat to medium. Add the onion, pepper, chilli and garlic. Cook until onion is softened, about 5 minutes. Return pork to pan. Add tomatoes, stock, chilli powder and salt. Simmer 1 hour, stirring occasionally. Stir in beans. Simmer until meat is tender and sauce is thickened, about 40 minutes. Garnish and serve.

**PER SERVING** 354Kcals, 38g protein, 10g fat, 2.5g saturated fat, 30g carbohydrates, 7g fibre, 1.9g salt

**2** of your **5 a day**

# roast loin of pork
## with carrots & apples

Pork loin and fibre-rich vegetables such as sweet potatoes and carrots are a great flavour combination.

**SERVES** 4  **PREPARATION** 20 minutes  **CHILL** 2 to 24 hours
**MARINATING** 2 hours  **COOKING** 45 minutes

125ml orange juice
grated zest of 1 orange
1 teaspoon honey
½ teaspoon ground cumin
¼ teaspoon cinnamon
¼ teaspoon chilli powder
650g boned pork loin, trimmed
1 tablespoon vegetable oil
2 medium sweet potatoes,
    peeled and diced
1 medium onion, diced
2 medium carrots, peeled and diced
2 medium apples, cored, peeled and
    cut into 3cm pieces
½ teaspoon salt
ground black pepper, to taste
120ml dry white wine
15g butter
chives, to garnish

**1** Combine orange juice, zest, honey, cumin, cinnamon and chilli powder in a large bowl. Add pork; turn to coat. Cover and chill for at least 2 hours or up to 24 hours, turning occasionally.

**2** Preheat oven to 180°C (160°C fan oven), gas 4. Heat oil in a large frying pan over medium-high heat. Add pork; brown on all sides, about 5 minutes. Transfer to a roasting tin.

**3** Place sweet potatoes, onion, carrots, apples, seasoning and wine in tin. Place pork on top of vegetables; brush with marinade. Cover with foil.

**4** Roast pork, about 40 minutes. The juices should run clear when a skewer is inserted into the meat. (A meat thermometer inserted in the centre should register 75°C.)

**5** Place pork on a cutting board. Rest 5 minutes. Stir butter into vegetables. Garnish and serve pork with vegetables.

**PER SERVING** 338Kcals, 36g protein, 11g fat, 4g saturated fat, 25g carbohydrates, 2.5g fibre, 0.6g salt

**2** of your **5 a day**

## on the menu

With their peppery taste, a salad of rocket leaves or watercress would be a good foil for the sweetness of the vegetables and fruits in this recipe. Pak choi would also work very well as an accompaniment.

# pork chops with wine and cabbage

In a cooked variation on sauerkraut, wine, garlic, vinegar and cloves give cabbage a wonderful rich flavour, a perfect foil for the savoury pork.

**SERVES** 4  **PREPARATION** 15 minutes  **COOKING** 55 minutes

1 tablespoon vegetable oil
4 pork chops, about 175g each
¾ teaspoon salt
ground black pepper, to taste
1 medium onion, thinly sliced
1 large carrot, peeled and
   coarsely chopped
2 garlic cloves, sliced
250ml white wine
1 small savoy cabbage, shredded
1 bay leaf
3 cloves
2 tablespoons white wine vinegar
1 teaspoon sugar

**1** Heat oil in a large non-stick frying pan over medium-high heat. Season chops with a little of the salt and some pepper. Add the chops to pan. Sauté until well browned on both sides, about 3 minutes each side. Transfer chops to a plate.

**2** Lower heat to medium. Add onion, carrot and garlic to pan. Sauté until onion is softened, about 5 minutes. Add the wine; bring to the boil. Stir in cabbage, bay leaf and cloves. Cover and simmer over medium-low heat until the cabbage is tender, 20 to 30 minutes. Remove bay leaf.

**3** Stir vinegar, sugar and remaining salt into the cabbage mixture. Add the pork chops. Cover. Simmer until pork is just cooked through, about 10 minutes.

**PER SERVING**  331Kcals, 33g protein, 17g fat, 5g saturated fat), 8g carbohydrates, 5g fibre, 0.7g salt

½ of your 5 a day

## did you know...

...that cabbage is one of the oldest cultivated vegetables? The great grandfather of the brassicas – which include cauliflower, broccoli, Brussels sprouts and kale – it probably originated close to the coasts of temperate northern Europe.

# irish stew

- MAKE AHEAD
- HEART HEALTHY

A classic dish gets a nutritional boost: the ratio of vegetables to meat has been increased.

**SERVES** 6   **PREPARATION** 20 minutes   **COOKING** 1 hour 30 minutes

2 teaspoons vegetable oil
500g boneless lamb shoulder,
    cut into 3cm chunks
4 red potatoes, unpeeled and coarsely chopped
3 medium carrots, peeled and cut
    into bite-sized chunks
2 medium onions, coarsely chopped
2 leeks, rinsed and coarsely chopped
1 large turnip, peeled and coarsely chopped
2 tablespoons plain flour
1 bay leaf
½ teaspoon dried rosemary
1 teaspoon salt
ground black pepper, to taste
150g fresh or frozen peas
bread, to serve

**1** Heat oil in a large flameproof casserole or non-stick deep frying pan over medium-high heat. Add meat in batches and brown on all sides, about 5 minutes each batch. Put in a bowl.

**2** Add all the vegetables to casserole or pan. Cook 10 minutes; stir occasionally. Stir in flour. Add 750ml water, bay leaf, rosemary and seasoning. Bring to the boil. Reduce heat. Add meat. Simmer, uncovered, until meat is tender, 50 to 60 minutes. Add peas. Simmer 5 minutes; serve with bread.

**PER SERVING** 314Kcals, 23g protein, 9g fat, 3g saturated fat, 37g carbohydrates, 6g fibre, 0.9g salt

**2** of your **5 a day**

# country lamb cobbler

- HEART HEALTHY

If you enjoy casseroles topped with pastry or dumplings, you'll love this low-fat version.

**SERVES** 4   **PREPARATION** 20 minutes   **COOKING** 1 hour

500g lean lamb steak, trimmed and
    cut into 3cm cubes
500g carrots, peeled and thickly sliced
4 large celery sticks, thickly sliced
500g leeks, trimmed and thickly sliced
375ml strong dry cider
500ml chicken stock
140g self-raising flour, sifted,
    plus extra for dusting
4 tablespoons chopped fresh parsley
    and sage combined
½ teaspoon salt
ground black pepper, to taste
125g soured cream
1 to 2 teaspoons semi-skimmed milk (optional)
300g frozen peas, thawed
rosemary, sage and thyme sprigs,
    tied together to make a bouquet garni

**1** Dry-fry lamb in a large flameproof casserole over medium-high heat until lightly browned, 6 to 8 minutes; stir frequently. Add carrots, celery and leeks. Cook 4 minutes; stir occasionally.

**2** Add cider and stock. Bring to the boil. Reduce heat to low; cover and simmer until vegetables are tender, 20 to 25 minutes.

**3** Meanwhile, preheat oven to 200°C (180°C fan oven), gas 6. To make pastry topping, combine the flour, parsley, sage and seasoning in a medium bowl. Stir in soured cream; mix to make a firm dough. If dough is too dry, add 1 or 2 tsp milk. Roll out to 1.5cm thickness. Cut into 16 triangles.

**4** Add peas and bouquet garni to casserole. Arrange pastry triangles on top, covering the surface.

**5** Bake until pastry topping is well risen and golden brown, 25 to 30 minutes. Remove bouquet garni.

**PER SERVING** 603Kcals, 42g protein, 24g fat, 11g saturated fat, 35g carbohydrates, 10g fibre, 1.9g salt

**4** of your **5 a day**

## on the **menu**

With all the vegetables, meat and pastry in the lamb cobbler, you need add very little to complete a meal. You might start with a pumpkin or asparagus soup and finish with fresh fruit and a selection of your favourite cheeses.

# fish & seafood

# tex-mex
# grilled prawn salad

• QUICK RECIPE

Avocado, prawns and olive oil are all rich in heart-protecting vitamin E.

**SERVES** 4  **PREPARATION** 15 minutes  **COOKING** 6 minutes

12 medium raw prawns, about 500g,
  peeled and deveined
¼ teaspoon salt
ground black pepper, to taste
non-stick cooking spray
115g cooked sweetcorn
  (fresh, drained canned or thawed frozen)
1 avocado, stoned, peeled and sliced
12 baby plum or cherry tomatoes, halved
½ red onion, finely chopped
2 tablespoons coarsely chopped,
  bottled pickled jalapeño (hot) chillies
2 tablespoons pickled jalapeño liquid
¾ teaspoon ground cumin
1 tablespoon olive oil
16 bite-sized tortilla chips
2 tablespoons roughly chopped coriander
65g soured cream
lettuce leaves, to serve

**1** Preheat grill to hot. Season prawns with salt and pepper. Coat with cooking spray.

**2** Grill prawns until curled and bright pink, 2 to 3 minutes each side. Allow to cool slightly.

**3** Combine sweetcorn, avocado, tomatoes, onion, pickled jalapeños and liquid, cumin and oil in a large bowl. Leave for 5 minutes. Fold in prawns, tortilla chips and coriander.

**4** Divide lettuce among four serving plates and top with salad. Spoon some soured cream on to each one. Serve.

**PER SERVING** 321Kcals, 25g protein, 18g fat, 5g saturated fat, 15g carbohydrates, 3g fibre, 1.3g salt

1 of your 5 a day

fresh ideas

Pickled jalapeños give the salad its hot punch. The pickling liquid will also spice up homemade salsas.

• QUICK RECIPE

# stir-fried prawns
# & mange-touts

The vitamin E in prawns and the vitamin C in mange-touts are a winning combination if you are looking to boost your immunity.

**SERVES** 4  **PREPARATION** 10 minutes  **COOKING** 8 minutes

1 tablespoon plus 2 teaspoons vegetable oil
125g mange-touts
1 small red pepper, seeded and very thinly sliced
¼ teaspoon salt
12 medium raw prawns, about 500g,
  peeled and deveined
3 spring onions, finely chopped
½ teaspoon crushed chilli flakes
2 garlic cloves, crushed
2.5cm piece fresh root ginger,
  peeled and finely chopped
2 tablespoons salt-reduced soy sauce
1 tablespoon freshly squeezed lemon juice
1 tablespoon grated lemon zest

**1** Heat the 2 tsp oil in a large non-stick frying pan or wok over medium heat. Add mange-touts, pepper and salt. Stir-fry until crisp-tender, about 3 minutes. Transfer to a plate.

**2** Heat remaining oil in the same pan. Add prawns, spring onions and crushed chilli flakes. Stir-fry 1½ minutes. Add garlic and ginger. Stir-fry 1 minute. Add soy sauce and lemon juice. Stir-fry until prawns are curled, bright pink and cooked through, about 1 minute.

**3** Add mange-touts and pepper to pan. Stir-fry just long enough to heat through, about 30 seconds. Stir in lemon zest; serve immediately.

**PER SERVING** 161Kcals, 24g protein, 5g fat, 0.8g saturated fat, 6g carbohydrates, 1.5g fibre, 1.6g salt

½ of your 5 a day

# prawns with fennel

Get plenty of vitamin B$_{12}$ from the prawns and a dose of vitamin C from the fennel, tomatoes and onion.

**SERVES** 4   **PREPARATION** 15 minutes   **COOKING** 25 minutes

1 tablespoon extra virgin olive oil
1 large onion, chopped
1 large bulb fennel, trimmed and chopped
1 garlic clove, crushed
400g can chopped tomatoes
125ml fish stock
½ tablespoon fennel seeds
finely grated zest and juice of ½ orange
salt and ground black pepper, to taste
200g long-grain rice
pinch of saffron threads, crushed
500g raw king prawns, peeled and deveined
basil leaves, shredded and whole, to garnish

**1** Heat oil in a large non-stick frying pan over medium heat. Add onion, fennel and garlic. Cook, stirring occasionally, until vegetables are soft, 5 minutes. Add tomatoes, fish stock, fennel seeds and orange zest and juice. Season with salt and pepper. Bring to the boil, stirring. Reduce heat to low and partially cover pan. Simmer 12 minutes.

**2** Meanwhile, cook rice according to pack instructions; add crushed saffron to the boiling water.

**3** Bring tomato sauce back to the boil. Place prawns on top of sauce. Cover pan tightly; cook over low heat until prawns are done, 3 to 4 minutes. Divide rice among serving bowls. Top with prawns and tomato sauce. Sprinkle with basil and serve.

**PER SERVING**  346Kcals, 29g protein, 4g fat, 0.5g saturated fat, 48g carbohydrates, 5g fibre, 1g salt

**3** of your 5 a day

# scallops florentine

'Florentine' is a way of denoting that a recipe contains spinach. This means it is rich in the vitamins, minerals and phytochemicals that make leafy green vegetables so very good for you.

**SERVES** 4   **PREPARATION** 10 minutes   **COOKING** 12 minutes

350g spinach
2 tablespoons olive oil
750g scallops
2 garlic cloves, crushed
fine strips of zest from ½ lemon
250ml chicken stock
150g frozen peas, thawed
1 tablespoon freshly squeezed lemon juice
¼ teaspoon salt
ground black pepper, to taste

**1** Steam spinach just until wilted, 3 minutes. Cool under cold running water. Squeeze dry.

**2** Heat oil in a large non-stick frying pan over high heat. Add scallops. Sauté until still slightly uncooked in centre, 2 minutes each side. (The centre will look translucent.) Transfer to a plate.

**3** Lower heat to medium. Add garlic and lemon zest to pan. Cook 30 seconds. Add stock and peas; simmer 3 minutes. Add spinach, scallops, lemon juice, salt and pepper. Cook until just heated through. Serve in shallow bowls or on plates.

**PER SERVING**  336Kcals, 51g protein, 10g fat, 2g saturated fat, 12g carbohydrates, 4g fibre, 1.7g salt

**1** of your 5 a day

## did you know...

...that scallops contain about twice the quantity of omega-3 fatty acids as tuna canned in water? Omega-3 fatty acids help to suppress inflammatory compounds in the body and improve cardio-vascular health.

## on the **menu**

Serve over – or with – steaming hot rice that's been cooked in chicken stock. Sliced ripe tomatoes make a good side dish. Serve fresh fruit for dessert.

# crab gumbo

Okra, a key component of this dish, contains a range of fibrous gums and pectins that help to lower cholesterol and protect against stomach ulcers.

**SERVES** 4 **PREPARATION** 10 minutes **COOKING** 35 minutes

2 tablespoons vegetable oil
250g okra, trimmed and cut into
   1.5cm thick slices
1 medium onion, coarsely chopped
1 medium red pepper, seeded and diced
1 medium green pepper, seeded and diced
100g piece baked ham, diced
2 garlic cloves, crushed
400g can chopped tomatoes
500ml chicken stock
500g crabmeat, ideally taken from the claws
¾ teaspoon Tabasco sauce
¼ teaspoon salt
ground black pepper, to taste

**1** Heat oil in a large pan over medium-high heat. Add the okra, onion, peppers and ham. Sauté until okra is tender and no longer sticky, about 10 minutes.

**2** Add garlic. Sauté 1 minute. Add tomatoes and chicken stock. Simmer, uncovered, 20 minutes.

**3** Stir crab, Tabasco, salt and pepper into the mixture, taking care not to break up the crab too much.
Gently heat through.

**PER SERVING** 330Kcals, 38g protein, 15g fat, 2.5g saturated fat, 13g carbohydrates, 5g fibre, 3g salt

**2** of your **5 a day**

## did you **know...**

...that gumbo got its name from the African word 'quinbombo', which means okra? What goes into a gumbo is pretty much up to the individual cook. However, okra is usually an ingredient in this spicy stew that's a classic in the southern states of the USA.

# scallop &
# cherry tomato sauté

• QUICK RECIPE
• HEART HEALTHY

Sizzling, protein-rich scallops and tiny tomatoes packed with vitamin C go direct from the pan to the dining table in literally minutes.

**SERVES** 4   **PREPARATION** 5 minutes   **COOKING** 10 minutes

500g scallops
4 teaspoons cornflour
2 teaspoons olive oil
3 garlic cloves, crushed
500g cherry tomatoes
170ml dry vermouth, white wine
  or chicken stock
salt and ground black pepper, to taste
15g fresh basil leaves, chopped

**1** Sprinkle scallops with 3 tsp of the cornflour, shaking off the excess. Heat oil in a large non-stick frying pan over medium heat. Add scallops and sauté until golden brown and cooked through, about 3 minutes. Using a draining spoon, transfer the scallops to a bowl.

**2** Add garlic to pan; cook 1 minute. Add tomatoes and cook until they begin to collapse, about 4 minutes. Add vermouth, wine or stock, seasoning and the basil. Bring to the boil; cook for about 1 minute.

**3** Blend remaining cornflour and 1 tbsp cold water in a small bowl. Add mixture to pan and cook, stirring, until sauce is slightly thickened, about 1 minute.

**4** Return scallops to pan. Reduce to a simmer; cook just until heated through, about 1 minute.

**PER SERVING** 248Kcals, 30g protein, 4g fat, 0.8g saturated fat, 14g carbohydrates, 1g fibre, 1.1g salt

**1** of your **5 a day**

## helpful **hint**

Almost any dish made with shellfish can also be made with a firm-fleshed fish. Fillet of monkfish, cut into bite-sized chunks, is a great substitute for prawns, scallops, lobster or crabmeat because it has a taste similar to that of shellfish. Salmon, swordfish and tuna can all be used as substitutes in recipes that call for shellfish.

# asian steamed fish

Low-fat fish and vitamin-packed vegetables are cooked using one of the most healthy of all cooking techniques – steaming.

**SERVES** 4  **PREPARATION** 15 minutes  **COOKING** 12 minutes

750g snapper or other firm-fleshed
   white fish fillets, in 4 pieces
2 tablespoons salt-reduced soy sauce
2 tablespoons white wine or sake
1 thin slice fresh ginger, peeled and
   cut into thin sticks
2 medium carrots, peeled and cut into
   5mm sticks lengthways
ground black pepper, to taste
60g mange-touts, cut in half lengthways
½ medium yellow pepper, seeded
   and cut into thin sticks
orange wedges, to serve (optional)

**1** Put fish in a baking dish that fits inside a large steamer basket or on a rack that will fit into a large frying pan or wok. Combine the soy sauce and white wine or sake and pour over the fish. Top with ginger, carrots and season with pepper.

**2** Fill pan with water to a depth of 2.5cm. Bring to a simmer. Put steamer basket or wire rack in pan. Place baking dish in the basket or on the rack. Cover pan or basket. Steam fish for 5 to 6 minutes. Add mange-touts and pepper to baking dish. Cover. Steam until fish flakes when touched with the tip of a knife and vegetables are crisp-tender, about 5 minutes. Serve with orange wedges, if you like.

**PER SERVING**  202Kcals, 38g protein, 3g fat, 0.6g saturated fat, 6.5g carbohydrates, 1.5g fibre, 1.4g salt

**1** of your **5 a day**

## did you know...

...that when it comes to counting cholesterol, mussels rate the lowest, with scallops next on the list. Of the shellfish, prawns are highest in cholesterol but they are still a low-fat source of protein.

# caribbean curry

The ginger, curry powder, chillies and allspice used here all contain health-protecting phytochemicals.

**SERVES** 4  **PREPARATION** 30 minutes  **COOKING** 30 minutes

2 teaspoons olive oil
6 thin spring onions, finely chopped
1 medium yellow pepper, seeded
   and coarsely chopped
1 tablespoon finely chopped, fresh root ginger
1½ teaspoons curry powder
¼ teaspoon crushed chilli flakes, or to taste
¼ teaspoon ground allspice
2 tablespoons salt-reduced soy sauce
1½ tablespoons brown sugar
400ml can reduced-fat coconut milk
3 tomatoes, quartered lengthways and seeded
250g swordfish steaks or monkfish fillet, skin or
   membrane removed, cut into 5cm chunks
250g medium raw prawns, peeled and
   deveined, tails intact
2 tablespoons roughly chopped fresh coriander
1 tablespoon freshly squeezed lime juice

**1** Heat oil in a large flameproof casserole over medium heat. Add spring onions, pepper and ginger. Sauté until softened, 5 minutes. Add curry powder, crushed chilli flakes and allspice. Sauté 2 minutes. Stir in soy sauce, brown sugar, coconut milk and tomatoes. Simmer gently, uncovered, for 15 minutes.

**2** Add fish and prawns to mixture. Simmer gently, uncovered, just until fish is cooked through, 5 to 8 minutes. Add coriander and lime juice. Serve at once.

**PER SERVING**  284Kcals, 25g protein, 15g fat, 10g saturated fat, 15g carbohydrates, 1.5g fibre, 1.6g salt

**2** of your **5 a day**

# salmon with chard and peppers

Swiss chard is rich in calcium and makes a bone-building base for a salmon fillet that's been laced with a terrific honey and mustard marinade.

**SERVES** 4  **PREPARATION** 15 minutes
**MARINATING** 30 minutes  **COOKING** 16 minutes

60ml bought grapefruit juice
1½ tablespoons Dijon mustard
1½ tablespoons honey
¼ teaspoon crushed chilli flakes
4 salmon fillets, about 175g each
750g Swiss chard, large stems removed
   and leaves cut into large pieces
3 tablespoons olive oil
½ each medium red and yellow pepper,
   seeded and finely chopped
ground black pepper, to taste

**1** In a baking dish large enough to hold fish fillets in a single layer, combine the juice, mustard, honey and crushed chilli flakes. Place salmon in dish, turning to coat both sides with the marinade. Chill, covered, for 30 minutes.

**2** Preheat grill to medium-high. Bring a large pan of water to the boil. Add Swiss chard. Return water to the boil and cook 3 minutes. Drain well. Squeeze out excess water.

**3** Heat olive oil in a large frying pan over medium heat. Add all the pepper. Sauté 1 minute. Add Swiss chard. Sauté until pepper and Swiss chard are tender, about 3 minutes. Remove pan from heat; keep mixture warm.

**4** Remove salmon from marinade. Place, skin side down, on the rack of a foil-lined grill pan. Add pepper. Reserve marinade.

**5** Grill salmon for 3 minutes. Brush with marinade. Grill until fish is opaque and flakes when touched with the point of a knife, 3 to 4 minutes. (If fish is browning too much, lower heat.) Serve on a bed of the vegetables.

**PER SERVING** 476Kcals, 41g protein, 30g fat, 5g saturated fat, 11g carbohydrates, 4.5g fibre, 1.2g salt

**2** of your **5 a day**

# baked cod casserole with potatoes, tomatoes

• HEART HEALTHY

A one-dish meal that's tailor-made for the health of your heart, combines lean fish, accompanied by an array of vitamin-rich vegetables.

**SERVES** 4  **PREPARATION** 20 minutes  **COOKING** 38 minutes

500g red potatoes, unpeeled,
    thickly sliced and quartered
1 medium red onion, thinly sliced
1 tablespoon olive oil
½ teaspoon salt
4 ripe tomatoes, seeded and
    coarsely chopped
3 garlic cloves, crushed
½ teaspoon dried oregano
75g rocket
500g cod, snapper or other thick, firm-fleshed
    white fish steaks, cut into 5cm chunks
ground black pepper, to taste

**1** Preheat oven to 180°C (160°C fan oven), gas 4. Combine potato, onion, oil and half the salt in a medium baking dish.

**2** Bake for 20 minutes, stirring mixture once.

**3** Stir tomatoes, garlic and oregano into potato mixture. Spread the rocket over the top in an even layer. Top with fish steaks. Add pepper and sprinkle with remaining salt.

**4** Bake, covered with foil, until fish is just cooked through, 15 to 18 minutes. Transfer fish and vegetable mixture to serving plates. Spoon pan juices over each serving.

**PER SERVING** 237Kcals, 25g protein, 4g fat, 0.5g saturated fat, 26g carbohydrates, 3g fibre, 0.8g salt

**1** of your **5 a day**

## helpful hint

Almost any baked fish will release some liquid during cooking, so don't be surprised if you find a puddle at the bottom of your casserole dish. Spoon these juices over the fish for extra flavour and moisture.

## roast trout & potatoes

• HEART HEALTHY

A bed of watercress adds vitamins and a slightly peppery flavour to the delicate taste of the trout.

**SERVES** 4 **PREPARATION** 20 minutes **COOKING** 50 minutes

750g potatoes, quartered
1 tablespoon olive oil
4 medium trout, about 300g each, cleaned
fresh tarragon sprigs
salt and ground black pepper, to taste
1 orange, cut into 16 half slices
1 lemon, cut into 16 half slices
60ml freshly squeezed orange juice
1 cucumber, peeled
175g low-fat plain yoghurt
2 tablespoons chopped fresh mint
150g watercress, washed and trimmed

**1** Preheat oven to 200°C (180°C fan oven), gas 6. Put potatoes in a large pan with enough water to cover. Bring to the boil. Reduce heat and simmer 5 minutes. Drain and return potatoes to pan. Drizzle with oil and toss to coat. Lay potato out on a baking sheet. Roast until tender, turning several times, about 25 minutes.

**2** Season inside of trout with tarragon, salt and pepper. Cut four 30cm squares of foil. Divide half the fruit slices among foil squares, lay fish on top and cover with remaining slices. Sprinkle orange juice over the top.

**3** Wrap fish in foil and seal packets. Lay packets on second baking sheet. Bake for 20 minutes. Meanwhile, coarsely grate the cucumber into a colander; press out excess water. Combine cucumber, yoghurt and mint in a small bowl. Arrange the fish and potatoes on serving plates. Spoon on cucumber raita and garnish with watercress and fruit slices.

**PER SERVING** 491Kcals, 56g protein, 13g fat, 2g saturated fat, 38g carbohydrates, 3.5g fibre, 0.7g salt

**1**
of your
**5 a day**

## barbecued tuna steaks with sweetcorn & tomato

• QUICK RECIPE
• HEART HEALTHY

Together, the tuna and vegetables in this dish provide antioxidant vitamins A, C and E. Tuna is also high in omega-3 fatty acids, which are thought to protect against heart disease.

**SERVES** 4 **PREPARATION** 20 minutes **COOKING** 10 minutes

600g tuna steaks, about 2.5cm thick
½ teaspoon salt
ground black pepper, to taste
150g apricot jam
1 tablespoon Dijon mustard
1 corn on the cob, husked and cut
    into 8 equal pieces
2 medium tomatoes, cored and each cut
    into 8 wedges
2 medium courgettes, each quartered lengthways
    and cut crossways into 5mm thick slices
2 garlic cloves, crushed
2 serrano chillies, seeded and finely chopped
4 teaspoons olive oil

**1** Preheat a medium-hot barbecue or grill. Season tuna steaks with ¼ tsp salt and some pepper. Combine jam and mustard in a small cup; spread one side of the tuna steaks with half the jam mixture.

**2** Place the corn, tomatoes and courgettes in the centre of each of four 30cm squares of foil, dividing them equally. Sprinkle the vegetables evenly with the garlic, remaining salt, more pepper, the chillies and the oil. Fold edges of foil over to form tightly sealed packets.

**3** Barbecue or grill the tuna and the vegetable packets for 4 minutes. Turn tuna over. Spread with remaining jam mixture. Cook until tuna is opaque in the centre and flakes when touched with the tip of a knife, 4 to 6 minutes. Open the vegetable packets carefully when serving, as the steam will escape and can burn. Serve with the tuna steaks.

**PER SERVING** 322Kcals, 39g protein, 11g fat, 2.5g saturated fat, 18g carbohydrates, 1.5g fibre, 1g salt

**1**
of your
**5 a day**

## on the **menu**

A crisp salad containing peppery watercress, sliced red cabbage and mixed green leaves makes a good accompaniment to this robust fish dish.

# pasta & noodles

You can try any combination of vegetables and herbs that you want for a pasta sauce. Sauté them in a little olive oil, add stock for liquid and sprinkle with Parmesan. Try the following combinations: rocket, leeks, broccoli and tarragon; aubergine, broccoli, garlic and thyme; green beans, mange-touts, fennel and parsley.

# pasta primavera

• HEART HEALTHY

This simple, colourful recipe gives you seven healthy vegetables in just one dish.

**SERVES** 4 **PREPARATION** 15 minutes **COOKING** 25 minutes

500g asparagus, trimmed
2 tablespoons olive oil
4 plum or round tomatoes, coarsely chopped
1 medium carrot, peeled and cut into thin slices
2 garlic cloves, thinly sliced
75g mushrooms, sliced
185ml vegetable or chicken stock
150g frozen peas, thawed
1 medium yellow courgette cut
    into 1.25cm thick slices
4 tablespoons shredded fresh basil
20g grated Parmesan cheese
250g fettuccine
salt and ground black pepper, to taste

**1** Blanch asparagus in boiling water 1 minute. Drain. Heat oil in a medium non-stick pan over medium heat. Add tomatoes, carrot and garlic. Cook 10 minutes. Add mushrooms and stock. Cook 10 minutes. Add asparagus, peas and courgette. Cook until vegetables are tender, about 2 minutes. Add basil and most of the Parmesan. Season with pepper. Cover; set aside.

**2** While sauce is cooking, cook pasta in a large pan of lightly salted boiling water until al dente, following pack instructions. Drain. Place in a serving bowl. Add vegetable sauce and toss to combine. Sprinkle with Parmesan.

**PER SERVING** 392Kcals, 19g protein, 10g fat, 2g saturated fat, 59g carbohydrates, 8g fibre, 0.3g salt

**4** of your **5 a day**

## did you know...

...that almost any dish that is made with fresh vegetables can be called primavera? The word means springtime in Italian.

# pasta with no-cook vegetable sauce

• QUICK RECIPE
• HEART HEALTHY

When a sauce is made from finely chopped raw vegetables, it retains all of the vitamin C and B that can be lost during lengthy cooking.

**SERVES** 4 **PREPARATION** 15 minutes **COOKING** 12 minutes

250g fusilli
1 medium courgette, cut into 5mm dice
1 medium yellow pepper,
    seeded and cut into 5mm dice
2 large tomatoes, cut into 5mm dice
2 tablespoons olive oil
4 tablespoons roughly chopped fresh basil
¾ teaspoon salt
ground black pepper, to taste
2 tablespoons grated Parmesan cheese

**1** Cook pasta in a large pan of lightly salted boiling water until al dente, following pack instructions.

**2** Combine the courgette, pepper, tomatoes, oil, basil, salt, pepper and Parmesan in a large serving bowl.

**3** Drain pasta. Add to vegetables in bowl. Toss to combine.

**PER SERVING** 321Kcals, 12g protein, 9g fat, 2.5g saturated fat, 50g carbohydrates, 3g fibre, 0.9g salt

**1** of your **5 a day**

## sausage & pepper medley pasta

• QUICK RECIPE

All kinds of peppers contain phytochemicals that protect against heart disease, stroke and cancer.

**SERVES** 4   **PREPARATION** 10 minutes   **COOKING** 15 minutes

2 tablespoons olive oil
250g lean pork sausages, in thin slices
2 medium onions, thinly sliced
2 large red or orange peppers, seeded
   and thinly sliced
1 large green pepper, seeded and thinly sliced
2 garlic cloves, minced
1 teaspoon dried basil
60g pitted black olives
1 tablespoon balsamic vinegar
¼ teaspoon salt
ground black pepper, to taste
250g fusilli or farfalle
20g grated Parmesan cheese

**1** Heat oil in a large non-stick frying pan over medium-high heat. Add sausages and onions. Sauté until onion is softened and light golden, about 5 minutes. Add peppers, garlic and basil. Sauté until peppers are very tender, 10 minutes. Remove from heat. Stir in olives, vinegar, ¼ tsp salt and pepper.

**2** Meanwhile, cook pasta in a large pan of lightly salted boiling water until al dente, following pack instructions. Drain; reserve 60ml of the cooking water. Toss pasta with sausage mixture and reserved water. Serve with Parmesan.

**PER SERVING** 543Kcals, 19g protein, 26g fat, 8g saturated fat, 62g carbohydrate, 6g fibre, 2.1g salt

**2** of your **5 a day**

## spirals with pan-roasted vegetables

• HEART HEALTHY

Roasting is one of the tastiest ways to cook vegetables and just one serving of this dish will give you more than a third of your daily dose of fibre.

**SERVES** 4   **PREPARATION** 20 minutes   **COOKING** 25 minutes

2 tablespoons olive oil
1 large red onion, cut into thin wedges
1 medium yellow pepper, seeded and chopped
600g butternut squash, peeled,
   seeded and cut into 2cm chunks
¼ teaspoon salt
2 tablespoons shredded fresh basil,
   plus extra to garnish
5 garlic cloves, crushed
150g baby plum or cherry tomatoes, halved
150g baby spinach leaves, tough stems removed
1 litre vegetable or chicken stock
250g pasta spirals

**1** Heat 1 tbsp oil in a large non-stick frying pan over medium heat. Add onion and pepper. Sauté until softened, about 5 minutes. Add squash, half the salt, the basil and half the garlic. Cover; cook, stirring occasionally, 8 minutes. Increase heat to high. Cook, uncovered, stirring occasionally, until the vegetables brown slightly and squash is just tender, about 7 minutes. Transfer mixture to a large bowl. Add tomatoes.

**2** Heat remaining oil in the pan over medium heat. Add the remaining garlic and salt, and all the spinach. Cook, stirring occasionally, until spinach wilts, about 2 minutes. Add spinach to the mixture in the bowl.

**3** Meanwhile, bring the stock and 475ml water to the boil in a large pan. Add pasta. Cook until al dente, following pack instructions. Reserve 125ml of the cooking liquid. Drain pasta and combine with vegetable mixture and reserved cooking liquid. Serve garnished with basil.

**PER SERVING** 410Kcals, 21g protein, 9g fat, 1.5g saturated fat, 68g carbohydrates, 7g fibre, 2.7g salt

**3** of your **5 a day**

## on the menu

This refreshing pasta dish doesn't require much more than a simple salad of mixed greens in a tangy vinaigrette and a chilled fruit salad for dessert to make a satisfying – and healthy – meal.

# creamy **farfalle** with green peas & **sun-dried** tomatoes

• QUICK RECIPE
• HEART HEALTHY

Peas add muscle-building protein to this dish along with B vitamins for energy production.

**SERVES** 4   **PREPARATION** 10 minutes   **COOKING** 15 minutes

250g farfalle
salt and ground black pepper, to taste
1 tablespoon olive oil
15g butter or margarine
2 medium onions, finely chopped
3 garlic cloves, crushed
½ teaspoon dried oregano
¼ teaspoon dried marjoram
1½ tablespoons plain flour
250ml vegetable or chicken stock
150g fresh or frozen peas
65g sun-dried tomatoes in oil,
    drained and thinly sliced
30g grated Parmesan cheese

**1** Cook pasta in a large pan of lightly salted boiling water until al dente, following pack instructions.

**2** Heat the oil and butter or margarine in a large non-stick frying pan over medium heat. Add onions, garlic, oregano and marjoram. Sauté until the onion is softened, about 5 minutes. Stir in flour until thoroughly combined. Whisk in the stock. Heat, stirring, until thickened, 2 to 3 minutes. Stir in peas and sun-dried tomatoes. Cook until peas are just tender, about 5 minutes. Remove from heat. Stir in 3 tbsp Parmesan.

**3** Drain pasta, reserving 125ml of the cooking water. Toss pasta with vegetable mixture and reserved water. Season with pepper and serve sprinkled with the remaining Parmesan.

**PER SERVING**   455Kcals, 17g protein, 19g fat, 5g saturated fat, 59g carbohydrates, 4.5g fibre, 0.9g salt

# linguine with **spinach** pesto

• QUICK RECIPE
• HEART HEALTHY

Adding spinach and peppers to a pesto sauce gives you an extra dose of the phytochemicals that offer valuable protection against age-related blindness.

**SERVES** 8   **PREPARATION** 15 minutes   **COOKING** 12 minutes

500g linguine
salt and ground black pepper, to taste
150g baby spinach leaves, tough stems removed
25g fresh basil leaves, finely chopped
3 garlic cloves
3 tablespoons walnuts
3 tablespoons olive oil
85ml freshly squeezed lemon juice
2 medium red peppers, seeded and cut into small dice
4 plum or round tomatoes, cut into small dice
20g grated Parmesan cheese

**1** Cook pasta in a large pan of lightly salted boiling water until al dente, following pack instructions.

**2** For the pesto, combine spinach, basil, garlic and walnuts in a food processor until finely chopped, or use a pestle and mortar. With the machine running, add olive oil, lemon juice, salt and pepper. Process or blend until smooth.

**3** Drain pasta. Transfer to a large serving bowl. Add spinach pesto, peppers and tomatoes. Toss gently to combine. Sprinkle with the Parmesan.

**PER SERVING**   317Kcals, 10g protein, 10g fat, 1.5g saturated fat, 49g carbohydrates, 3g fibre, 0.5g salt

# thai beef with green omelette

Basil, coriander and pepper bring hints of oriental flavour to this noodle, steak and omelette stir-fry.

**SERVES** 4  **PREPARATION** 15 minutes  **COOKING** 13 minutes

2 tablespoons sunflower or groundnut oil
1 green pepper, seeded and finely diced
4 eggs
1 teaspoon sesame oil
4 tablespoons chopped fresh coriander
8 fresh basil leaves, shredded
2 lemongrass stalks, chopped
1 garlic clove, chopped
250g lean frying steak, cut into fine strips
1 red pepper, seeded and cut into fine strips
200g mange-touts
6 spring onions
2 tablespoons fish sauce or soy sauce
400g Thai ribbon noodles, cooked according to the
   pack instructions, or use ready-to-wok noodles

**1** Preheat grill to high. Heat 1 tbsp oil in a large frying pan over medium-high heat. Add green pepper and cook for 2 to 3 minutes. Beat the eggs, 1 tsp sesame oil, coriander and basil together. Pour the mixture over the pepper, making sure the herbs are evenly distributed. Cook until egg has set and browned underneath, about 2 minutes. Put the pan under the hot grill to set the top of the omelette, about 2 minutes. Slide the omelette on to a board.

**2** Heat remaining oil in the same pan (or in a wok) over high heat and add the lemongrass, garlic and steak. Stir-fry until the beef is browned and cooked, about 3 minutes. Reduce the heat, if necessary. Add red pepper and mange-touts. Stir-fry for 3 minutes. Add spring onions, fish sauce or soy sauce and noodles. Stir-fry until the noodles are hot.

**3** Cut the omelette in half, then into thin strips. Divide the stir-fry among four large pasta bowls or plates and share the omelette strips among them.

**PER SERVING**  649Kcals, 37g protein, 23g fat, 6g saturated fat, 78g carbohydrate, 5.5g fibre, 2.6g salt

**2** of your **5 a day**

# penne with
# griddled aubergine

• HEART HEALTHY

Salting, and then griddling instead of frying, keeps the aubergine from absorbing too much oil and reduces the total fat content of the pasta dressing.

**SERVES** 4 **PREPARATION** 15 minutes
**STANDING TIME** 30 minutes **COOKING** 25 minutes

500g aubergine, cut lengthways
   into 2cm thick slices
salt and ground black pepper, to taste
2 tablespoons olive oil
4 garlic cloves, thinly sliced
750g plum or round tomatoes, halved,
   seeded and coarsely chopped
1 teaspoon chopped fresh oregano
   or ½ teaspoon dried
2 teaspoons balsamic vinegar
½ teaspoon sugar
non-stick cooking spray
250g penne
20g shaved or grated Parmesan cheese

**1** Sprinkle aubergine slices with ¼ tsp salt. Leave for a least 30 minutes to draw out liquid.

**2** Heat oil in a large non-stick frying pan over medium-low heat. Add garlic. Cook, stirring, 1 minute.

**3** Add tomatoes, oregano and ¼ tsp salt. Increase heat to medium. Cook until tomato is just softened, about 6 minutes. Stir in vinegar and sugar. Cook a further 30 seconds.

**4** Preheat a ridged griddle or grill to medium-high. Rinse aubergine slices; pat dry. Lightly coat both sides of aubergine with cooking spray.

**5** Griddle or grill aubergine until softened and, if griddling, dark grill marks score the surface, about 5 minutes each side. Set aside to cool slightly.

**6** Meanwhile, cook the pasta in a large pan of lightly salted boiling water until al dente, following pack instructions. Drain. Toss with the tomato mixture. Season with pepper. Coarsely chop aubergine. Add to pasta mixture. Stir in Parmesan. Serve.

**PER SERVING** 352Kcals, 12g protein, 10g fat, 2.5g saturated fat, 57g carbohydrates, 6g fibre, 0.6g salt

**3** of your **5 a day**

## on the menu

Serve with sliced smoked mozzarella cheese (available from specialist cheese shops) and Italian bread toasted and topped with roasted garlic (see page 278).

# pasta with prawns & cherry tomatoes

As well as having a wonderfully strong, sweet flavour, cherry tomatoes are an excellent source of vitamin C and vitamin A in the form of beta carotene.

**SERVES** 4　**PREPARATION** 10 minutes　**COOKING** 12 minutes

250g orecchiette or medium pasta shells
salt and ground black pepper, to taste
2 tablespoons olive oil
500g medium raw prawns, shelled and
　deveined, tails intact
3 garlic cloves, crushed
4 canned anchovy fillets
½ teaspoon crushed chilli flakes, or to taste
600g red cherry or baby plum tomatoes, halved
3 tablespoons fresh oregano leaves or 1 teaspoon
　dried, plus extra leaves to garnish (optional)
60g pitted green olives
2 tablespoons drained capers

**1** Cook pasta shells in a large pan of lightly salted boiling water until al dente, following pack instructions.

**2** Heat 1 tbsp oil in a large non-stick frying pan over medium-high heat. Add prawns and 2 crushed garlic cloves. Sauté until prawns just turn pink and curl, 2 to 3 minutes. Transfer to a plate.

**3** Heat remaining oil in the same pan. Add remaining garlic, the anchovies and crushed chilli flakes. Sauté until garlic has softened, about 30 seconds. Do not let it brown. Add the tomatoes and oregano. Sauté until tomato is softened, 3 to 4 minutes. Add cooked prawns, olives and capers.

**4** Drain pasta well. Toss with prawn and tomato mixture. Sprinkle with black pepper. Garnish with oregano, if using.

**PER SERVING** 418Kcals, 32g protein, 11g fat, 2g saturated fat, 52g carbohydrates, 4g fibre, 1.9g salt

1 of your 5 a day

# pasta salad with rocket & mozzarella

Rocket is a vitamin-packed, leafy base for a topping of penne, olives and fresh, and sun-dried tomatoes.

**SERVES** 4　**PREPARATION** 15 minutes　**COOKING** 10 minutes

250g penne
salt and ground black pepper, to taste
350g red and yellow cherry tomatoes, halved
½ small red onion, thinly sliced
125g rocket, chopped
100g hard mozzarella cheese, cut into 15mm cubes
4 sun-dried tomatoes, finely chopped and soaked
　in boiling water for 10 minutes
2 tablespoons pitted black olives, chopped
1 tablespoon olive oil
1 tablespoon balsamic vinegar

**1** Cook pasta in a large pan of lightly salted boiling water until al dente, following pack instructions. Drain; rinse under cold running water.

**2** Combine the cherry tomatoes, onion, rocket, mozzarella, sun-dried tomatoes, olives and cold pasta in a large bowl.

**3** Whisk the olive oil, balsamic vinegar, ½ tsp salt and some pepper in a small bowl. Add to pasta mixture. Toss well.

**PER SERVING** 343Kcals, 13g protein, 10g fat, 4g saturated fat, 52g carbohydrates, 3g fibre, 0.9g salt

1 of your 5 a day

## on the **menu**

To round off the meal, serve it with a salad of mixed lettuce leaves with a dressing of your choice and a crisp baguette. Finish up with a variety of apples and cheeses for dessert.

The tomatoes, pepper and white wine in Angel Hair with Clams & Roasted Pepper are classic foils for many types of seafood. You can substitute any firm-fleshed white fish for the scallops or use crab instead of the clams.

# angel hair with clams & roasted pepper

Peppers rich in cancer-fighting antioxidants are a foil for clams and scallops while a good amount of parsley adds more beta carotene and vitamin C to the mix.

**SERVES** 4   **PREPARATION** 10 minutes   **COOKING** 25 minutes

2 tablespoons olive oil
250g scallops
2 garlic cloves
125ml dry white wine
pinch of crushed chilli flakes
500g clams, scrubbed
400g can chopped tomatoes
1 large roasted red pepper from a jar,
   sliced
15g fresh flat-leaf parsley,
   roughly chopped
350g angel hair pasta
salt and ground black pepper, to taste

**1** Heat oil in a large non-stick pan over medium-high heat. Add scallops. Cook until almost cooked through, about 4 minutes. Transfer to a plate.

**2** Add garlic to pan. Cook 15 seconds. Add wine, crushed chilli flakes and clams. Cover. Reduce heat to medium. Cook until clams have all opened, about 8 minutes. Transfer clams with draining spoon to bowl. Discard any clams that have not opened.

**3** Add tomatoes to the pan. Simmer until reduced and thickened, about 15 minutes. Stir in the roasted pepper, clams, scallops and parsley.

**4** Cook angel hair pasta in a large pan of lightly salted boiling water until al dente, following pack instructions. Drain well. Add to sauce in pan. Season with pepper. Serve at once.

**PER SERVING** 493Kcals, 32g protein, 9g fat, 1.5g saturated fat, 75g carbohydrates, 4g fibre, 0.7g salt

1 of your 5 a day

# linguine with shiitake mushrooms

Use either shiitake or chestnut mushrooms to add an earthy taste to a sauce of ham, pepper and tomatoes.

**SERVES** 6   **PREPARATION** 10 minutes   **COOKING** 18 minutes

2 tablespoons olive oil
1 medium yellow pepper, trimmed,
   seeded and cut into small dice
250g shiitake mushroom caps, cut into thin strips,
   or chestnut mushrooms, sliced
125g lean ham, finely chopped
2 garlic cloves, crushed
2 x 400g cans whole tomatoes,
   drained and chopped
½ teaspoon dried basil
salt and ground black pepper, to taste
350g linguine
grated Parmesan cheese (optional)

**1** Heat oil in a large non-stick pan over medium-high heat. Add pepper, mushrooms, ham and garlic. Sauté until mushrooms are tender, 6 to 8 minutes. Add tomatoes and basil. Cook until thickened, about 10 minutes. Add a little salt and pepper to taste.

**2** Meanwhile, cook pasta in a large pan of lightly salted boiling water until al dente, following the pack instructions. Drain. Add to sauce in pan. Serve with Parmesan, if you like.

**PER SERVING** 290Kcals, 13g protein, 6g fat, 1g saturated fat, 49g carbohydrates, 4g fibre, 0.9g salt

2 of your 5 a day

• QUICK RECIPE

# tagliatelle with blue cheese

A rather smart version of cauliflower cheese uses broccoli for extra nutritional value, noodles and blue cheese for a more sophisticated sauce.

**SERVES** 4   **PREPARATION** 10 minutes   **COOKING** 15 minutes

250g spinach tagliatelle
salt and ground black pepper, to taste
250g broccoli florets, cut small
250g cauliflower florets, cut small
175g blue cheese, rind removed, diced
freshly grated nutmeg

**1** Cook pasta in large pan of lightly salted boiling water until al dente, following pack instructions. Add broccoli and cauliflower for the last 3 minutes of cooking time. Drain pasta and vegetables in a large colander.

**2** Rinse pan and return to a low heat. Add blue cheese. Cook, stirring often, until cheese melts into a smooth sauce.

**3** Add pasta and vegetables; stir gently to coat well and heat through. Season to taste with nutmeg, salt and pepper.

**PER SERVING**  435Kcals, 23g protein, 17g fat, 10g saturated fat, 49g carbohydrates, 4.5g fibre, 0.9g salt

# asian noodle salad

• QUICK RECIPE
• MAKE AHEAD

A Thai-style seasoning of basil, mint and coriander adds vitamin C and carotenoids to a dish already packed with vitamins, minerals, fibre and phytochemicals from its great mix of vegetables.

**SERVES** 6   **PREPARATION** 15 minutes   **COOKING** 10 minutes

350g wholewheat linguine
salt and ground black pepper, to taste
250g mange-touts, halved lengthways
3 medium carrots, peeled,
   cut into 5cm lengths,
   and thinly sliced lengthways
50g fresh basil leaves
15g fresh mint leaves
4 tablespoons fresh coriander leaves
2 garlic cloves
2 tablespoons toasted sesame oil
1 tablespoon vegetable oil
¼ teaspoon crushed chilli flakes
salt and ground black pepper
1 medium red pepper, seeded and thinly sliced
3 spring onions, finely chopped
2 tablespoons chopped unsalted
   dry-roasted peanuts

**1** Cook linguine in a large pan of lightly salted boiling water until al dente, following pack instructions. Add mange-touts and carrots for the last 2 minutes of cooking. Drain in a colander. Rinse under cold running water. Drain well.

**2** Put basil, mint, coriander, garlic, sesame oil, vegetable oil, crushed chilli flakes, ¼ tsp salt and black pepper in a food processor or a mortar and blend to form a paste.

**3** Combine linguine, mange-touts, carrots, pepper, spring onions, herb paste and ¼ tsp salt in a large bowl. Serve at room temperature or chilled. Garnish with peanuts.

**PER SERVING**  300Kcals, 11g protein, 10g fat, 1.5g saturated fat, 47g carbohydrates, 7g fibre, 0.6g salt

## on the **menu**

This salad stands alone as a lunch dish or even a light supper dish. For a more substantial dish, add some shredded cooked chicken, pork or beef. This salad also makes a good side dish to go with roasted or grilled meat or poultry.

# tortellini with squash & ricotta

A hearty, warming dish that will be a favourite to serve during the colder months.

**SERVES** 4   **PREPARATION** 15 minutes   **COOKING** 30 minutes

1 tablespoon olive oil
1 medium onion, finely chopped
750g butternut squash, seeded,
    peeled and cut into 2cm cubes
125ml vegetable or chicken stock
1 teaspoon dried sage
salt and ground black pepper, to taste
350g cheese tortellini
130g ricotta cheese
40g grated pecorino or Parmesan cheese
1 tablespoon finely chopped flat-leaf parsley,
    plus sprigs to garnish

**1** Heat oil in a large non-stick pan over medium heat. Add onion. Cook until golden, about 10 minutes. Add squash, stock, sage, ½ tsp salt and some black pepper. Cook, covered, until squash is just tender, about 20 minutes.

**2** Meanwhile, cook tortellini in a large pan of lightly salted water until al dente, following pack instructions. Drain. Toss with ricotta in a large bowl.

**3** Add squash, most of the pecorino or Parmesan cheese and the parsley to tortellini mixture. Toss gently. Sprinkle with remaining cheese. Garnish and serve.

**PER SERVING**  370Kcals, 18g protein, 19g fat,
9g saturated fat, 36g carbohydrates, 5g fibre, 2g salt

**2** of your **5 a day**

## helpful hint

Pecorino is an Italian hard cheese suitable for grating. Made from sheep's milk, its flavour is sharper than that of Parmesan, a hard grating cheese made from cow's milk. The two cheeses are interchangeable in many recipes, or you can combine them. Both are best freshly grated; you can now buy freshly grated Parmesan from supermarkets.

# meat tortellini with pepper sauce

• QUICK RECIPE

Convenience food can be a healthy option when you make smart choices: roasted peppers in jars provide significant amounts of beta carotene and vitamin C.

**SERVES** 4   **PREPARATION** 5 minutes   **COOKING** 10 minutes

350g meat-filled tortellini
salt and ground black pepper, to taste
280g jar roasted red peppers
2 garlic cloves
2 tablespoons olive oil
1 tablespoon salt-reduced soy sauce
15g cold butter, cut into small pieces
3 tablespoons shredded fresh basil leaves

**1** Cook tortellini in a large pan of lightly salted boiling water until al dente, following pack instructions.

**2** Purée peppers and their liquid, the garlic, oil and soy sauce in a food processor or blender. Transfer to a medium pan. Season with pepper. Simmer over low heat for 10 minutes.

**3** Drain tortellini. Just before serving, whisk cold butter into the purée and stir in the basil. Add tortellini. Toss to combine.

**PER SERVING**  275Kcals, 9g protein, 16g fat, 7g saturated fat, 23g carbohydrates, 3g fibre, 1.5g salt

½ of your 5 a day

## on the menu

Serve Meat Tortellini with Pepper Sauce with an accompaniment of lightly sautéed broccoli. Finish the meal with a refreshing fruit sorbet.

# cannelloni with spinach & mushrooms

• MAKE AHEAD

A filling of ricotta, mozzarella and spinach, and a sauce of tomatoes and mushrooms makes cannelloni into a healthy and delicious one-dish meal.

**SERVES** 4   **PREPARATION** 25 minutes   **COOKING** 40 minutes

8 cannelloni
salt and ground black pepper, to taste
2 teaspoons olive oil
1 small onion, finely chopped
250g frozen chopped spinach, thawed
260g ricotta cheese
120g coarsely grated hard mozzarella cheese
20g grated Parmesan cheese
1 teaspoon dried basil
¼ teaspoon garlic powder
330g tomato pasta sauce
300g mushrooms, sliced
basil leaves, to garnish (optional)

**1** Preheat oven to 180°C (160°C fan oven), gas 4. Cook cannelloni in a large pan of lightly salted boiling water for 8 minutes. Drain. Leave to cool slightly.

**2** Heat 1 tsp oil in a medium non-stick frying pan over medium heat. Add onion. Sauté until softened, 5 minutes. Briefly drain spinach in a colander; retain some liquid on the leaves. Combine spinach, ricotta, mozzarella, Parmesan, basil, garlic powder and ¼ tsp salt in a large bowl.

**3** Spread 50ml tomato sauce evenly over the base of a 32 x 22 x 5cm baking dish. Fill each cannelloni tube from both ends with spinach mixture. Arrange in baking dish in a single layer. Top with the remaining tomato sauce. Cover with foil. Cook until heated through, about 30 minutes.

**4** About 5 minutes before the end of the cooking time, heat the remaining oil in a frying pan over medium heat. Add the mushrooms and sauté until just slightly softened, 2 minutes. Serve cannelloni topped with mushrooms and garnished with basil, if you like.

**PER SERVING**  380Kcals, 23g protein, 19g fat, 10g saturated fat, 31g carbohydrates, 2g fibre, 1.9g salt

**2** of your **5 a day**

# parsnip and lentil shells

• MAKE AHEAD

Nutty-tasting fibre and protein-rich lentils are partnered with sweet parsnip for an unusual filling.

**SERVES** 4   **PREPARATION** 15 minutes   **COOKING** 1 hour 5 minutes

24 large pasta shells for stuffing, about 160g
300g parsnips, peeled and diced
500ml boiling water
225g red lentils
2 tablespoons olive oil
2 red peppers, seeded and finely sliced into strips
½ teaspoon sugar
2 x 400g cans chopped tomatoes
grated zest of 1 lemon and juice of ½ lemon
salt, to taste
6 tablespoons chopped fresh parsley
1 spring onion, chopped
100g Stilton cheese, crumbled or chopped

**1** Boil pasta shells in a large pan of water until just tender, 12 to 15 minutes. Drain and rinse under cold water. Set aside.

**2** Preheat oven to 220°C (200°C fan oven), gas 7. Put parsnips in a pan and add the boiling water. Cover and simmer 5 minutes. Add lentils, cover and cook over low heat until lentils are tender and water has been absorbed, 15 to 20 minutes.

**3** Meanwhile, heat oil in a pan over medium heat. Add peppers. Stir well, cover and cook until tender, 10 minutes. Stir in sugar, tomatoes, lemon juice. Pour into large baking dish or roasting tin.

**4** Beat a little salt into lentil mixture. Add 5 tbsp parsley, the lemon zest and spring onion. Fill the shells with the mixture. Put them on the tomato mixture. Sprinkle with Stilton. Bake until the cheese has melted and begins to brown, 15 minutes. Garnish with the remaining parsley and serve.

**PER SERVING** 577Kcals, 28g protein, 17g fat, 7g saturated fat, 83g carbohydrate, 10g fibre, 0.8g salt

**5** of your **5 a day**

# baked pasta with garlic & spinach

Here's an easy way to include more garlic in your diet and boost your immune system.

**SERVES** 8   **PREPARATION** 15 minutes   **COOKING** 45 minutes

non-stick cooking spray
500g penne or rigatoni
salt and ground black pepper, to taste
1 tablespoon olive oil
6 garlic cloves, thinly sliced
1 red pepper, seeded and chopped
250g frozen chopped spinach,
   thawed and squeezed dry
800g passata
260g ricotta cheese
120g grated hard mozzarella cheese
Kalamata olives and parsley, to garnish

**1** Preheat oven to 180°C (160°C fan oven), gas 4. Lightly coat a large baking dish with non-stick cooking spray. Cook penne in a large pan of lightly salted boiling water until tender, following pack instructions.

**2** Heat oil in a medium non-stick frying pan over medium-low heat. Add garlic and pepper. Sauté until golden, about 5 minutes. Add spinach and heat through, about 5 minutes. Transfer to a large bowl. Stir in passata and ricotta.

**3** Drain penne and add to bowl with black pepper. Transfer to baking dish. Top with mozzarella. Cover with foil.

**4** Bake for 25 minutes. Remove foil. Bake until lightly golden, about 10 minutes. Garnish with olives and parsley.

**PER SERVING**  370Kcals, 16g protein, 11g fat, 5g saturated fat, 55g carbohydrates, 2.5g fibre, 1.4g salt

**1** of your **5 a day**

---

# creamy macaroni cheese with tomatoes

Old-fashioned comfort food gets a flavour and vitamin boost from grated carrots and sliced tomatoes.

**SERVES** 8   **PREPARATION** 15 minutes   **COOKING** 30 minutes

non-stick cooking spray
500g macaroni
salt and ground black pepper, to taste
3 tablespoons vegetable oil
4 spring onions, coarsely chopped
35g plain flour
1 litre semi-skimmed milk, warmed
1 medium carrot, peeled and coarsely grated
2 tablespoons Dijon mustard
175g coarsely grated mature Cheddar cheese
40g grated Parmesan cheese
2 medium tomatoes, cored and sliced
60g fresh wholemeal breadcrumbs

**1** Preheat oven to 190°C (170°C fan oven), gas 5. Lightly coat a 33 x 22 x 5cm baking dish with non-stick cooking spray. Cook macaroni in a large pan of lightly salted boiling water until al dente, following pack instructions. Drain well; return to the pan.

**2** Heat oil in a large non-stick pan over medium heat. Add the spring onions and ¼ tsp salt. Cook, stirring occasionally, for 3 minutes. Gradually stir in flour. Cook 1 minute. Gradually stir in 250ml milk until thoroughly blended, then gradually stir in the remaining milk. Bring to the boil. Lower heat. Simmer, stirring, until lightly thickened, 2 to 3 minutes. Stir in the carrot and pepper to taste. Remove from heat. Stir in mustard, Cheddar and half the Parmesan.

**3** Fold sauce into the macaroni. Transfer mixture to baking dish. Place the tomatoes in single layer over the top. Combine remaining Parmesan and breadcrumbs; sprinkle over tomatoes. Bake until the filling is bubbling and the topping is lightly browned, about 20 minutes. Leave to stand 10 minutes.

**PER SERVING**  470Kcals, 20g protein, 16g fat, 8g saturated fat, 62g carbohydrates, 3g fibre, 1g salt

**½** of your **5 a day**

Use any short to medium stubby pasta shape in this macaroni cheese recipe; trottole, rigatoni, short fusilli, spirali, conchiglie, penne or farfalle are suitable. For children, try using fun shapes such as letters of the alphabet, animals and stars.

# vegetables, pulses & grains

## on the **menu**

These high-protein stuffed courgettes can be the centrepiece of a lunch or a dinner with the addition of wholegrain rolls and a salad of red and yellow cherry tomatoes.

# stuffed courgette gratin

• HEART HEALTHY

These courgette 'boats' filled with ricotta and Gruyère cheese are a good source of bone-building calcium.

**SERVES** 4   **PREPARATION** 15 minutes   **COOKING** 23 minutes
**REST** 10 minutes

4 medium courgettes
salt and ground black pepper, to taste
260g ricotta cheese
1 large egg, lightly beaten
30g Gruyère cheese, coarsely grated
1 teaspoon plain flour
½ teaspoon dried thyme
400g can sweetcorn, drained and rinsed
2 teaspoons vegetable oil
4 spring onions, thinly sliced
1 plum or round tomato, seeded
   and coarsely chopped
fresh parsley leaves, to garnish (optional)

**1** Preheat grill to medium-high. Cover a baking tray with foil.

**2** Cook courgettes in a large pan of lightly salted boiling water until softened, about 5 minutes. Drain. Rinse under cold running water.

**3** Halve courgettes lengthways. Scoop out centres, leaving a shell about 8mm thick. Coarsely chop flesh. Place courgette shells on baking tray.

**4** In a medium bowl, combine ricotta, egg, Gruyère, flour, thyme, ¼ tsp salt, black pepper and sweetcorn.

**5** Heat oil in a medium non-stick frying pan over medium-high heat. Add chopped courgettes, spring onions and tomato. Sauté until light golden and mixture is dry, about 8 minutes. Leave to cool slightly. Stir into the ricotta mixture. Spoon into the courgette halves.

**6** Grill until heated through and the filling is lightly browned, about 10 minutes. Leave to stand 10 minutes. Garnish, if you like, and serve.

**PER SERVING** 262Kcals, 15g protein, 13g fat, 7g saturated fat, 20g carbohydrates, 4g fibre, 1.3g salt

• MAKE AHEAD

# couscous-stuffed peppers

Chickpeas and couscous combine to give this low-calorie dish a high protein score.

**SERVES** 6   **PREPARATION** 20 minutes   **COOKING** 30 minutes

6 large peppers (a mixture of colours)
salt and ground black pepper, to taste
1 tablespoon vegetable oil
1 small courgette, finely chopped
2 garlic cloves, crushed
1 tablespoon freshly squeezed lemon juice
100g couscous soaked in 200ml boiling water
400g can chickpeas, drained and rinsed
1 medium ripe tomato, seeded
   and finely chopped
1 teaspoon dried oregano
75g feta cheese, crumbled

**1** Preheat oven to 180°C (160°C fan oven), gas 4. Slice tops off peppers to make lids. Scoop out seeds and membranes; discard. Simmer the peppers and lids in a large pan of lightly salted boiling water, covered, for 5 minutes. Drain, set aside.

**2** Heat oil in a medium pan over medium heat. Add courgette and garlic. Sauté 2 minutes. Stir in lemon juice. Cook 1 minute and remove from heat. Stir in the couscous, chickpeas, tomato, oregano, ½ tsp salt, pepper and feta.

**3** Fill each pepper with couscous mixture. Place upright in a shallow baking dish. Cover with pepper lids. Bake until filling is heated through, about 20 minutes.

**PER SERVING** 192Kcals, 8g protein, 7g fat, 2g saturated fat, 26g carbohydrate, 4.5g fibre, 0.8g salt

# barley risotto
## with asparagus & mushrooms

To reduce saturated fat, olive oil replaces the butter usually used in this Italian-style dish.

**SERVES** 4    **PREPARATION** 15 minutes    **COOKING** 40 minutes

840ml vegetable or chicken stock
2 tablespoons olive oil
1 medium onion, finely chopped
250g mixed mushrooms, coarsely chopped
2 garlic cloves, crushed
200g pearl barley
250g asparagus, trimmed and cut into
   bite-sized pieces, leaving tips whole
40g grated Parmesan cheese

**1** Heat the stock and 500ml water in a medium pan to just below a simmer. Cover; keep at a simmer.

**2** Heat oil in a large, deep, non-stick frying pan over medium heat. Sauté onion until slightly softened, about 3 minutes. Add chopped mushrooms and garlic. Sauté until mushrooms soften, 5 minutes. Stir in the barley. Stir in 500ml hot stock mixture. Simmer, covered, 15 minutes.

**3** Blanch asparagus tips in the stock liquid in the pan for 2 minutes. Transfer to a plate with a slotted spoon.

**4** Add more hot stock to the barley mixture, a ladleful at a time, stirring frequently. Each addition of liquid must be fully absorbed before any more is added. When adding the last of the stock, stir in asparagus stems and Parmesan. Serve the risotto topped with asparagus tips.

**PER SERVING** 354Kcals, 19g protein, 12g fat, 3.5g saturated fat, 48g carbohydrates, 2g fibre, 1.2g salt

**1** of your **5 a day**

# vegetable lattice pie

A multitude of favourite vegetables and a hint of cheese are crammed into a vitamin-packed pie.

**SERVES** 6    **PREPARATION** 20 minutes
**COOKING** 55 minutes    **REST** 10 minutes

25g butter
2 medium celery sticks, coarsely chopped
1 medium onion, coarsely chopped
1 large carrot, peeled and cut
   into small chunks
1 small red pepper, seeded
   and coarsely chopped
¾ teaspoon dried thyme
3 tablespoons plain flour
250ml vegetable stock
75g broccoli florets, cut small
100g cauliflower florets, cut small
6 baby white onions or the bulbs
   of spring onions
60g Cheddar cheese, cut into small cubes
375g shortcrust pastry, thawed if frozen
flour, for dusting

**1** Melt butter in a large non-stick pan over medium heat. Add celery, chopped onion, carrot, pepper and thyme. Sauté until vegetables are tender, 10 minutes.

**2** Stir in the flour until thoroughly combined. Stir in stock. Increase heat to medium-high. Add broccoli, cauliflower and onions. Bring to the boil. Lower heat and simmer, uncovered, 15 minutes. Remove pan from heat. (If making filling ahead, leave it to cool to room temperature. Cover and chill.)

**3** Preheat oven to 200°C (180°C fan oven), gas 6. Spread the vegetable mixture in a 23cm pie dish. Top with cheese. Brush the dish edge with water. Cover with latticed pastry (see Hint) or roll out pastry, cover pie, trim edges and cut six long slits in top to let the steam escape. Put the dish on a baking sheet.

**4** Bake until pastry is golden and filling is bubbling, 25 to 30 minutes. Leave to stand 10 minutes before serving.

**PER SERVING** 392Kcals, 10g protein, 25g fat, 10g saturated fat, 35g carbohydrates, 3g fibre, 1.1g salt

**1** of your **5 a day**

## helpful **hint**

To make a lattice pie crust, roll out dough 10 or 15cm wide and longer than the pie plate by 5 cm. Cut into thin strips (10 or 12 will be enough). Starting at the edge of the plate, weave the strips over the pie, lifting up those made in one direction where necessary, to enable you to weave strips in the other direction. Neatly trim the ends.

# carrot-courgette soufflé

An impressive and sophisticated dish – and a good way to get more antioxidants into your diet.

**SERVES** 8   **PREPARATION** 15 minutes   **COOKING** 1 hour 5 minutes

500g carrots, peeled and cut
    into 1.5cm thick slices
non-stick cooking spray
2 tablespoons vegetable oil
1 small onion, coarsely chopped
2 tablespoons plain flour
125ml semi-skimmed milk
4 large eggs, separated
1 medium courgette, grated
½ teaspoon salt
ground black pepper, to taste
¼ teaspoon freshly grated nutmeg

**1** Steam carrots until tender in a medium pan over simmering water, about 20 minutes. Purée in blender.

**2** Preheat oven to 200°C (180°C fan oven), gas 6. Coat a 2 litre soufflé dish with non-stick cooking spray.

**3** Heat oil in a small pan over medium heat. Add onion. Sauté until softened, about 5 minutes. Stir in the flour. Cook, stirring occasionally, 1 minute. Stir in milk. Bring to the boil, stirring constantly. Transfer to a large bowl. Stir in carrot and egg yolks. Fold in courgette. Stir in salt, pepper and nutmeg.

**4** Whisk egg whites in a medium bowl until soft peaks form. Fold whites, a third at a time, into vegetable mixture. Spoon into the prepared dish. Bake until puffed and golden, 30 to 40 minutes. Serve at once.

**PER SERVING** 124Kcals, 6g protein, 7g fat, 1.5g saturated fat, 10g carbohydrates, 2g fibre, 0.4g salt

**1** of your **5 a day**

## helpful hint

The slightest amount of fat from butter, oil or egg yolk will prevent egg whites from forming soft peaks when whipped. To avoid this, make sure the bowl is clean and the egg whites are carefully separated, with not a speck of yolk.

# vegetable tart provençale

- MAKE AHEAD
- HEART HEALTHY

A thyme-flavoured pastry case makes a tasty container for nutrition-packed vegetables: tomatoes, onions and courgettes containing vitamin C, antioxidants, beta carotene and lycopene, to fight against cancer and heart disease.

**SERVES** 4  **PREPARATION** 20 minutes  **COOKING** 45 minutes

non-stick cooking spray
2 large white onions, cut into thin wedges
210g plain flour, plus extra for dusting
1½ teaspoons fresh thyme leaves,
    chopped
½ teaspoon salt
85ml iced water
2 tablespoons olive oil
2 large courgettes, about 200g each
4 medium tomatoes, cut into thin wedges
2 tablespoons grated Parmesan cheese

**1** Coat a large non-stick frying pan with non-stick cooking spray and set over medium-high heat until hot. Reduce heat to medium-low. Add onions; sauté until very soft and golden, 20 minutes. Transfer to a plate.

**2** Preheat oven to 200°C (180°C fan oven), gas 6. Mix flour, thyme and half the salt in a large bowl. Mix in water and oil until a soft dough forms. Lightly sprinkle work surface with flour and roll out dough into a 35 x 25cm rectangle or 32cm round. Fold in half and transfer to 32 x 22cm tart pan or 28cm round tart pan with removable base. Trim the edges.

**3** Cut courgettes diagonally into long, 2.5cm thick slices. Coat frying pan again with cooking spray and set over medium heat. Add courgettes and sauté until golden, 5 to 7 minutes.

**4** Arrange courgettes, tomatoes and onions in rows on the pastry base, standing them up and overlapping them slightly. Sprinkle with remaining salt and the Parmesan. Bake until crust is golden, about 20 minutes. Serve warm.

**PER SERVING** 314Kcals, 11g protein, 9g fat, 2.5g saturated fat, 49g carbohydrates, 4g fibre, 0.7g salt

**3** of your **5 a day**

## did you know...

...that 'provençale' refers to Provence, on the Mediterranean in southern France? The region produces, olives, onions, tomatoes, garlic and dozens of herbs such as rosemary, thyme and marjoram in profusion and they are the basis of a flavoursome, robust cuisine that is loved around the world.

## did you know...

...that tofu is made by coagulating the protein of soya beans into curds? It has a high calcium, high protein and high fat content. With no flavour of its own, tofu absorbs the flavours of other ingredients and adds a silken texture to dishes.

# fried rice with • HEART HEALTHY
# tofu & vegetables

Incorporate high-quality vegetable protein from tofu into your diet with this fresh, light dish.

**SERVES** 4   **PREPARATION** 20 minutes
**MARINATING** 1 hour   **COOKING** 20 minutes

250ml dry white wine or vegetable stock
60ml salt-reduced soy sauce
2 tablespoons honey
2.5cm piece fresh root ginger,
   peeled and grated
350g firm tofu, cut into 2.5cm cubes
200g long-grain rice
non-stick cooking spray
2 garlic cloves, crushed
500g frozen mixed stir-fry vegetables,
   slightly thawed
5 spring onions, cut into 5cm pieces
¼ teaspoon pepper
1 large egg, lightly beaten

**1** Combine wine or stock, 1 tbsp of the soy sauce, the honey and 1 tsp gated ginger in a large plastic bag. Add tofu. Press out excess air; close bag. Shake bag gently to coat tofu with marinade. Marinate in fridge 1 hour; turn occasionally.

**2** Cook the rice according to pack instructions; keep warm. Lightly coat a wok or large frying pan with non-stick cooking spray. Set over high heat until hot but not smoking.

**3** Stir-fry garlic and remaining ginger until fragrant, about 1 minute. Add mixed vegetables, half the spring onions, the rice, the remaining soy sauce and the pepper. Stir-fry until mixed vegetables are heated through, about 4 minutes. Push ingredients to one side of wok, and then pour in beaten egg. Cook until almost set. Cut into strips.

**4** Pour marinade into a small pan. Boil over high heat for 2 minutes. Add tofu and marinade to wok. Stir-fry until tofu is heated through, about 4 minutes. Sprinkle with spring onions.

**PER SERVING** 362Kcals, 21g protein, 8g fat, 1.5g saturated fat, 53g carbohydrates, 3.5g fibre, 1.7g salt

# thai-style stir-fry • QUICK RECIPE

Ginger, chillies, garlic and spring onions give powerful antioxidant protection against chronic disease.

**SERVES** 4   **PREPARATION** 15 minutes   **COOKING** 6 minutes

125ml vegetable stock
60ml freshly squeezed lime juice
2 tablespoons salt-reduced soy sauce
2 teaspoons sugar
2 teaspoons cornflour
2 tablespoons vegetable oil
4 garlic cloves, crushed
2.5cm piece fresh root ginger,
   peeled and finely chopped
2 serrano or jalapeño chillies,
   seeded and finely chopped
1 medium red pepper, seeded and
   cut into small squares
4 spring onions, thinly sliced
1 medium courgette, diced
125g baby corn
125g Chinese leaves, shredded
500g firm tofu, cut into 1.25cm cubes

**1** Whisk the stock, lime juice, soy sauce, sugar and cornflour in a small bowl until smooth.

**2** Heat 2 tsp oil in a non-stick wok or large frying pan over medium-high heat. Add garlic, ginger and chillies. Stir-fry 30 seconds. Add to stock mixture.

**3** Heat remaining oil in wok. Add pepper, spring onions and courgette. Stir-fry until crisp-tender, 2 to 3 minutes. Add corn and Chinese leaves. Stir-fry 1 minute. Add tofu and stock mixture. Cover and simmer 2 minutes. Serve at once.

**PER SERVING** 261Kcals, 17g protein, 14g fat, 2g saturated fat, 19g carbohydrates, 2g fibre, 1g salt

# four-bean **chilli** **bake** with polenta topping

• MAKE AHEAD

Polenta and beans contain plenty of fibre, while the mixture of vegetables add vitamins, folate and antioxidants to fight disease.

**SERVES** 6 **PREPARATION** 15 minutes
**COOKING** 50 minutes **REST** 15 minutes

1 tablespoon vegetable oil
1 medium onion, finely chopped
1 medium red pepper, seeded and coarsely chopped
3 garlic cloves, crushed
2 medium carrots, peeled and cut into small dice
2 small courgettes, halved lengthways
   and cut crossways into thin slices
2 tablespoons chilli powder
2 teaspoons cumin
2 x 400g cans tomatoes,
   drained and roughly chopped
400g can black beans or black-eyed beans,
   drained and rinsed
400g red kidney beans, drained and rinsed
400g can pinto or cannellini beans, drained and rinsed
400g can chickpeas, drained and rinsed
250g polenta
½ teaspoon salt
180g Cheddar cheese, coarsely grated
fresh coriander sprigs, to garnish

**1** Heat oil in a large non-stick pan over medium heat. Add onion and pepper. Cook until softened, 5 minutes. Stir in garlic. Cook 30 seconds. Add carrots. Cover; cook 2 minutes. Add courgettes, chilli powder and cumin. Cook 1 minute. Stir in tomatoes. Bring to the boil, lower heat and simmer, partially covered, for 15 minutes, stirring occasionally.

**2** Stir in the three types of beans and the chickpeas. Heat through. Remove half the bean mixture; chill or freeze in an airtight dish to use for another meal.

**3** Preheat oven to 200°C (180°C fan oven), gas 6. Bring 1 litre water to the boil in a medium pan. Combine 250ml water, the polenta and salt in a medium bowl. Gradually stir the polenta mixture into the boiling water. Simmer gently, stirring constantly, until polenta is no longer gritty, 5 minutes.

**4** Spread half the polenta over the base of a 20 x 20 x 5cm baking dish. Spoon the remaining chilli mixture over polenta. Reserve 2 tbsp cheese. Sprinkle the remainder over the chilli. Spread remaining polenta on top. Sprinkle evenly with the remaining cheese.

**5** Bake until filling is bubbling and the top is golden brown, about 20 minutes. Leave to stand 15 minutes. Cut into rectangles to serve. Garnish with coriander.

**PER SERVING** 548Kcals, 28g protein, 15g fat, 7g saturated fat, 76g carbohydrates, 16g fibre, 3g salt

**3** of your **5 a day**

# chilli with beans, tomatoes & sweetcorn

• HEART HEALTHY

Clear your arteries with the fibre from two kinds of beans, the vitamin C in the carrots and the vitamins C, B$_6$ and folate found in the peppers.

**SERVES** 6   **PREPARATION** 15 minutes   **COOKING** 45 minutes

2 tablespoons vegetable oil
1 large onion, finely chopped
1 medium red pepper, seeded
   and coarsely chopped
1 small carrot, peeled and diced
1 small celery stick, diced
4 garlic cloves, crushed
3 tablespoons chilli powder
2 tablespoons paprika
2 teaspoons dried oregano
1 teaspoon ground cumin
2 x 400g cans tomatoes with their liquid,
   roughly chopped
2 x 400g cans cannellini beans,
   drained and rinsed
400g can black beans or red kidney beans,
   drained and rinsed
60ml salt-reduced soy sauce
300g frozen sweetcorn
fresh coriander leaves, to garnish

**1** Heat oil in a large non-stick pan over medium-high heat. Add onion, pepper, carrot, celery and garlic. Cook until vegetables are softened, about 5 minutes. Stir in chilli powder, paprika, oregano and cumin. Cook 1 minute.

**2** Add tomatoes, beans, 250ml water and soy sauce to pan. Simmer, uncovered, 30 minutes, stirring occasionally. Stir in sweetcorn. Simmer a further 10 minutes. Garnish and serve.

**PER SERVING** 293Kcals, 15g protein, 6g fat, 0.8g saturated fat, 49g carbohydrates, 13g fibre, 2.9g salt

**4** of your **5 a day**

**fresh ideas**
Although black beans, white beans and sweetcorn are a hearty foundation for this protein-rich vegetarian chilli, any bean will do. You can also substitute an equal amount of canned (or cooked from dry) lentils for the beans used in this recipe. If you use lentils, add them with the sweetcorn for the final 10 minutes of cooking.

# open grilled vegetable sandwich

Fresh asparagus and big chunky mushrooms provide a wide range of the B vitamins that your body needs for maximum energy production.

**SERVES** 4   **PREPARATION** 15 minutes   **COOKING** 14 minutes

2 tablespoons olive oil
1 tablespoon balsamic vinegar
¼ teaspoon salt
ground black pepper, to taste
4 large, flat mushrooms, stems removed
1 small bunch asparagus,
   trimmed and halved
1 large red pepper, halved and seeded
4 large slices Italian bread, such as ciabatta
100g goat's cheese

**1** Preheat grill to high. Whisk olive oil, balsamic vinegar, salt and pepper in a small bowl. Brush mushrooms, asparagus and pepper with the mixture.

**2** Grill vegetables, turning once, until tender. Allow about 10 minutes for asparagus and pepper, and about 12 minutes for mushrooms. Peel off the skin and slice pepper when it is cool enough to handle.

**3** Turn off grill. Place bread on grill rack and grill until warm, about 2 minutes.

**4** Spread bread with goat's cheese. Put mushrooms on each slice. Top with pepper and asparagus. Serve warm.

**PER SERVING** 250Kcals, 11g protein, 14g fat, 6g saturated fat, 21g carbohydrates, 3g fibre, 1g salt

**1** of your **5 a day**

# mixed salad greens pizza

Don't serve pizza with a salad on the side; combine the two to create a light and healthy one-dish meal.

**SERVES** 4   **PREPARATION** 20 minutes   **COOKING** 20 minutes

2 tablespoons polenta
1 large ready-made pizza base,
   thawed if frozen
20g grated Parmesan cheese
2 tablespoons balsamic vinegar
1 tablespoon Dijon mustard
1 teaspoon soft light brown sugar
¼ teaspoon salt
350g plum or round tomatoes,
   cut into thin wedges
1 medium red onion, halved and thinly sliced
240g hard mozzarella, coarsely grated
200g mixed salad leaves

**1** Preheat oven to 220°C (200°C fan oven), gas 7. Sprinkle a large baking sheet with polenta and place pizza base on top. Sprinkle Parmesan over the top. Bake until Parmesan starts to brown and pizza begins to puff, about 15 minutes.

**2** Whisk vinegar, mustard, brown sugar and salt in a large bowl. Add tomatoes and onion, and toss to combine. Set aside.

**3** Top pizza with mozzarella and return to oven. Bake until cheese has melted and pizza base is crisp, about 5 minutes.

**4** Add salad leaves to tomato mixture; toss to coat. Scatter salad over hot pizza and serve.

**PER SERVING** 465Kcals, 21g protein, 18g fat, 9g saturated fat, 57g carbohydrates, 3g fibre, 1.5g salt

**2** of your **5 a day**

## on the menu

Pizza needs little, if any, accompaniment and is a sustaining meal in itself. Serve with fruit juice diluted with sparkling water and topped with mint.

# vegetable
# side dishes

# roasted asparagus with parmesan

• QUICK RECIPE

Make this simple dish with the freshest new season asparagus. Remember to always store fresh asparagus in the fridge or it will lose half its vitamin C and much of its flavour in just two or three days.

**SERVES** 4   **PREPARATION** 10 minutes   **COOKING** 12 minutes

500g asparagus, trimmed
1 medium red pepper, seeded and
   cut lengthways into thin strips
1 tablespoon olive oil
1 tablespoon balsamic vinegar
30g Parmesan cheese, in one piece
ground black pepper, to taste

**1** Preheat oven to 240°C (220°C fan oven), gas 9. Place asparagus and pepper strips in a large shallow baking dish. Drizzle with the oil and toss to coat.

**2** Roast until crisp-tender, 10 to 12 minutes, turning occasionally. Transfer to a serving dish.

**3** Sprinkle with vinegar. Toss to coat. Using a vegetable peeler, shave cheese into thin curls over vegetables. Season with pepper.

**PER SERVING** 104Kcals, 7g protein, 6g fat,
2g saturated fat, 6g carbohydrates, 3g fibre, 0.2g salt

**2** of your **5 a day**

## helpful hint

Roasted vegetables are an ideal accompaniment for roast meat or poultry. When the roast goes into the oven, prepare the vegetables and place them in a roasting tin with oil and seasonings. When the roast comes out of the oven, turn up the heat and put in the vegetables. They will have enough time to cook while the roast poultry or meat rests before it's ready to carve. Turn the vegetables once or twice to brown them evenly.

# stir-fried asparagus & mange-touts

• QUICK RECIPE

This green vegetable medley is loaded with nutrients that are essential for giving infants the best start in life and at the same time prevent age-related diseases.

**SERVES** 4   **PREPARATION** 10 minutes   **COOKING** 4 minutes

1 tablespoon olive oil
500g asparagus, trimmed, stalks cut diagonally into
   2.5cm lengths, leaving tips about 5cm long
125g mange-touts
4 spring onions, thinly sliced
¼ teaspoon salt
ground black pepper, to taste
1 small garlic clove
crushed zest of ½ lemon, cut into thin strips
2 tablespoons finely chopped fresh parsley

Heat oil in a large non-stick frying pan or wok over medium-high heat. Add asparagus, mange-touts, spring onions, salt and pepper. Stir-fry until vegetables are almost crisp-tender, 2 to 3 minutes. Add garlic, zest and parsley. Stir-fry 1 minute.

**PER SERVING** 70Kcals, 5g protein, 3.5g fat, 0.5g
saturated fat, 4g carbohydrates, 2.5g fibre, 0.3g salt

**2** of your **5 a day**

# balsamic beetroot with pecan nuts

• QUICK RECIPE

High in natural sugars, beetroot takes on both delicate and more feisty flavours and is a great energy booster.

**SERVES** 4 **PREPARATION** 5 minutes **COOKING** 10 minutes

3 tablespoons chopped pecan nuts
2 tablespoons balsamic vinegar
1 teaspoon sugar
2 teaspoons butter or margarine
3 medium beetroots, steamed, peeled
 and sliced or 250g pack cooked beetroot
 without vinegar, sliced

**1** Toast the pecan nuts in a medium non-stick frying pan over medium heat, stirring often, until browned, about 4 minutes. Take care not to burn. Transfer to a plate.

**2** Heat the vinegar, sugar and butter or margarine in the same pan over medium-low heat. Add the beetroots. Cook, stirring often, until heated through and all the liquid is absorbed, about 5 minutes. Top with pecan nuts. Serve.

**PER SERVING** 122Kcals, 2.5g protein, 7g fat, 2g saturated fat, 12g carbohydrates, 2.5g fibre, 0.3g salt

**1** of your **5 a day**

• QUICK RECIPE

# creamy broccoli & cauliflower

Rich in antioxidants, the carrot juice in the creamy sauce makes it every bit as healthy as the vegetables.

**SERVES** 4 **PREPARATION** 10 minutes **COOKING** 15 minutes

125ml carrot juice
3 tablespoons soured cream
150g broccoli florets
210g cauliflower florets

**1** Bring the carrot juice to the boil in a small pan over high heat. Boil until reduced by about half, about 8 minutes. Remove from heat. Whisk in soured cream.

**2** Steam broccoli and cauliflower until crisp-tender, about 5 minutes. Transfer to a serving dish. Serve with the soured cream sauce.

**PER SERVING** 56Kcals, 3.5g protein, 3g fat, 1.5g saturated fat, 4g carbohydrates, 1.5g fibre, 0.01g salt

**½** of your **5 a day**

## helpful hint

Beetroot stains are often difficult to remove from cutting boards. To save your work surfaces, peel steamed beetroots by first cutting off both ends over the sink and then holding the beetroot under cold running water while you peel off the skins. Coat the cutting board lightly with non-stick cooking spray before slicing. This may not prevent staining altogether, but it will help.

## on the **menu**

Drizzle the broccoli and cauliflower with the creamy
sauce, or serve the sauce separately in a small bowl
so that guests can use it as a dip.

# stir-fried pak choi with mange-touts

- QUICK RECIPE
- HEART HEALTHY

Pak choi has more of the disease-fighting antioxidant beta carotene than other types of cabbage. It is low in calories, has no fat and is a rich source of fibre and vitamin C. Crunchy mange-touts are a good partner.

**SERVES** 4   **PREPARATION** 10 minutes   **COOKING** 10 minutes

2 teaspoons olive oil
1 medium carrot, peeled and
   cut into matchsticks
3cm piece fresh root ginger,
   peeled and cut into slivers
500g pak choi, cut into very thin slices
250g mange-touts, trimmed
finely grated zest of ½ orange
4 tablespoons orange juice
1 tablespoon brown sugar
1 tablespoon salt-reduced soy sauce
½ teaspoon salt
1 teaspoon cornflour blended
   with 1 tablespoon water

**1** Heat 60ml water and the oil in a large non-stick frying pan over medium heat. Add carrot and ginger. Cook, stirring frequently, until carrot is crisp-tender, about 3 minutes.

**2** Add pak choi, mange-touts, orange zest and juice, brown sugar, soy sauce and salt. Cover and cook 3 minutes, or until pak choi begins to wilt.

**3** Uncover and cook, stirring frequently, until pak choi is crisp-tender, about 2 minutes. Stir in the cornflour mixture and cook, stirring constantly, until vegetables are evenly coated, about 1 minute.

**PER SERVING**  116Kcals, 6g protein, 3g fat, 0.5g saturated fat, 18g carbohydrates, 4g fibre, 1.3g salt

**2** of your **5 a day**

## fresh ideas

When you're cooking a member of the cabbage family – and that includes Brussels sprouts, broccoli, pak choi and cauliflower – you can always use the seasoning from one dish to flavour another one. For example, any of these vegetables can be lightly steamed and served with the simple mustard sauce that accompanies the Brussels sprouts and potato mixture (right).

• QUICK RECIPE

# mustard-glazed
# brussels sprouts
# & new potatoes

The slight sharpness of Brussels sprouts provide a taste contrast to the mellow new potatoes.

**SERVES** 4   **PREPARATION** 10 minutes   **COOKING** 15 minutes

300g Brussels sprouts, halved if large
350g red or white new potatoes,
   unpeeled and halved if large
1 tablespoon olive oil
1 shallot or ¼ onion, finely chopped
60g lean ham or prosciutto,
   trimmed and chopped
2 teaspoons Dijon mustard
¼ teaspoon salt
ground black pepper, to taste

**1** Steam Brussels sprouts and new potatoes until tender, 8 to 10 minutes. Drain.

**2** Heat oil in large non-stick frying pan over medium-high heat. Add shallot or onion. Sauté until softened, 2 to 3 minutes. Stir in ham or prosciutto and mustard. Add Brussels sprouts, potatoes, salt and pepper. Heat through, about 2 minutes. Serve at once.

**PER SERVING** 142Kcals, 7.5g protein, 5g fat, 0.8g saturated fat, 19g carbohydrates, 4g fibre, 0.9g salt

½ of your 5 a day

## on the **menu**

Mustard-Glazed Brussels Sprouts & New Potatoes makes a good accompaniment to roast turkey or duck. A mixed green salad will lighten the menu. Serve grapes or slices of melon for dessert.

Many apples are suitable both for cooking and eating, but some varieties work better in recipes than others. Cooking apples, such as Bramley, cook to a soft purée and are ideal for pies but are not suitable for dishes like this one. Dessert apples that are firmer and more tart are best for dishes such as this – Granny Smith and Braeburn are both good. They can withstand longer cooking times without disintegrating.

# braised cabbage with apple & caraway

• QUICK RECIPE
• HEART HEALTHY

A terrific mixture of interesting flavours and textures, from sweet to nutty. The protective phytochemicals in cabbage are particularly effective against hormone-related diseases such as breast cancer.

**SERVES** 4   **PREPARATION** 15 minutes   **COOKING** 15 minutes

2 tablespoons chopped walnuts (optional)
2 teaspoons vegetable oil
1 small onion, finely chopped
¾ teaspoon caraway seeds
500g green cabbage, cored
    and thinly sliced
1 tablespoon rice wine vinegar
    or cider vinegar
½ teaspoon salt
2 small crisp red apples such as Royal Gala,
    cored and cut into small cubes
1 teaspoon honey

**1** Toast walnuts in a wok or large non-stick frying pan over medium heat, stirring often, until browned, about 3 minutes. Set aside. Heat oil in wok over medium heat. Add onion and caraway seeds. Sauté until onion is softened, about 5 minutes.

**2** Stir in cabbage, vinegar and salt. Cover. Cook until cabbage begins to wilt, about 4 minutes. Uncover. Increase heat to high. Add apples and honey. Cook, stirring frequently, until apple is crisp-tender and most of the liquid has evaporated, 4 to 6 minutes. Transfer to a serving plate. Top with walnuts and serve.

**PER SERVING** 134Kcals, 4g protein, 7g fat, 0.8g saturated fat, 14g carbohydrates, 4.5g fibre, 0.5g salt

½ of your 5 a day

## helpful hint

One secret to successful stir-frying is to get the wok or frying pan very hot before adding the oil. This helps to prevent food from sticking. Stir-fry vegetables in small batches rather than piling them into the pan. If they're crowded, they will start to steam and lose the crisp-tender texture that is characteristic of a stir-fry.

# chinese leaves with ginger

• QUICK RECIPE

A lively alternative to a more straightforward cabbage-based dish, given extra crunch and spice.

**SERVES** 4   **PREPARATION** 10 minutes   **COOKING** 6 minutes

1 tablespoon vegetable oil
2.5cm piece fresh root ginger,
    peeled and finely chopped
450g Chinese leaves or pak choi,
    coarsely chopped
¼ teaspoon salt
60ml vegetable or chicken stock
1 tablespoon chopped roasted peanuts

**1** Heat a wok or large non-stick frying pan over high heat. Add oil and ginger. Cook 30 seconds. Add Chinese leaves or pak choi. Stir-fry 2 minutes. Add salt and stock. Cover. Cook until almost wilted, about 2 minutes.

**2** Remove pan from heat. Leave, covered, 1 minute. Sprinkle with peanuts and serve.

**PER SERVING** 78Kcals, 4g protein, 5g fat, 1g saturated fat, 5g carbohydrates, 2.5g fibre, 0.4g salt

1 of your 5 a day

## carrots **parmesan**

There's plenty of vitamin A in every serving, in the protective form of beta carotene.

**SERVES** 6 **PREPARATION** 6 minutes **COOKING** 30 minutes

2 tablespoons olive oil
500g carrots, peeled and
    cut diagonally into thin slices
¼ teaspoon salt
ground black pepper, to taste
2 tablespoons grated Parmesan cheese

**1** Heat oil in a medium non-stick pan over medium-low heat. Add carrots. Cover. Cook just until carrots are tender, about 15 minutes.

**2** Increase heat to medium. Cook, uncovered, until lightly browned, stirring occasionally, about 15 minutes. Season with salt and pepper. Sprinkle with Parmesan just before serving.

**PER SERVING** 83Kcals, 2g protein, 5g fat, 1.5g saturated fat, 7g carbohydrates, 2g fibre, 0.3g salt

**1** of your **5 a day**

## on the **menu**

Carrots Parmesan is a simple yet sophisticated dish. Serve with baked ham and new potatoes, with strawberries and fresh pineapple for dessert.

• QUICK RECIPE
• HEART HEALTHY

# roasted carrots
## with rosemary

Eating carrots can reduce cholesterol levels, in turn decreasing the risk of heart disease.

**SERVES** 6 **PREPARATION** 10 minutes **COOKING** 20 minutes

500g large carrots, peeled and
    cut into matchsticks
¼ teaspoon salt
1½ teaspoons olive oil
1 teaspoon fresh rosemary leaves
    or ½ teaspoon dried, plus fresh
    sprigs to garnish (optional)

**1** Preheat oven to 200°C (180°C fan oven), gas 6. Mound carrot sticks on a baking tray. Sprinkle with salt and drizzle with oil. Toss gently to coat. Spread out in a single layer.

**2** Roast 10 minutes. Stir in rosemary. Roast until crisp-tender and lightly browned in places, 7 to 10 minutes. Garnish, if you like, and serve.

**PER SERVING** 35Kcals, 0.5g protein, 1g fat, 0.2g saturated fat, 6.5g carbohydrates, 2g fibre, 0.2g salt

**1** of your **5 a day**

• QUICK RECIPE
• HEART HEALTHY

# braised carrot,
## celery & fennel

Low in calories, celery is also a source of fibre
and potassium. Both raw or cooked, its taste
complements a range of other vegetables.

**SERVES** 4   **PREPARATION** 10 minutes   **COOKING** 18 minutes

4 large carrots, peeled,
    halved lengthways and cut
    into thin 5cm long pieces
3 celery sticks, cut into thin 5cm long pieces
1 small red onion, sliced
½ fennel bulb, cored and thinly sliced
420ml chicken stock
salt and pepper, to taste
2 teaspoons butter
roughly chopped fresh parsley, to garnish

**1** In a large pan over medium-high heat, gently simmer carrots,
celery, onion and fennel in the stock, covered, until the
vegetables are tender, about 15 minutes.

**2** Uncover pan. Boil until liquid has reduced slightly,
2 to 3 minutes. Season to taste with salt and pepper.
Stir in the butter and serve garnished with parsley.

**PER SERVING** 84Kcals, 5g protein, 3g fat, 2g saturated
fat, 10g carbohydrates, 3g fibre, 0.7g salt

**1** of your **5 a day**

## helpful **hint**

Combining vegetables can make a simple side dish
into something much more exciting. Make sure you
choose vegetables that will cook in the same amount
of time. Try parsnips and carrots, for example, or
courgettes and tomatoes. Others can be matched if
you parboil the one that needs more cooking, such as
potato, before combining it with one that cooks faster,
such as leeks. Use seasonings that suit both
vegetables.

# carrot & parsnip purée

• QUICK RECIPE
• MAKE AHEAD

When buying parsnips, select ones about the size of a medium carrot for the best flavour.

**SERVES** 4 **PREPARATION** 10 minutes **COOKING** 20 minutes

4 medium carrots, peeled and chopped
2 medium parsnips, peeled and chopped
½ teaspoon salt
15g butter or 1 tablespoon vegetable oil
1 teaspoon grated orange zest

**1** Combine carrots, parsnips and salt in a medium pan with enough water to barely cover the vegetables. Simmer, uncovered, until vegetables are very tender and most of the liquid has evaporated, about 20 minutes.

**2** Drain vegetables. Transfer to food processor or blender. Add butter or oil and orange zest. Process to a smooth purée.

**PER SERVING** 95Kcals, 1.5g protein, 4g fat, 2g saturated fat, 14g carbohydrates, 4.5g fibre, 0.6g salt

**1** of your **5 a day**

• QUICK RECIPE

# baby vegetables with orange sauce

Zingy orange and lively capers bring lots of extra flavour to small and tender vegetables.

**SERVES** 4 **PREPARATION** 5 minutes **COOKING** 15 minutes

12 baby turnips or 8 small turnips,
  halved, about 600g
8 baby leeks, about 175g, trimmed
250g baby corn
150g small Tenderstem broccoli spears
grated zest and juice of 1 orange
25g butter
2 tablespoons capers, drained

**1** Put the turnips in a large pan with plenty of boiling water to cover. Bring to the boil over high heat, reduce heat and cover; simmer 10 minutes. Turn the heat to high and add the leeks, baby corn and broccoli. Return to the boil, reduce the heat and cover. Simmer until the vegetables are just tender, 3 to 4 minutes. Drain and put into a serving dish.

**2** Add the orange zest, juice and butter to the pan and bring to the boil over high heat, whisking vigorously. Boil for 30 seconds to reduce the juice slightly. Remove from heat, stir in capers and pour over vegetables.

**PER SERVING** 120Kcals, 6g protein, 6.5g fat, 3.5g saturated fat, 11g carbohydrate, 7g fibre, 0.8g salt

**3** of your **5 a day**

**fresh ideas**

• Use pistachio oil instead of butter and add pistachio nuts, then serve the baby vegetables cold.
• Make the dish into a light lunch by adding smoked chicken or shavings of smoked cheese and serve with walnut bread.

## did you **know...**

...that baby vegetables can either be fully ripe miniature varieties of a vegetable or immature vegetables picked before they are fully grown? The flavour of these vegetables is generally more delicate than that of their larger relatives. Although not a baby vegetable, Tenderstem broccoli works well here; it has no woody stalks so the whole stem is succulent.

# irish mashed potatoes with cabbage & leeks

• HEART HEALTHY

Add cabbage and leeks to simple mashed potato to boost its flavour and nutritional value.

**SERVES** 8   **PREPARATION** 15 minutes   **COOKING** 50 minutes

1kg floury potatoes, such as Cara,
   unpeeled and quartered
835ml chicken stock
500g leeks, rinsed and thinly sliced
250ml semi-skimmed milk
3 garlic cloves, crushed
1 bay leaf
500g green cabbage, cored and thinly sliced
¼ teaspoon freshly grated nutmeg
¼ teaspoon salt
white pepper, to taste
25g unsalted butter
4 tablespoons roughly snipped fresh chives

**1** Place potatoes in a large pan. Pour in stock and add water to cover. Boil potatoes until tender, 20 to 25 minutes.

**2** Put leeks, milk, garlic and bay leaf in a large pan. Cover. Bring to the boil and simmer until leek is softened, 20 minutes. Drain; reserve leeks, and the milk and garlic liquid separately. Discard bay leaf.

**3** In the same pan, put cabbage and 60ml water. Cover. Boil gently until tender, 10 to 15 minutes. Drain. Squeeze cabbage dry; chop finely.

**4** Drain potatoes; transfer to a large bowl. Add milk and garlic and mash well. Stir in leeks, cabbage, nutmeg, salt, pepper and butter. Top with chives.

**PER SERVING** 185Kcals, 10g protein, 5g fat, 3g saturated fat, 28g carbohydrates, 4.5g fibre, 0.7g salt

**1** of your **5 a day**

## helpful hint

When a recipe calls for white pepper rather than black, it may be as much for its appearance as for its flavour. Chefs often use white pepper on pale-coloured foods. A white peppercorn is a ripened black peppercorn with a milder flavour.

# celeriac, kale & leek gratin

• QUICK RECIPE

Kale is packed with vitamins and beta carotene and is perfect with celeriac and feta cheese.

**SERVES** 6   **PREPARATION** 10 minutes   **COOKING** 20 minutes

1 celeriac, about 750g, peeled,
   halved and cut into 1cm thick slices
2 tablespoons olive oil
2 leeks, rinsed and sliced
200g curly kale, shredded
150ml apple juice
2 thick slices white bread,
   cut into 1cm dice
200g feta cheese, chopped
2 tablespoons sunflower seeds
6 tablespoons semi-skimmed milk
2 tablespoons chopped fresh parsley

**1** Put the celeriac in a large pan and cover with boiling water. Bring to the boil, reduce the heat to medium, cover and simmer until celeriac is tender, 5 minutes. Drain.

**2** Add the oil and leeks to the pan and cook, uncovered, over high heat for 2 minutes, stirring until the leeks are slightly softened. Stir in the kale, reduce heat to medium and cook, stirring, for 3 minutes. Add the apple juice. Boil for about 2 minutes to leave the vegetables moist and juicy but not too wet.

**3** Spread out the kale mixture in a large gratin dish or roasting tin. Arrange the celeriac on top in two rows, overlapping the slices slightly.

**4** Preheat grill to medium. Mix the bread, feta and sunflower seeds in a large bowl. Sprinkle the milk evenly over and turn mixture lightly with a large spoon or spatula, without mashing the bread. Sprinkle over the vegetables and grill on a low rack away from the heat source until the topping is crisp and browned, 5 to 8 minutes. Sprinkle with parsley and serve.

**PER SERVING** 230Kcals, 11g protein, 14.5g fat, 5.5g saturated fat, 15g carbohydrate, 7g fibre, 1.7g salt

**3** of your **5 a day**

**fresh ideas**

The celeriac gratin would also taste good with Lancashire, Wensleydale, Cheshire or white Stilton cheese instead of feta.

# ginger candied
## sweet potatoes

There is twice the daily requirement for vitamin A in a single serving of this unusual sweet side dish.

**SERVES** 4   **PREPARATION** 10 minutes   **COOKING** 25 minutes

2 tablespoons honey
1½ tablespoons vegetable oil
500g orange sweet potatoes,
   peeled and cut into 2cm pieces
½ teaspoon grated lemon zest
½ teaspoon grated fresh root ginger
¼ teaspoon salt

**1** Heat honey and oil in a medium non-stick pan over medium heat until bubbling, about 1 minute. Add the sweet potatoes. Cover. Cook over low heat until sweet potatoes begin to give off liquid, about 5 minutes. Add lemon zest and ginger. Cook, covered, until potato is just tender, a further 10 to 15 minutes. Be sure not to overcook.

**2** Uncover pan. Add salt. Boil over medium-high heat until potato is thickly glazed, about 5 minutes.

**PER SERVING** 180Kcals, 1.5g protein, 6g fat, 1g saturated fat, 32g carbohydrates, 3g fibre, 0.4g salt

**1** of your **5 a day**

• HEART HEALTHY

# spicy swede
## & potatoes

A golden onion raita brings a cool, fresh flavour to a selection of spiced root vegetables.

**SERVES** 4   **PREPARATION** 10 minutes   **COOKING** 24 minutes

2 spring onions, finely sliced
1 tablespoon chopped fresh mint
300ml plain low-fat yoghurt
3 tablespoons sunflower or groundnut oil
2 onions, halved and sliced
¼ teaspoon turmeric
750g swede, cut into 2cm cubes
700g potatoes, peeled and cut into 2cm cubes
40g fresh root ginger, peeled and finely chopped
1 tablespoon cumin seeds
salt, to taste
4 tablespoons chopped fresh coriander to garnish

**1** For the raita, mix the spring onions and mint into the yoghurt. Cover and chill. Heat 1 tbsp oil in a pan over medium-high heat and add the onions. Cook, stirring occasionally, until lightly browned, about 10 minutes. Stir in turmeric. Leave to cool. Lightly fork the onions into yoghurt mixture.

**2** Cook swede in a pan of boiling water to cover for 5 minutes. Add potatoes and cook until just tender, 5 to 7 minutes. Drain well.

**3** Heat remaining oil in the pan. Add ginger and cumin. Cook for 2 minutes. Stir in the vegetables with a little salt and the coriander. Garnish and serve with the raita.

**PER SERVING** 310Kcals, 10g protein, 11g fat, 2g saturated fat, 49g carbohydrate, 6.5g fibre, 0.3g salt

**3** of your **5 a day**

# baked sweet potato fries

• QUICK RECIPE

Fries cooked in the oven are the way to go when you are trying to cut back on fat. These baked sweet potato sticks are so full of flavour, that you will never be able to tell the difference.

**SERVES** 4  **PREPARATION** 7 minutes  **COOKING** 20 minutes

non-stick cooking spray
500g orange sweet potatoes, peeled
    and cut into 1cm thick 'fries'
1 tablespoon vegetable oil
¼ teaspoon salt
ground black pepper, to taste

**1** Preheat oven to 220°C (200°C fan oven), gas 7. Lightly coat a large baking sheet with non-stick cooking spray.

**2** Combine sweet potatoes, oil, salt and pepper in a large bowl. Toss to coat. Spread on the baking sheet in a single layer.

**3** Bake 10 minutes. Turn fries over. Continue baking until tender and lightly browned, about 10 more minutes.

**PER SERVING**  133Kcals, 1.5g protein, 3g fat, 0.5g saturated fat, 27g carbohydrates, 3g fibre, 0.4g salt

**1** of your **5 a day**

## on the menu

Baked Sweet Potato Fries go especially well with pork in the form of ham, sausages, chops or roasts and taste good with vegetable burgers, too.

# helpful **hint**

Twice-Baked Stuffed Sweet Potatoes can be made up to a
day ahead. Bake and stuff the potatoes as directed. Place
in a shallow dish, cover loosely and chill. Remove from the
fridge 30 minutes before baking as directed in the recipe.

# twice-baked stuffed sweet potatoes

• MAKE AHEAD

Use a half-and-half combination of butter and oil to maintain a rich flavour in the mash while reducing the quantity of unhealthy saturated fat.

**SERVES** 4 **PREPARATION** 10 minutes
**COOKING** 1 hour 10 minutes, plus cooling

2 large orange sweet potatoes,
    about 750g total weight
225g canned crushed pineapple, drained
1 tablespoon vegetable oil
15g butter
1 tablespoon brown sugar
1 teaspoon grated orange zest
½ teaspoon salt
2 tablespoons chopped pecan nuts

**1** Preheat oven to 180°C (160°C fan oven), gas 4. Pierce each sweet potato twice with the tip of a knife. Put on a baking tray.

**2** Bake until soft, about 50 minutes. Set aside until cool enough to handle but still very warm. Reduce heat to 170°C (150°C fan oven), gas 3.

**3** Cut potatoes in half lengthways. Scoop out flesh and place in medium bowl, being careful not to tear skin. Reserve skins. Add pineapple, oil, butter, sugar, zest and salt to potato flesh. Mix with an electric mixer or whisk until slightly fluffy.

**4** Place skin shells on baking tray. Fill with potato mixture, mounding it a little. Bake for 15 minutes. Sprinkle with pecan nuts. Bake for a further 5 minutes.

**PER SERVING** 307Kcals, 3g protein, 12g fat, 3g saturated fat, 51g carbohydrates, 5g fibre, 0.7g salt

**3** of your **5 a day**

fresh ideas
Roasted tomatoes will keep for several days in the fridge. Eat them as they are or use in pasta sauces and salads.

# roasted tomatoes with garlic & herbs

Slow-roasting fresh tomatoes in olive oil concentrates lycopene, the cancer-fighting phytochemical, and makes it more readily available to the body.

**SERVES** 4 **PREPARATION** 10 minutes **COOKING** 3 hours

1.5kg plum tomatoes, halved lengthways
2 tablespoons olive oil
5 garlic cloves, finely chopped
25g fresh basil, finely chopped
2 tablespoons finely chopped fresh rosemary
1 teaspoon sugar
1 teaspoon salt

**1** Preheat oven to 130°C (110°C fan oven), gas 1–2. Line a Swiss-roll tin with foil.

**2** Put tomato halves in a large bowl and toss with the oil, garlic, basil, rosemary, sugar and salt. Put, cut side up, in prepared pan. Bake for about 3 hours, or until they have collapsed and their skins have wrinkled. Serve at room temperature or chilled.

**PER SERVING** 122Kcals, 3g protein, 7g fat, 1g saturated fat, 13g carbohydrates, 3.5g fibre, 1.1g salt

**4** of your **5 a day**

## vegetables with a **balsamic** glaze

Boost your supply of vitamins B and C with this colourful Mediterranean-style combination of griddled vegetables.

**SERVES** 4   **PREPARATION** 10 minutes   **COOKING** 14 to 28 minutes

non-stick cooking spray, if grilling
1 large red pepper, seeded and
   cut into 2cm wide strips
1 medium courgette, sliced
1 medium red onion, sliced
2 large, flat mushrooms, stems removed and caps
   cut into 2cm wide strips
2 tablespoons extra virgin olive oil
1 teaspoon dried oregano
1 tablespoon balsamic vinegar
¼ teaspoon salt
ground black pepper, to taste

**1** Preheat a ridged griddle or grill to high. Lightly coat the grill rack, if using, with non-stick cooking spray.

**2** Combine pepper, courgette, onion and mushrooms in a large bowl. Sprinkle with oil and oregano. Toss to coat.

**3** Put a batch of vegetables in the griddle, or place all the vegetables on the grill rack in a single layer. Griddle or grill until crisp-tender and lightly flecked with brown, 6 to 8 minutes. Turn over; cook until done, about 5 minutes.

**4** Arrange vegetables on a platter. Mix the balsamic vinegar, salt and pepper in a small bowl. Brush over vegetables. Serve warm or at room temperature.

**PER SERVING**  85Kcals, 1.5g protein, 6g fat, 1g saturated fat, 6g carbohydrates, 1.5g fibre, 0.3g salt

**2** of your **5 a day**

## **courgettes** with parsley, garlic & lemon

There's a substantial helping of vitamin C in every serving of this simple side dish.

**SERVES** 4   **PREPARATION** 5 minutes   **COOKING** 8 minutes

2 teaspoons olive oil
600g courgettes, halved lengthways and cut
   thinly crossways to make half-moons
4 garlic cloves, crushed
¼ teaspoon salt
2 tablespoons roughly chopped fresh parsley
2 teaspoons freshly squeezed lemon juice

**1** Heat oil in a large non-stick frying pan over medium-high heat. Add courgettes. Sauté 3 minutes. Add garlic. Sauté until courgettes are crisp-tender, 3 to 5 minutes.

**2** Remove pan from heat. Stir in salt, parsley and lemon juice. Serve warm or at room temperature.

**PER SERVING**  40Kcals, 3g protein, 2g fat, 0.5g saturated fat, 3g carbohydrates, 1.5g fibre, 0.3g salt

**1** of your **5 a day**

## helpful **hint**

Cut vegetables for griddling into pieces that are of uniform size and no more than 2cm thick. This way, they will cook quickly and evenly. To test the griddle is hot, splash some water on to the surface; it should splutter and evaporate.

## on the menu

Griddled vegetables go well with sardines or tuna. Griddling and grilling intensifies all the flavours. Serve with crusty bread and finish the meal with Ruby Mincemeat Tarts topped with whipped cream.

## did you know...

...that Asian oyster sauce, which is made from boiled oysters, doesn't have a fishy flavour? There are many vegetarian brands on the market made from mushrooms that can be used with equal success.

# asian vegetables with oyster sauce

• QUICK RECIPE

Soy sauce, oyster sauce, lime juice, garlic, ginger and basil give a taste of Thailand to an exciting selection of lightly cooked fresh vegetables.

**SERVES** 8   **PREPARATION** 20 minutes   **COOKING** 6 minutes

1 tablespoon salt-reduced soy sauce
1 tablespoon oyster sauce
2 tablespoons freshly squeezed lime juice
1 tablespoon sugar
2 tablespoons vegetable oil
4 garlic cloves, crushed
2 serrano or jalapeño chillies,
   seeded and thinly sliced diagonally
3 spring onions, thinly sliced
1 medium red pepper, seeded
   and cut into small pieces
125g mange-touts
1 large aubergine, cut into small cubes
125g mushrooms, stems removed
   and caps cut into wedges
2.5cm piece fresh root ginger,
   peeled and finely chopped
3 small heads baby pak choi,
   cored and thinly sliced
15g fresh basil leaves, shredded

**1** Combine soy sauce, oyster sauce, lime juice and sugar in a small bowl.

**2** Heat oil in a large non-stick frying pan over medium-high heat. Add garlic and chillies. Stir-fry 30 seconds. Add the spring onions, pepper, mange-touts, aubergine, mushrooms and ginger. Stir-fry 2 minutes. Add pak choi. Stir-fry until wilted, about 1 minute. Add soy mixture. Stir-fry until all the vegetables are crisp-tender, about 1 minute. Stir in basil and serve at once.

**PER SERVING** 61Kcals, 2.5g protein, 3g fat, 0.5g saturated fat, 6g carbohydrates, 2g fibre, 0.5g salt

**1** of your **5 a day**

• QUICK RECIPE

# spring vegetable sauté with tarragon

Yellow courgettes with a strong, bright colour contain more beta carotene than paler ones.

**SERVES** 4   **PREPARATION** 15 minutes   **COOKING** 4 minutes

125g mange-touts
1 small bunch asparagus, trimmed and
   cut into 10cm pieces
15g butter
1 tablespoon vegetable oil
1 bunch spring onions, cut into 5cm lengths
1 medium yellow courgette, thinly sliced
½ teaspoon salt
ground black pepper, to taste
1 teaspoon chopped tarragon or ½ teaspoon dried

**1** Blanch the mange-touts and asparagus in boiling water for 1 minute. Drain. Heat butter and oil in a large non-stick frying pan over medium-high heat. Add spring onions and courgette. Sauté for about 1 minute.

**2** Add mange-touts, asparagus, salt and pepper. Cover. Cook until vegetables are heated through, about 2 minutes. Stir in tarragon. Serve at once.

**PER SERVING** 90Kcals, 3g protein, 6g fat, 2g saturated fat, 6g carbohydrates, 2g fibre, 0.6g salt

**1** of your **5 a day**

# satay-roasted roots

• HEART HEALTHY

A peanut dressing is a superb way to make crisply roasted vegetables that are low in fat.

**SERVES** 4   **PREPARATION** 10 minutes   **COOKING** 35 minutes

600g potatoes, unpeeled and halved
650g swede, peeled and cut into 12 wedges
4 parsnips, about 500g, peeled and halved
4 small onions, about 250g, halved
4 tablespoons smooth peanut butter
1 garlic clove, crushed
2 teaspoons toasted sesame oil
4 spring onions, thinly sliced
grated zest of 1 lemon, fruit cut into wedges
chopped flat-leaf parsley, to garnish

**1** Put the potatoes, swede, parsnips and onions in a large pan with boiling water to cover. Simmer 10 minutes.

**2** Preheat oven to 230°C (210°C fan oven), gas 8. Mix the peanut butter, garlic and sesame oil in a bowl. Gradually stir in 5 tbsp water from the vegetables to make a dressing. Drain the vegetables and put into a roasting tin. Add the dressing and mix to coat. Roast for 25 to 30 minutes, until crisp and browned in places, turning once. Serve sprinkled with spring onions, lemon zest and parsley, with lemon wedges on the side.

**PER SERVING** 360Kcals, 11g protein, 12g fat, 2.5g saturated fat, 56g carbohydrate, 12g fibre, 0.3g salt

**4** of your 5 a day

# bulghur wheat with spring vegetables

• MAKE AHEAD
• HEART HEALTHY

As well as complex carbohydrates, bulghur wheat also contains protein, niacin, insoluble fibre and vitamin E, to keep your cardiovascular system healthy.

**SERVES** 6   **PREPARATION** 45 minutes   **COOKING** 10 minutes

225g bulghur wheat
850ml boiling water
2 tablespoons olive oil
3 tablespoons freshly squeezed
   lemon juice
1 teaspoon salt
ground black pepper, to taste
2 leeks, halved lengthways,
   rinsed and cut crossways
   into 2cm pieces
2 garlic cloves, crushed
12 asparagus spears, trimmed and
   cut into 5cm lengths
150g frozen peas
15g fresh mint leaves, chopped,
   plus mint sprigs to garnish

**1** Combine bulghur wheat and boiling water in a large heatproof bowl. Leave to stand until bulghur is tender, about 30 minutes; stir after 15 minutes. Drain bulghur in a large, fine-meshed sieve to remove any remaining liquid.

**2** Whisk 1 tbsp oil, the lemon juice, salt and pepper in a large bowl. Add bulghur and fluff with a fork.

**3** Heat remaining oil in a medium frying pan over low heat. Add leeks and garlic; cook until leeks are tender, about 5 minutes. Transfer to the bowl containing bulghur.

**4** In a steamer set over a pan of boiling water, steam the asparagus until tender, about 4 minutes. Add peas during the final 30 seconds. Add vegetables and mint to bulghur mixture; toss to combine. Serve at room temperature or chilled.

**PER SERVING** 200Kcals, 6.5g protein, 5g fat, 0.7g saturated fat, 33g carbohydrates, 2g fibre, 0.8g salt

**½** of your 5 a day

## did you know...

...that bulghur wheat is made from parboiled wheat kernels that have been dried and cracked? It is good for stuffings and pilafs but is traditionally used for tabbouleh and other salads.

# white beans
## & swiss chard

• MAKE AHEAD

Beans protect your heart with plenty of soluble fibre that helps to lower cholesterol.

**SERVES** 8  **PREPARATION** 10 minutes  **COOKING** 25 minutes

250g Swiss chard
2 tablespoons olive oil
1 small onion, finely chopped
1 medium carrot, peeled and finely chopped
1 teaspoon dried oregano
1 bay leaf
2 garlic cloves, crushed
250ml vegetable or chicken stock
3 x 400g cans cannellini or butter beans,
   drained and rinsed
½ teaspoon salt
ground black pepper, to taste
40g grated Parmesan cheese

**1** Remove tough stems from Swiss chard and finely chop. Coarsely chop leaves.

**2** Heat oil in a large non-stick frying pan over medium heat. Add onion, carrot, oregano and bay leaf. Sauté until onion and carrot are very soft, about 8 minutes. Add garlic. Sauté for 30 seconds.

**3** Add the Swiss chard and stock to the pan. Cook, stirring occasionally, until Swiss chard begins to wilt, about 2 minutes. Stir in beans. Simmer, covered, 10 minutes. Uncover and cook until Swiss chard is tender, 5 minutes. Season with salt and pepper. Remove bay leaf. Sprinkle with Parmesan.

**PER SERVING**  192Kcals, 12g protein, 5g fat, 1.5g saturated fat, 25g carbohydrates, 8g fibre, 1.9g salt

**2** of your 5 a day

**fresh ideas**
Instead of cannellini beans, you can use another type of white bean or, for a nutty flavour, try making this dish with chickpeas. Vary the herbs, too. Fresh thyme, parsley or chervil all work well.

• MAKE AHEAD  • HEART HEALTHY

# mediterranean
## rice with green peas
## & sun-dried tomatoes

Combining rice and peas will help to boost the muscle-building protein in any meal.

**SERVES** 6  **PREPARATION** 15 minutes  **COOKING** 20 minutes

420ml vegetable or chicken stock
300g fresh or frozen peas
50g soft sun-dried tomatoes, thinly sliced
¼ teaspoon salt
ground black pepper, to taste
200g long-grain rice

**1** Bring stock to the boil in a medium pan over high heat. Add peas, tomatoes and seasoning. Bring back to the boil. Add rice and stir. Cover. Lower heat to a bare simmer. Cook until liquid is just absorbed and rice is tender, about 15 minutes.

**2** Remove pan from heat. Leave rice mixture to stand, covered, for 10 minutes. Uncover. Fluff up with a fork.

**PER SERVING**  216Kcals, 9g protein, 6g fat, 0.8g saturated fat, 33g carbohydrates, 2.5g fibre, 0.7g salt

**½** of your 5 a day

# vegetable fried rice

- MAKE AHEAD
- HEART HEALTHY

You'll get a good balance of vitamins and minerals from this veg-heavy version of an oriental classic.

**SERVES** 6  **PREPARATION** 20 minutes  **COOKING** 15 minutes

60ml chicken or vegetable stock

2½ tablespoons salt-reduced soy sauce

1½ teaspoons toasted sesame oil

1½ tablespoons vegetable oil

2 medium carrots, peeled and cut into matchstick pieces

1 medium red pepper, seeded and coarsely chopped

4 spring onions, thinly sliced (darker green tops reserved for garnish)

4cm piece fresh root ginger, peeled and finely chopped

100g quartered white, brown or shiitake mushrooms

2 garlic cloves, crushed

150g Chinese leaves, sliced

¼ teaspoon salt

280g long-grain rice, cooked and chilled

**1** Whisk stock, soy sauce and sesame oil in a small bowl.

**2** Heat vegetable oil in a wok or large, deep non-stick frying pan over medium-high heat. Add carrots, pepper, white and pale green parts of spring onions and the ginger. Cook just until crisp-tender, stirring once, about 5 minutes.

**3** Add the mushrooms and garlic. Cook, stirring occasionally, 5 minutes. Add Chinese leaves and salt. Cook, stirring, just until the Chinese leaves are slightly wilted, about 3 minutes. Stir in rice and soy sauce mixture. Cook, stirring occasionally, until rice is heated through, about 3 minutes. Slice darker green spring onion stems. Sprinkle over rice before serving.

**PER SERVING**  211Kcals, 4.5g protein, 7g fat, 1g saturated fat, 36g carbohydrates, 2g fibre, 0.9g salt

## on the **menu**

Vegetable Fried Rice becomes a substantial main dish if you add chopped cooked turkey, chicken, ham, pork or scrambled egg to the mix.

# rice with kale & butternut squash

Butternut squash is packed with antioxidants and fibre. Here it combines with the dark green goodness of kale and raisins to give an unexpected sweetness.

**SERVES** 6   **PREPARATION** 15 minutes   **COOKING** 16 minutes

500g kale, tough stems removed
100g basmati rice
1 tablespoon curry powder
250g butternut squash, peeled,
   seeded, and cut in 2.5cm pieces
40g raisins
250ml reduced-fat coconut milk
185ml water
1 teaspoon salt

**1** Blanch the kale leaves in boiling water for 1 minute. Drain. Heat a large non-stick frying pan over medium-low heat. Add rice. Toast, stirring frequently, until lightly browned, about 3 minutes. Add curry powder. Cook, stirring, 1 minute.

**2** Add kale, squash, raisins, coconut milk, water and salt. Cover and simmer until the liquid is absorbed and the rice and squash are tender, about 12 minutes. Remove from the heat. Leave to stand, covered, for 5 minutes.

**PER SERVING**  163Kcals, 5g protein, 6g fat, 4g saturated fat, 23g carbohydrates, 3g fibre, 0.7g salt

**1 of your 5 a day**

## did you know...

...that rice rarely, if ever, causes food allergies and is a staple for half the world's population? Basmati rice is particularly suitable for pilafs, as the grains stay dry and separate during cooking.

• MAKE AHEAD
• HEART HEALTHY

# tomato chutney

Tomatoes contain chlorogenic acid, which may help to guard against certain cancers.

**MAKES** 750ml  **PREPARATION** 20 minutes
**COOKING** 25 minutes  **CHILL** 24 hours

850g plum or round tomatoes,
    seeded and coarsely chopped
2 medium celery sticks, coarsely chopped
1 medium red onion, coarsely chopped
85g sultanas
75g soft light brown sugar
85ml cider vinegar
4cm piece fresh root ginger,
    peeled and finely chopped
2 tablespoons chopped jalapeño
    chillies in vinegar
¼ teaspoon ground allspice
¼ teaspoon salt
14 baby plum or small cherry tomatoes,
    quartered

**1** In a large non-aluminium pan, combine the tomatoes, celery, onion, sultanas, brown sugar, vinegar, ginger, chillies, allspice

and salt. Bring to the boil. Simmer, uncovered, stirring occasionally, until ingredients are tender and most of the liquid has evaporated, 20 to 25 minutes.

**2** Remove pan from heat. Stir in baby plum or cherry tomatoes. Leave to cool to room temperature. Transfer to a covered dish and chill for at least 24 hours. Store in a sealed container in the fridge for up to one week.

**PER TABLESPOON**  16Kcals, 0.2g protein, 0g fat, 0g saturated fat, 4g carbohydrate, 0.3g fibre, trace salt

## on the menu

There are many types of chutney, but they mostly feature a single vegetable or fruit simmered in a spicy blend of seasonings. In this recipe, you can try substituting 2 chopped unripe (hard) mangoes for the plum tomatoes. To make mango chutney, leave out the celery and baby tomatoes and then follow the recipe as directed. Chutney goes well with grilled meats, grains, rice, curries and potato dishes. It also makes an excellent appetiser served with cream cheese on crackers or wedges of toasted pitta bread.

# squash pickle

• MAKE AHEAD
• HEART HEALTHY

Ginger, cinnamon and peppercorns add sweet and spicy flavours to the pickles as well as health-protective phytochemicals.

**MAKES** 2 litres  **PREPARATION** 25 minutes  **COOKING** 20 minutes

strips of lemon zest from 1 lemon
1kg sugar
750ml cider vinegar
5cm piece fresh root ginger,
    peeled and finely chopped
2 cinnamon sticks
20 black peppercorns
1 tablespoon salt
about 1.75kg butternut squash, peeled, seeded,
    and cut into 5cm long rectangular pieces

**1** Combine lemon zest, sugar, vinegar, ginger, cinnamon sticks, peppercorns and salt in a large non-aluminium pan. Simmer, stirring to dissolve sugar, for 5 minutes. Add the squash. Simmer, stirring occasionally, until crisp-tender, about 15 minutes.

**2** Transfer squash pickles to sterilised jars, using a draining spoon. You will need eight 250ml jars or four 500ml jars. Pour in cooking liquid to within 5mm of the top of each jar. Seal and use within one week.

**PER TABLESPOON** 34Kcals, 0.1g protein, 0g fat, 0g saturated fat, 9g carbohydrate, 0.2g fibre, 0.1g salt

# sweetcorn & pepper relish

• QUICK RECIPE
• MAKE AHEAD
• HEART HEALTHY

Canned sweetcorn contains ferulic acid, an antioxidant that destroys naturally occurring toxins in the body.

**SERVES** 6  **PREPARATION** 10 minutes  **COOKING** 5 minutes

375ml white vinegar
50g sugar
¾ teaspoon mustard powder
¼ teaspoon salt
2 spring onions, thinly sliced
½ small orange pepper, seeded and diced
½ small yellow pepper, seeded and diced
420g can sweetcorn, drained

**1** In a small non-aluminium pan, combine vinegar, sugar, mustard and salt. Simmer 5 minutes. Remove from heat.

**2** Stir in spring onions, peppers and sweetcorn. Cool. Store in a sealed container in the fridge for up to one week. Serve relish chilled or at room temperature.

**PER SERVING** 125Kcals, 2g protein, 0.8g fat, 0.1g saturated fat, 26g carbohydrate, 1g fibre, 0.6g salt

**fresh ideas** To spice up this simple relish, add a tablespoon or two of finely chopped jalapeño or other chillies.

# fresh, grilled
## & roasted salads

## endive & watercress salad with almonds

• QUICK RECIPE

Watercress and endive are super sources of beta carotene. Here they are enlivened with a creamy, spicy dressing with a hint of ginger and curry.

**SERVES** 6   **PREPARATION** 10 minutes

85g low-fat plain yoghurt
1 tablespoon low-fat mayonnaise
2 teaspoons honey
1 teaspoon Dijon mustard
¼ teaspoon curry powder
pinch of ground ginger
350g watercress, tough stems removed
1 large head endive, halved lengthways and
   cut crossways into 1cm thick slices
1 red dessert apple, halved, cored and thinly sliced
2 tablespoons slivered almonds, toasted

For the dressing, whisk yoghurt, mayonnaise, honey, mustard, curry powder and ginger in a small bowl. Combine watercress, endive and apple in a large bowl. Add the dressing; toss to combine. Sprinkle with almonds.

**PER SERVING**  73Kcals, 4g protein, 4g fat, 0.5g saturated fat, 5g carbohydrates, 2g fibre, 0.15g salt

**1** of your **5 a day**

## helpful hint

To toast nuts or seeds, place in a small, dry frying pan. Cook over medium heat, shaking the pan often, until they just begin to colour. Remove from the pan and cool before using.

## cucumber, radish & mange-touts salad

• QUICK RECIPE
• HEART HEALTHY

Mange-touts and radishes are both great sources of folate and vitamin C, nutrients that work together to protect the health of your heart.

**SERVES** 4   **PREPARATION** 10 minutes   **COOKING** 3 minutes

175g mange-touts
salt
1 tablespoon rice vinegar
2 teaspoons sugar
2 teaspoons soy sauce
1 teaspoon toasted sesame oil
2 cucumbers, scored lengthways
   and thinly sliced
2 bunches of radishes, thinly sliced
1 tablespoon sesame seeds,
   toasted (optional)

**1** Cook mange-touts in a pan of lightly salted boiling water until crisp-tender, 2 to 3 minutes. Drain. Rinse under cold running water.

**2** For the vinaigrette, whisk the vinegar, sugar, soy sauce, sesame oil and a pinch of salt in a bowl until sugar and salt are dissolved.

**3** Combine the mange-touts, cucumbers and radishes in a large bowl. Add vinaigrette; toss to combine. Sprinkle with sesame seeds, if you like.

**PER SERVING**  81Kcals, 4g protein, 3g fat, 0.5g saturated fat, 9g carbohydrates, 2.5g fibre, 0.4g salt

**2** of your **5 a day**

## did you know...

...that radishes were cultivated thousands of years ago in China? They were so highly prized in ancient Greece that gold replicas were made of them.

## on the **menu**

This salad makes a good first course to a main meal of grilled chicken and corn on the cob. Serve juicy wedges of chilled watermelon for a refreshing dessert.

# asparagus, tomato & mange-touts with ginger

This elegant, fresh-tasting salad is an excellent source of folate, beta carotene and vitamin C, key nutrients for fighting cancer and heart disease.

**SERVES** 6  **PREPARATION** 10 minutes  **COOKING** 10 minutes

25g walnuts
1 tablespoon soy sauce
2 teaspoons rice vinegar
2 teaspoons freshly squeezed lemon juice
1 teaspoon toasted sesame oil
3 tablespoons vegetable oil
2 spring onions, finely chopped
2.5cm piece fresh root ginger,
    peeled and finely chopped
125g mange-touts
salt
500g thin asparagus, trimmed
1 head cos lettuce, cored and
    separated into leaves
4 medium tomatoes, cut into wedges

**1** Toast the walnuts in a small pan over medium heat, stirring often, until browned, about 3 minutes. Chop coarsely and set aside. For the dressing, whisk soy sauce, rice vinegar, lemon juice and sesame oil in a small bowl. Whisk in vegetable oil, then stir in spring onions and ginger.

**2** Cook the mange-touts in a pan of lightly salted boiling water until crisp-tender, 2 to 3 minutes. Transfer to a colander with a draining spoon. Rinse under cold running water.

**3** Add asparagus to the boiling water in the pan. Cook until crisp-tender, 3 to 4 minutes. Drain in the colander. Rinse under cold running water. Toss mange-touts and asparagus in a large bowl with just enough dressing to coat lightly.

**4** Arrange 3 or 4 cos leaves on each serving plate. Top with mange-touts, asparagus and tomato. Garnish with walnuts. Pass remaining dressing separately.

**PER SERVING**  127Kcals, 5g protein, 10g fat,
1g saturated fat, 6g carbohydrates, 3g fibre, 0.4g salt

**2** of your **5 a day**

---

• HEART HEALTHY

# beef & pasta salad

Lightly grilled steak is a good source of iron, here paired with super-healthy broccoli and tomatoes.

**SERVES** 4  **PREPARATION** 15 minutes  **COOKING** 20 minutes

250g small pasta shapes of your choice
salt
500g broccoli florets
300g well-trimmed sirloin steak
325g low-fat plain yoghurt
3 tablespoons low-fat mayonnaise
1 tablespoon balsamic vinegar
20g basil leaves
500g tomatoes, quartered
1 medium red onion, thinly sliced

**1** Cook pasta in a large pan of lightly salted boiling water until al dente, following pack instructions. Add the broccoli florets during the last 2 minutes of cooking; drain.

**2** Preheat grill to high. Grill steak for 4 minutes each side for medium, or until done as you like. Place on a cutting board; slice thinly across the grain, on the diagonal.

**3** For the dressing, combine yoghurt, mayonnaise, vinegar, basil and ½ tsp salt in a food processor or blender; whiz until smooth. Pour dressing into a large serving bowl.

**4** Add the steak and any juices that have accumulated on the cutting board; toss to coat. Add pasta, broccoli, tomatoes and onion to bowl and toss again. (Can be made ahead and chilled. Bring back to room temperature before serving.)

**PER SERVING**  473Kcals, 35g protein, 10g fat,
3g saturated fat, 62g carbohydrates, 7g fibre, 1g salt

**3** of your **5 a day**

• QUICK RECIPE
• MAKE AHEAD
• HEART HEALTHY

# green salad with garlic & ginger

Crisp, fat-free and delicately flavoured, these lightly steamed vegetables taste good eaten hot or cold.

**SERVES** 4  **PREPARATION** 20 minutes  **COOKING** 4 minutes

250g broccoli
250g baby pak choi or other Chinese leaves
4 spring onions
250g sugar snap peas, trimmed
1 garlic clove, crushed
1 teaspoon finely grated ginger
1 tablespoon fish sauce
1 teaspoon brown sugar

**1** Fill a steamer or pan with water to just below the base of a steamer basket. Bring water to the boil.

**2** Cut broccoli into small florets, trimming stalks to about 2cm. Peel remaining stalks and cut diagonally into thin slices. Trim pak choi and slice stems. Trim spring onions and slice thinly on the diagonal.

**3** Combine broccoli, pak choi, spring onions and sugar snap peas in a large bowl. Add garlic and ginger; toss well. Transfer to steamer basket. Steam, covered, until vegetables are crisp-tender, 3 to 4 minutes.

**4** Place vegetables in a serving dish. Combine fish sauce and sugar in a small cup, stirring until sugar has dissolved. Drizzle over the vegetables. Serve hot or chill briefly in the fridge before serving.

**PER SERVING**  70Kcals, 7g protein, 1g fat, 0.2g saturated fat, 7g carbohydrates, 4g fibre, 0.9g salt

**2** of your **5 a day**

• QUICK RECIPE

# cos lettuce with chunky tomato vinaigrette

Enliven a leafy green salad with chunks of sharply flavoured feta cheese and an exciting dressing laced with basil and tomatoes.

**SERVES** 6  **PREPARATION** 12 minutes

2 large ripe tomatoes, halved,
   seeded and coarsely chopped
15g fresh basil leaves
2 tablespoons tomato ketchup
2 tablespoons olive oil
1 tablespoon balsamic vinegar
1 small garlic clove, crushed
½ teaspoon salt
1 large head cos lettuce,
   torn into bite-sized pieces
35g feta cheese, crumbled

For the vinaigrette, place tomatoes, basil, tomato ketchup, oil, vinegar, garlic and salt in a food processor or blender. Pulse until blended but still chunky. Toss the lettuce with vinaigrette in a large bowl. Sprinkle with feta cheese. Serve at once.

**PER SERVING**  61Kcals, 1.5g protein, 5g fat, 1.5g saturated fat, 2g carbohydrates, 0.5g fibre, 0.6g salt

**½** of your **5 a day**

**fresh ideas**

Chunky Tomato Vinaigrette also makes a flavoursome topping for grilled meats and chicken or pasta. It can be made several hours before it's needed and chilled. To dress up a simple pasta dish, chop some mozzarella and add with salami and black olives.

# carrot-almond salad & raspberry vinaigrette

• QUICK RECIPE

A salad of lightly cooked carrots gets extra texture from almonds, a rich source of folate and vitamin E.

**SERVES** 4  **PREPARATION** 15 minutes  **COOKING** 8 minutes

2 tablespoons raspberry vinegar
1 tablespoon olive oil
1 tablespoon honey
¼ teaspoon salt
¼ teaspoon ground black pepper
500g carrots, peeled and thinly sliced on the diagonal
30g slivered or sliced almonds
1 spring onion, thinly sliced

**1** For the vinaigrette, whisk the vinegar, oil, honey, salt and pepper in a small bowl. Steam carrots over a medium pan of simmering water until just tender, about 8 minutes. Rinse under cold running water. Drain.

**2** Toss the carrots, almonds, spring onion and vinaigrette in a medium bowl. Serve at once.

**PER SERVING** 126Kcals, 2.5g protein, 7g fat, 0.9g saturated fat, 13g carbohydrates, 3.5g fibre, 0.3g salt

**1** of your **5 a day**

## did you know...

...that there are two varieties of almonds, only one of which you can eat? Edible almonds are sweet while the inedible bitter almond contains a form of cyanide.

# three-vegetable salad with curry vinaigrette

Indoles, phytochemicals found in cauliflower and other kinds of cruciferous vegetables, may help against hormone-related cancers, while green beans contain vitamin A for good vision.

**SERVES** 4  **PREPARATION** 10 minutes  **COOKING** 8 minutes

2 teaspoons curry powder
60ml freshly squeezed lime juice
salt
3 tablespoons vegetable oil
250g green beans, trimmed and
   halved crossways
1 small cauliflower, separated into
   small florets, stalks removed
150g sweetcorn, thawed frozen
shredded lime zest, to garnish (optional)

**1** Put curry powder in a small, dry pan and toast, stirring frequently, over low heat until fragrant, about 1 minute. For the vinaigrette, whisk lime juice, curry powder and ¼ tsp salt in a small bowl. Whisk in vegetable oil.

**2** Cook beans in a large pan of lightly salted boiling water until crisp-tender, about 3 minutes. Transfer with a draining spoon to a colander. Rinse under cold running water. Add cauliflower to the boiling water. Cook until crisp-tender, about 4 minutes. Drain in colander. Rinse under cold running water.

**3** Toss beans, cauliflower, sweetcorn and vinaigrette in a large bowl. Garnish if you like and serve at room temperature or chilled.

**PER SERVING**  170Kcals, 7g protein, 10g fat, 1.5g saturated fat, 12g carbohydrates, 4g fibre, 0.3g salt

**2** of your **5 a day**

## helpful **hint**

Toasting curry powder in a dry frying pan removes the raw taste and boosts the flavour. Other spices, such as cumin and chilli powder, benefit from toasting, too. They can be added to foods that don't require further cooking.

# griddled
## salad mix

A really scrumptious salad of vegetables briefly cooked on the griddle is full of taste and colour – and as a bonus will help to keep your heart healthy too.

**SERVES** 6   **PREPARATION** 25 minutes   **COOKING** 15 minutes

1 medium aubergine
1 small fennel bulb, trimmed
1 medium yellow courgette
1 medium green courgette
½ teaspoon salt
non-stick cooking spray
1 small red pepper, halved lengthways and seeded
3 tomatoes, halved lengthways and seeded
2 tablespoons olive oil
2 garlic cloves, crushed
1 teaspoon finely chopped fresh marjoram
   or ½ teaspoon dried
1½ tablespoons balsamic vinegar

**1** Preheat a ridged griddle. Slice the aubergine, fennel and courgettes lengthways into 1cm thick pieces. Sprinkle with half the salt. Coat with cooking spray.

**2** Griddle pepper, skin side down, until the skin is blackened and blistered, 3 to 4 minutes. Griddle aubergine, fennel and courgettes on one side until griddle marks are dark brown but vegetables are still very firm, about 4 minutes. Turn over and griddle until browned and just tender, about 3 minutes for courgettes and 5 to 6 minutes longer for aubergine and fennel.

**3** Coat cut sides of tomatoes with cooking spray. Griddle, cut sides down, just until light grill marks appear, 3 minutes.

**4** Heat the oil in a small frying pan over medium heat. Add garlic, marjoram and remaining salt. Sauté 1 minute.

**5** Peel griddled pepper, if you like, and cut into thin strips. Cut the remaining vegetables into bite-sized chunks. Transfer to a medium bowl. Add olive oil mixture and vinegar. Toss to coat. Serve at room temperature.

**PER SERVING** 80Kcals, 2g protein, 4.5g fat, 0.7g saturated fat, 9g carbohydrates, 3.5g fibre, 0.4g salt

**2** of your **5 a day**

# wilted
## spinach salad

Use multigrain bread to make croutons and add extra interest with sautéed onions and crumbs of bacon.

**SERVES** 4   **PREPARATION** 5 minutes   **COOKING** 5 minutes

250g baby spinach leaves
2 tablespoons olive oil
1 red onion, thinly sliced
60ml tomato juice
1 tablespoon freshly squeezed lemon juice
1 teaspoon Dijon mustard
1 small garlic clove, crushed
¼ teaspoon salt
pinch of ground black pepper
2 slices rindless, unsmoked back bacon cooked and crumbled
2 slices multigrain bread, trimmed, toasted, and cut into small cubes
   for croutons

**1** Put spinach in large bowl. Heat the olive oil in a large non-stick frying pan over medium heat. Add onion. Sauté for 1 minute. Stir in tomato juice, lemon juice, mustard, garlic, salt and pepper. Bring just to the boil. Remove from heat.

**2** Pour hot dressing over spinach and toss to coat. Top with bacon and croutons. Serve warm.

**PER SERVING** 145Kcals, 6g protein, 9g fat, 2g saturated fat, 12g carbohydrates, 2g fibre, 1.92g salt

**1** of your **5 a day**

# roasted **aubergine** & **tomato** salad

Brushing vegetables with a little oil and roasting them is generally a healthier option than frying, particularly with aubergines, which soak up oil like a sponge.

**SERVES** 4    **PREPARATION** 15 minutes    **COOKING** 20 minutes

non-stick cooking spray
500g aubergine, cut crossways into thin slices
500g plum or round tomatoes, thinly sliced
2 tablespoons olive oil
salt and ground black pepper, to taste
1 garlic clove
1 tablespoon red wine vinegar
15 small basil leaves

**1** Preheat oven to 240°C (220°C fan oven), gas 9. Line a large baking dish with foil. Coat lightly with non-stick cooking spray. Place aubergine and tomato slices in a single layer on the foil. Brush with half the oil. Sprinkle with salt and pepper.

**2** Roast until aubergine is softened and golden, 20 minutes. Leave to cool.

**3** For the dressing, crush the garlic in a small bowl. Add the remaining oil and all the vinegar, and whisk until blended. Overlap slices of tomato and aubergine on a serving plate and intersperse with basil leaves. Brush with dressing.

**PER SERVING**  92Kcals, 2g protein, 6g fat, 1g saturated fat, 7g carbohydrates, 4g fibre, 3g salt

# sweet potato salad with **raisins** & **orange** dressing

On average, one medium sweet potato provides more than 100 per cent of the recommended daily allowance for vitamin A and about 80 per cent of the vitamin C you need.

**SERVES** 4    **PREPARATION** 25 minutes    **COOKING** 20 minutes

non-stick cooking spray
500g orange sweet potatoes, peeled, quartered lengthways and cut crossways into thin slices
3 tablespoons olive oil
about 1 tablespoon freshly squeezed lemon juice
1 tablespoon freshly squeezed orange juice
1 teaspoon honey
¼ teaspoon salt
¼ teaspoon ground black pepper
250g salad leaves, torn into pieces
1 navel orange, peeled and segmented
1 small red onion, thinly sliced crossways
3 tablespoons raisins

**1** Preheat oven to 200°C (180°C fan oven), gas 6. Line a large baking dish with foil and lightly coat with non-stick cooking spray. Toss the sweet potatoes in the baking dish with half the oil to coat, then spread in an even layer. Roast until tender and lightly browned, about 20 minutes.

**2** Whisk the remaining oil, lemon juice, orange juice, honey, salt and pepper in a small bowl. Taste dressing and add an extra 1 tsp lemon juice, if you like.

**3** Toss warm potatoes and dressing in a serving bowl. Add salad leaves, orange segments, onion and raisins. Toss to combine.

**PER SERVING**  244Kcals, 3g protein, 9g fat, 1.4g saturated fat, 40g carbohydrates, 4.5g fibre, 0.4g salt

**fresh ideas**

To make Sweet Potato Salad into a main course lunch dish, add slices of fresh mozzarella cheese, cubes of feta or another soft cheese of your choice before you drizzle on the dressing. Or, serve with slices of cooked chorizo sausage.

# potato salad with sun-dried tomatoes & basil

- QUICK RECIPE
- MAKE AHEAD
- HEART HEALTHY

Everyone's favourite party food, this salad supplies plenty of vitamin C, courtesy of all three vegetables.

**SERVES** 6  **PREPARATION** 10 minutes  **COOKING** 15 minutes

750g small new potatoes,
   unpeeled and halved
salt
2 tablespoons low-fat mayonnaise
2 teaspoons Dijon mustard
60ml buttermilk
2 spring onions, thinly sliced lengthways
25g chopped soft sun-dried tomatoes
   (not oil-packed)
8 basil leaves, shredded or finely chopped
ground black pepper, to taste

**1** Cook potatoes in a large pan of lightly salted boiling water until tender, 10 to 15 minutes. Drain well.

**2** For the dressing, combine mayonnaise and mustard in a small bowl. Stir in the buttermilk.

**3** Combine potatoes, spring onions, sun-dried tomatoes, basil, ½ tsp salt and pepper to taste in a large bowl. Add dressing. Toss to coat.

**PER SERVING** 119Kcals, 2.5g protein, 3g fat, 0.3g saturated fat, 21g carbohydrates, 1g fibre, 0.5g salt

½ of your 5 a day

## did you know...

...that the name coleslaw comes from a Dutch word, 'koolsla', which means cabbage salad? Recipes for this salad have always been open to improvisation from the basic cabbage to the dressing (mayonnaise to vinaigrette and many combinations in between).

# carrot-broccoli slaw

- QUICK RECIPE
- MAKE AHEAD

Use broccoli instead of cabbage and add a sprinkling of almonds to make an alternative version of coleslaw.

**SERVES** 6  **PREPARATION** 10 minutes  **COOKING** 2 minutes

25g slivered almonds
3 tablespoons low-fat mayonnaise
1 tablespoon white wine vinegar
stalks of 1 large broccoli
   (florets reserved for another use)
3 medium carrots, peeled and grated
3 tablespoons roughly chopped fresh parsley
ground black pepper, to taste

**1** Toast the almonds in a small pan over medium heat, stirring often, until browned, about 2 minutes. For the dressing, whisk the mayonnaise and vinegar in a small bowl.

**2** Peel the broccoli stalks, then grate in a food processor or by hand. Combine broccoli, carrots and dressing in a large bowl. Stir in almonds, parsley and pepper.

**PER SERVING** 80Kcals, 3g protein, 5g fat, 0.5g saturated fat, 5g carbohydrates, 3g fibre, 0.2g salt

1 of your 5 a day

# sweetcorn, tomato & basil salad

• QUICK RECIPE

A phytochemical in sweetcorn helps to protect your eyes against age-related macular degeneration, which leads to blindness.

**SERVES** 6 **PREPARATION** 15 minutes

1 tablespoon olive oil
1 teaspoon balsamic vinegar
¼ teaspoon salt
300g sweetcorn, fresh or frozen, thawed
2 large ripe tomatoes, seeded and coarsely chopped
15g fresh basil leaves, finely chopped, plus leaves to garnish
½ red onion, finely chopped

Whisk oil, vinegar and salt in a large bowl. If you're using fresh sweetcorn, blanch the kernels for 30 seconds in a large pan of boiling water before adding them to the salad. Stir in the sweetcorn. Gently stir in tomatoes, basil and onion. Serve.

**PER SERVING** 75Kcals, 2g protein, 3g fat, 0.5g saturated fat, 10g carbohydrates, 1g fibre, 0.2g salt

**1** of your **5 a day**

## fresh ideas

A fresh vegetable salad, which is a lot like a salsa, can be made from various different kinds of vegetables and vinaigrettes. Parboil vegetables that require it. Try carrots, celery, spring onions and dill; turnips, peas, peppers and chives; and red onions, potatoes, radishes and parsley.

## on the menu

Serve this simple, fresh salad with grilled fish or poultry and Baked Sweet Potato Fries (page 193). Finish the meal with a slice of Carrot-Pineapple Cake (page 245) and an espresso coffee.

# breads & muffins

# sweet potato muffins with pecan streusel

Nuts can provide a useful supply of protein in a vegetarian diet.

**MAKES** 12 muffins **PREPARATION** 20 minutes
**COOKING** 20 minutes, plus cooling

135g soft light brown sugar
280g plain flour
1½ teaspoons cinnamon
salt
25g butter, cut up
40g chopped pecan nuts
non-stick cooking spray
1 teaspoon baking powder
1 teaspoon bicarbonate of soda
¾ teaspoon ground ginger
250g orange sweet potato,
   cooked and mashed
90g honey
60ml vegetable oil
1 tablespoon finely grated orange zest
2 large eggs, lightly beaten
125ml buttermilk

**1** For the pecan streusel, combine 60g sugar, 35g flour, ½ tsp cinnamon and a pinch of salt in a medium bowl. Cut in the butter until the mixture is crumbly. Using your fingertips, rub mixture briefly to blend the butter. Stir in pecan nuts. Chill the streusel mixture.

**2** Preheat oven to 180°C (160°C fan oven), gas 4. Coat a 12 hole muffin tin with non-stick cooking spray. Combine the remaining flour, the baking powder, bicarbonate of soda, ginger, remaining cinnamon and ½ tsp salt in a small bowl.

**3** Combine the sweet potato, remaining sugar, honey, oil and zest in a medium bowl. Add eggs and buttermilk, and beat until well blended. Add flour mixture, stirring until just evenly moistened. Spoon into muffin cups, filling each one two-thirds full. Sprinkle with pecan streusel.

**4** Bake until tops of muffins spring back to the touch, about 20 minutes. Cool in the pan on a wire rack before turning out.

**PER MUFFIN** 255Kcals, 5g protein, 10 fat, 2.5g saturated fat, 40g carbohydrates, 1.5g fibre, 0.6g salt

**¼** of your **5 a day**

## did you know...

...that muffin batter can be prepared, spooned into muffin pans and chilled overnight? All you need to do in the morning is pop the pan into a preheated oven to have delicious fresh muffins to eat for breakfast.

# carrot-raisin muffins

Sunflower seeds are rich in heart-protecting vitamin E. They also include selenium, copper, fibre, iron, zinc, folate and vitamin $B_6$.

**MAKES** 12 muffins    **PREPARATION** 10 minutes
**COOKING** 15 minutes, plus cooling

non-stick cooking spray (optional)
140g plain flour
70g wholemeal flour
100g caster sugar
2 teaspoons baking powder
¼ teaspoon salt
½ teaspoon cinnamon
¼ teaspoon ground allspice
¼ teaspoon freshly grated nutmeg
135g unsweetened apple sauce
60ml vegetable oil
2 large eggs, lightly beaten
1 large carrot, peeled and finely grated
80g raisins
2 tablespoons sunflower seeds

**1** Preheat oven to 200°C (180°C fan oven), gas 6. Coat a 12 hole muffin tin with non-stick cooking spray or line with paper cake cases.

**2** Mix flours, sugar, baking powder, salt, cinnamon, allspice and nutmeg in a medium bowl.

**3** Combine the apple sauce, oil and eggs in a large bowl. Fold in the carrot and raisins. Add flour mixture, stirring just until evenly moistened. Spoon into muffin cups, filling each one two-thirds full. Sprinkle with sunflower seeds.

**4** Bake until a skewer inserted in the centre of a muffin comes out clean, about 15 minutes. Cool muffins in the pan on a wire rack before turning out. Serve warm.

**PER MUFFIN** 181Kcals, 24g protein, 6.5g fat, 1g saturated fat, 28g carbohydrates, 1.5g fibre, 0.3g salt

¼ of your 5 a day

## helpful hint

The rule of thumb with muffins is not to overmix the batter. To make sure that the finished result is light and well risen, stir the ingredients with a wooden spoon until just combined. Muffins are very versatile. Savoury or sweet, they're perfect for breakfast and as a snack food at any time.

# sweet potato scones

• QUICK RECIPE
• MAKE AHEAD

These scones are heart friendly. They're low in saturated fat because they're made with oil instead of butter.

**MAKES** 12 scones   **PREPARATION** 12 minutes   **COOKING** 15 minutes

245g plain flour, plus extra for dusting
¼ teaspoon salt
1 tablespoon baking powder
pinch of freshly grated nutmeg
250g orange sweet potato, cooked and mashed
60ml vegetable oil
60ml semi-skimmed milk
1 large egg, lightly beaten
2 tablespoons soft light brown sugar

**1** Preheat oven to 220°C (200°C fan oven), gas 7. Sift flour, salt, baking powder and nutmeg into a small bowl.

**2** Stir together sweet potato, oil, milk, egg and sugar in a medium bowl. Stir in flour mixture until just evenly moistened.

**3** Turn dough out on to a floured work surface. Pat out to a 2cm thick round. Cut into rounds with a 6cm biscuit cutter. Place rounds on a baking sheet about 2.5cm apart. Gather up remaining dough. Pat into a circle; cut out remaining scones.

**4** Bake until golden, 12 to 15 minutes. Serve warm.

**PER SCONE**  142Kcals, 3g protein, 5g fat, 0.8g saturated fat, 23g carbohydrates, 1g fibre, 0.49g salt

# tomato scones

• QUICK RECIPE
• MAKE AHEAD

Lovely savoury scones are made with yoghurt and enlivened with sun-dried tomatoes and spring onions.

**MAKES** 12 scones   **PREPARATION** 12 minutes
**COOKING** 12 minutes, plus cooling

non-stick cooking spray
1 medium tomato, seeded and
    finely chopped
280g plain flour
1 tablespoon baking powder
½ teaspoon salt
260g low-fat plain yoghurt
85ml olive oil
1 spring onion, finely chopped
2 soft sun-dried tomatoes,
    finely chopped

**1** Preheat oven to 220°C (200°C fan oven), gas 7. Lightly coat a baking sheet with non-stick cooking spray. Drain tomato on kitchen paper.

**2** Combine flour, baking powder and salt in a medium bowl. Combine yoghurt and oil in a small bowl; stir into flour mixture until just evenly moistened.

**3** Stir fresh tomato, spring onion and sun-dried tomatoes into flour mixture. Drop dough, about 3 tbsp at a time, on to the prepared baking sheet, to make 12 scones.

**4** Bake until the tops are golden brown, about 12 minutes. Serve warm or at room temperature.

**PER SCONE**  166Kcals, 3g protein, 8g fat, 1g saturated fat, 20g carbohydrates, 1g fibre, 0.5g salt

## helpful **hint**

To make Sweet Potato Scones even healthier for your heart, substitute 2 egg whites for the whole egg. Use plain wholemeal flour in place of some or all of the white flour.

**fresh ideas**

Baking powder, vegetable oil and yoghurt are the ingredients that produce a soft, flaky scone. To make the tops browner, brush the scones with milk or oil before baking. To add more flavour to savoury scones, include 2 tablespoons of finely chopped ham, chives or mild chillies in the batter. Scones freeze well so it's well worth making a double batch and storing some for later.

• MAKE AHEAD

# cranberry-walnut
# pumpkin bread

Walnuts and walnut oil contain 'good fats' that help to keep your arteries clear and your heart healthy. A generous helping of superfood cranberries adds a taste and texture contrast.

**MAKES** 1 loaf (about 16 slices)  **PREPARATION** 15 minutes
**COOKING** 45 minutes, plus cooling

non-stick cooking spray
175g plain flour
1 teaspoon ground ginger
1 teaspoon cinnamon
¾ teaspoon bicarbonate of soda
¼ teaspoon salt
260g pumpkin or squash,
  cooked and puréed
150g soft dark brown sugar
60ml walnut oil or vegetable oil
2 large eggs, lightly beaten
1 teaspoon vanilla extract
50g walnuts, coarsely chopped
60g sweet dried cranberries

**1** Preheat oven to 180°C (160°C fan oven), gas 4. Lightly coat a 23 x 13cm loaf tin with non-stick cooking spray.

**2** Sift together flour, ginger, cinnamon, bicarbonate of soda and salt in a medium bowl. Stir pumpkin or squash, sugar, oil, eggs and vanilla extract until smooth in another medium bowl. Stir into flour mixture until just evenly moistened. Stir in the walnuts and cranberries. Spoon into prepared tin.

**3** Bake until a cocktail stick inserted into the centre comes out clean, about 45 minutes. Turn out on to a wire rack to cool.

**PER SLICE** 144Kcals, 3g protein, 6g fat, 1g saturated fat, 18g carbohydrates, 0.8g fibre, 0.3g salt

**¼ of your 5 a day**

**fresh ideas** Quick breads such as Cranberry-Walnut Pumpkin Bread make welcome gifts. They're called quick breads because they don't contain yeast, so no rising time is required. This means that you can prepare a loaf for the oven in minutes.

• MAKE AHEAD

# carrot-ginger
# scones

The classic scone gets a beta carotene boost from grated carrot and an injection of flavour from ginger.

**MAKES** 8 scones  **PREPARATION** 15 minutes
**COOKING** 20 minutes, plus cooling

non-stick cooking spray
210g plain flour, plus extra for dusting
50g plus 2 teaspoons caster sugar
1½ teaspoons baking powder
½ teaspoon salt
¼ teaspoon bicarbonate of soda
2 tablespoons crystallised ginger
75g chilled butter, cut into small pieces
1 large carrot, peeled and grated
125ml buttermilk

**1** Preheat oven to 200°C (180°C fan oven), gas 6. Lightly coat a large baking sheet with non-stick cooking spray.

**2** Combine the flour, 50g sugar, the baking powder, salt and bicarbonate of soda in a food processor. Pulse to combine. Add ginger; pulse until finely ground. Add butter; pulse until the mixture resembles coarse breadcrumbs. Transfer to a bowl.

**3** Add carrot to flour mixture. Fold in buttermilk until just evenly moistened. Scrape dough on to a floured work surface. Knead briefly until dough just holds together. Pat out to a 2.5cm thick round. Sprinkle top with remaining 2 tsp sugar.

**4** Cut dough into eight equal wedges. Arrange 2.5cm apart on the prepared baking sheet. Bake until golden, 18 to 20 minutes. Transfer to a wire rack to cool.

**PER SCONE** 223Kcals, 3g protein, 10g fat, 6g saturated fat, 33g carbohydrates, 1g fibre, 0.8g salt

**¼ of your 5 a day**

# carrot-flecked
## corn bread

The addition of grated carrots transforms an ordinary swift corn bread into a nutritious superfood.

**MAKES** 9 squares **PREPARATION** 10 minutes **COOKING** 25 minutes, plus cooling

2 tablespoons vegetable oil
280g instant polenta
45g plain flour
2 teaspoons baking powder
1 teaspoon bicarbonate of soda
2 tablespoons caster sugar
1 teaspoon salt
435ml buttermilk
1 large egg, lightly beaten
2 medium carrots, peeled and finely grated

**1** Preheat oven to 200°C (180°C fan oven), gas 6. Swirl oil in a 20 x 20 x 5cm baking tin. Preheat tin in oven for 5 minutes.

**2** Combine the polenta, flour, baking powder, bicarbonate of soda, sugar and salt in a large bowl. Stir in the buttermilk, egg and carrots. Carefully pour in oil from baking tin. Mix well. Pour batter into hot tin.

**3** Bake until a cocktail stick inserted into the centre comes out clean, about 25 minutes. Cool in tin for 10 minutes. Turn out on to a wire rack and cool slightly before cutting.

**PER SQUARE** 200Kcals, 6g protein, 5g fat, 0.7g saturated fat, 33g carbohydrates, 1g fibre, 1.1g salt

**1/4 of your 5 a day**

## did you know...

...that buttermilk is produced by adding live cultures to semi-skimmed milk? This thickens the milk and gives it a pleasant creamy, tangy flavour. Buttermilk is a useful ingredient in baking, particularly in scones and muffins.

# red pepper & **green**
## **chilli** spoon bread

Just dig in to enjoy this unusual moist bread made with eggs and polenta and which includes plenty of sweetcorn alongside the peppers and chillies.

**SERVES** 6 **PREPARATION** 20 minutes **COOKING** 55 minutes

vegetable oil, for greasing
170g instant polenta
250ml semi-skimmed milk
1 teaspoon salt
15g butter
100g green chillies in vinegar, drained
1 medium red pepper, seeded and cut
    into small chunks
150g sweetcorn, fresh, drained canned,
    or thawed frozen
3 large eggs, separated

**1** Preheat oven to 190°C (170°C fan oven), gas 5. Coat a medium casserole with vegetable oil.

**2** In a small pan, bring 350ml water and the polenta to the boil. Lower heat. Simmer, stirring frequently, 3 minutes. Transfer to a medium bowl. Place milk, salt, butter, chillies, pepper and sweetcorn in the pan; heat until butter melts. Cool slightly. Lightly beat egg yolks and stir in. Stir into polenta.

**3** Whisk egg whites in a medium bowl until stiff peaks form. Fold into polenta mixture. Pour into prepared casserole.

**4** Bake until centre is firm and top is browned, 50 minutes. Serve at once.

**PER SERVING** 222Kcals, 10g protein, 7g fat, 3g saturated fat, 30g carbohydrates, 1.5g fibre, 1g salt

**1/4 of your 5 a day**

# wholemeal pumpkin rolls with honey

- MAKE AHEAD
- HEART HEALTHY

Wholemeal flour and a purée of pumpkin add antioxidant vitamins and fibre to these sweet rolls.

**MAKES** 24 rolls   **PREPARATION** 30 minutes   **RISING** about 2 hours 30 minutes   **COOKING** 12 minutes, plus cooling

220g pumpkin seeds
1 sachet (7g) active dried yeast
125ml lukewarm water
90g honey
430g pumpkin or squash,
   cooked and puréed
2 tablespoons olive oil,
   plus extra for greasing
600g strong white bread flour
140g strong wholemeal bread flour
2 teaspoons salt

**1** Toast the seeds in a small pan over medium heat, stirring often, until browned, about 2 minutes. Set aside. Sprinkle yeast over lukewarm water in a large bowl. Leave until foamy, about 5 minutes. Add honey; stir until it dissolves. Stir in pumpkin or squash and oil. Stir in flours and salt to form a dough.

**2** Place dough on a lightly floured work surface. Knead until smooth and elastic, about 10 minutes, adding more flour as needed to prevent sticking. Work in pumpkin seeds. Place dough in a lightly oiled bowl. Turn to coat. Cover loosely with cling film. Leave to rise in a warm place until doubled in size, about 1 hour 30 minutes.

**3** Line two baking sheets with foil. Knock back the dough. Form into 24 rolls. Put on prepared baking sheets. Cover loosely with oiled cling film. Leave to rise in a warm place until doubled in size, about 1 hour.

**4** Preheat oven to 200°C (180°C fan oven), gas 6. Uncover rolls. Bake until puffed and golden, and rolls sound hollow when tapped underneath, about 12 minutes. Serve warm.

**PER ROLL**   177Kcals, 5.5g protein, 6g fat, 1g saturated fat, 28g carbohydrates, 2g fibre, 0.4g salt

¼ of your 5 a day

**fresh ideas**

Some cooks prefer to use fresh yeast instead of dried but, at the end of the day, there is little difference between the results achieved. The dry variety is almost twice as concentrated as fresh. Whichever type you choose, remember that yeast is a living organism. It will thrive between 32°C and 46°C and die in temperatures above 60°C.

# wholemeal winter loaf

- MAKE AHEAD
- HEART HEALTHY

Wheatgerm and bran in wholemeal flour supply vitamin E and fibre that are lost in processing white flour. Pumpkin and squash add extra fibre.

**MAKES** 2 loaves (about 12 slices each)  **PREPARATION** 25 minutes
**RISING** 2 hours **COOKING** 30 minutes, plus cooling

490g strong wholemeal bread flour
420g strong white bread flour,
    plus extra for dusting
1 teaspoon easy-blend yeast
170ml semi-skimmed milk
180g honey
2 teaspoons salt
2 large eggs, lightly beaten
390g pumpkin or squash,
    cooked and puréed
2 tablespoons olive oil, pus extra for greasing
2 bunches spring onions, coarsely chopped
2 tablespoons chopped fresh rosemary
150g sunflower seeds

**1** Combine the flours in a large bowl. Put 350g flour mixture in another large bowl with the yeast.

**2** Heat milk, 125ml water and the honey in a medium pan until just warm. Stir into flour-yeast mixture. Add salt and eggs. Beat with electric beaters on low speed for 30 seconds; scrape down side of bowl constantly. Beat on high speed 3 minutes.

**3** Add pumpkin or squash, oil, spring onions, rosemary, sunflower seeds and remaining flour mixture, beating until mixture is well combined.

**4** Place dough on a lightly floured work surface. Knead until smooth and elastic, 6 to 8 minutes, adding more plain flour as needed to prevent sticking. Shape dough into a ball. Place in a lightly oiled bowl. Turn to coat. Cover loosely with oiled cling film. Leave dough to rise in a warm place until doubled in size, about 1 hour.

**5** Knock back dough. Turn out on to lightly oiled surface. Divide in half. Leave to rest for 10 minutes.

**6** Lightly oil two 23 x 13cm loaf tins. Pat each half of the dough into a loaf shape. Put in loaf tins. Cover loosely with oiled cling film. Leave to rise in a warm place until almost doubled in size, about 50 minutes.

**7** Preheat oven to 190°C (170°C fan oven), gas 5. Bake until the loaves sound hollow when tapped underneath, about 30 minutes. Turn on to a wire rack to cool.

**1/4** of your **5 a day**

**PER SLICE** 205Kcals, 7g protein, 5g fat, 1g saturated fat, 34g carbohydrates, 3g fibre, 0.4g salt

## helpful hint

Store plain white or self-raising flour at cool room temperature for up to six months. Wholemeal and other wholegrain flours are slightly higher in fat and can turn rancid more quickly. Store them in the fridge for up to six months or the freezer for up to a year. Return to room temperature before using in baked goods.

# potato bread with poppy seeds

**• MAKE AHEAD**
**• HEART HEALTHY**

Poppy seeds on a glazed surface give an attractive finish to the crust of this loaf. The potato provides plenty of potassium and vitamins C and $B_6$.

**MAKES** 1 loaf (about 12 slices)  **PREPARATION** 25 minutes
**RISING** 2 hours  **COOKING** 45 minutes, plus cooling

3 tablespoons caster sugar
60ml lukewarm water
1 sachet (7g) active dried yeast
250g potato, cooked and mashed
250ml semi-skimmed milk
25g butter
1½ teaspoons salt
560g strong white bread flour
oil, for greasing
1 large egg beaten with 1 tablespoon milk, for glaze
2 teaspoons poppy seeds

**1** Stir 1 tbsp sugar into the water in a small bowl. Sprinkle the yeast over the top. Leave until foamy, about 5 minutes. Stir to dissolve yeast.

**2** Stir potato, milk, remaining sugar, the butter and salt in a small pan. Heat to just warm the mixture and melt the butter. Using a rubber spatula, push mixture into a large bowl through a sieve to remove any lumps in the potato. Stir in yeast mixture and 420g flour to form a dough.

**3** Sprinkle remaining flour on work surface. Turn out dough and knead, working in flour, until smooth and elastic, about 10 minutes. Add more flour as needed to prevent sticking. Place dough in a lightly oiled bowl. Turn to coat. Cover loosely with oiled cling film. Leave to rise in a warm place until doubled in size, about 1 hour 15 minutes.

**4** Lightly oil a 23 x 13cm loaf tin. Knock back dough. Knead briefly. Press into loaf tin. Cover with oiled cling film. Leave to rise in a warm place until doubled in size, about 45 minutes.

**5** Preheat oven to 180°C (160°C fan oven), gas 4. Brush top of loaf with egg glaze. Sprinkle with poppy seeds. Using a serrated knife, cut a 1cm deep slit lengthways down the middle of the loaf.

**6** Bake until browned and loaf has pulled away slightly from edges of pan, 40 to 45 minutes. Turn out on to a wire rack. Cool for at least 1 hour before slicing.

**PER SLICE** 232Kcals, 6g protein, 5g fat, 2g saturated fat, 44g carbohydrates, 1.52g fibre, 0.6g salt

# tomato-rye bread with rosemary & garlic

The red pigment in tomato juice gives this bread its sunny colour while herbs and garlic add extra taste.

**MAKES** 1 loaf (about 12 slices)  **PREPARATION** 30 minutes
**RISING** 2 hours  **COOKING** 50 minutes, plus cooling

125ml tomato juice
1 tablespoon olive oil, plus extra for greasing
1 teaspoon salt
½ teaspoon dried rosemary
2 garlic cloves, crushed
1 sachet (7g) active dried yeast
125ml lukewarm water
80g rye flour
280g strong white bread flour, plus extra for dusting
30g sun-dried tomatoes (not oil-packed), finely chopped

**1** Bring tomato juice, 120ml water, oil, salt, rosemary and garlic to a simmer in a small pan. Transfer to a medium bowl. Cool until lukewarm.

**2** Sprinkle yeast over lukewarm water in a small bowl. Leave until foamy, 5 minutes. Stir to dissolve.

**3** Add yeast mixture to tomato juice mixture. Gradually stir in rye flour. Gradually knead in plain flour until dough comes together and is workable (dough will be sticky). Knead in the sun-dried tomatoes. Turn dough out on to a floured work surface. Knead for 1 minute. Leave to rest for 10 minutes.

**4** Knead dough again on lightly floured surface until smooth and elastic, about 10 minutes; add more plain flour as needed if dough is very sticky (dough should be slightly sticky). Place dough in a lightly oiled bowl. Turn to coat. Cover loosely with oiled cling film. Leave to rise in a warm place until doubled in size, about 1 hour.

**5** Knock back dough. Lightly coat a 23 x 13cm loaf tin with olive oil. Place dough in tin, patting it into the corners. Cover loosely with oiled cling film. Leave to rise in a warm place until doubled in size (risen above top of pan), about 1 hour.

**6** Preheat oven to 190°C (170°C fan oven), gas 5. Bake until the loaf sounds hollow when tapped underneath, 40 to 50 minutes. Turn out on to a wire rack. Cool loaf completely before slicing.

**PER SLICE** 119Kcals, 3g protein, 2g fat, 0.2g saturated fat, 23g carbohydrates, 1.5g fibre, 0.4g salt

**¼** of your **5 a day**

# onion
# bread sticks

• MAKE AHEAD
• HEART HEALTHY

Freshly sautéed onions add a zesty taste and an attractive decoration to twisted bread sticks.

**MAKES** 12 bread sticks   **PREPARATION** 25 minutes
**RISING** 1 hour   **COOKING** 30 minutes, plus cooling

290g pack pizza base mix
flour, for dusting
2 tablespoons olive oil, plus extra for greasing
2 medium onions, very thinly sliced
coarse salt and ground black pepper, to taste

**1** Lightly oil two large baking sheets. Make up pizza base mix as pack instructions and knead for 5 minutes. Roll or pat dough out on a lightly floured surface to make a 30 x 15cm rectangle. Cut evenly into 12 bread sticks, each 15cm long. Gently twist each stick. Place on baking sheets. Cover loosely with oiled cling film. Leave to rise in a warm place until doubled in size, about 1 hour.

**2** Heat oil in a large non-stick frying pan over medium heat. Sauté onions until very soft and golden, about 12 minutes.

**3** Preheat oven to 200°C (180°C fan oven), gas 6. Place one oven rack at the lowest position and another at the highest.

**4** Just before baking, distribute sautéed onions over surface of each bread stick, taking care not to deflate dough. Sprinkle each stick with a little salt and pepper.

**5** Bake for 16 minutes, swapping the sheets over halfway through. Transfer to a wire rack to cool.

**PER BREAD STICK** 138Kcals, 3g protein, 4g fat, 0.5g saturated fat, 24g carbohydrates, 1g fibre, 0.2g salt

**¼**
of your
**5 a day**

# focaccia with
# tomatoes & parsley

• MAKE AHEAD
• HEART HEALTHY

Focaccia is a flat bread, rather like a pizza, but is softer and thicker. Tomatoes, peppers and Parmesan cheese are welcome additions.

**SERVES** 8   **PREPARATION** 25 minutes   **RISING** 2 hours
**COOKING** 40 minutes, plus cooling

2 teaspoons caster sugar
500ml lukewarm water
1 sachet (7g) active dried yeast
15g fresh parsley, chopped
3½ tablespoons olive oil, plus extra for greasing
1½ teaspoons salt
½ teaspoon dried sage
700g strong white bread flour, plus extra for dusting
2 garlic cloves, crushed
3 medium tomatoes, thinly sliced
1 large yellow pepper, seeded and cut into thin strips
2 tablespoons grated Parmesan cheese

**1** Stir sugar into lukewarm water in a large bowl. Sprinkle yeast over the top. Leave until foamy, about 5 minutes. Stir to dissolve yeast.

**2** Reserve 2 tbsp parsley. Stir the remaining parsley, 3 tbsp oil, salt and sage into yeast mixture. Add 280g flour; mix vigorously. Stir in remaining flour to make a stiff dough.

**3** Lightly flour a work surface. Knead dough until smooth and elastic, about 10 minutes; add more flour as needed to prevent sticking. Place dough in a lightly oiled bowl. Turn to coat. Cover loosely with oiled cling film. Leave to rise in a warm place until doubled in size, about 1 hour 15 minutes.

**4** Lightly oil a 43 x 28cm Swiss roll tin. Knock back dough. Knead briefly. Pat into a rectangle to fit into tin. Cover dough loosely with oiled cling film. Leave to rise in a warm place until doubled in size, about 40 minutes.

**5** Preheat oven to 200°C (180°C fan oven), gas 6. Place oven rack in lowest position. Make dimples in dough with fingertips. Brush with oil. Sprinkle with garlic and arrange tomato slices over the top. Top with pepper strips. Sprinkle with Parmesan cheese.

**6** Bake focaccia on lowest rack until browned at the edges, 35 to 40 minutes. Transfer to a wire rack. Sprinkle with reserved parsley. Leave to cool for at least 20 minutes.

**PER SERVING** 380Kcals, 10g protein, 7g fat, 1.5g saturated fat, 71g carbohydrates, 3g fibre, 0.8g salt

**½**
of your
**5 a day**

fresh ideas

Focaccia is delicious used for sandwiches. Try slices of mozzarella and tomato. Prosciutto – very thin slices of cured or air-dried ham – also tastes excellent in focaccia with tomato or thinly sliced red pepper.

# cakes,
## cookies & desserts

# secret-ingredient chocolate cake

Cocoa, flour, sugar and eggs are all ingredients you'd expect to find in a cake. The surprise healthy addition here is healthy tomato juice.

**SERVES** 16 **PREPARATION** 20 minutes
**COOKING** 30 minutes, plus cooling

non-stick cooking spray
185ml tomato juice
75g unsweetened cocoa powder
315g plain flour
1 teaspoon bicarbonate of soda
½ teaspoon baking powder
¼ teaspoon salt
315g caster sugar
125ml vegetable oil
3 large eggs
1½ teaspoons vanilla extract
30g plain chocolate
2 tablespoons semi-skimmed milk
125g low-fat soft cheese
350g icing sugar, sifted
170g seedless raspberry jam

**1** Preheat oven to 180°C (160°C fan oven), gas 4. Coat two 23cm round sandwich tins with non-stick cooking spray.

**2** Bring the tomato juice and 60ml water to the boil in a small pan. Whisk in 60g cocoa powder until completely dissolved. Remove from heat.

**fresh ideas**
Instead of a thick layer of icing, you can take this cake from tea party to dinner party by topping it generously with freshly whipped cream and a sprinkling of fresh raspberries or sliced strawberries.

**3** Sift together flour, bicarbonate of soda, baking powder and salt in a medium bowl.

**4** Beat sugar, oil, eggs and 1 tsp vanilla extract in a large bowl to combine. Beat in cocoa mixture. Beat in flour mixture until just evenly moistened. Divide batter between tins.

**5** Bake until a skewer inserted into the centre of each cake comes out clean, 25 to 30 minutes. Transfer tins to a wire rack. Leave cakes to cool for 10 minutes. Turn cakes out on to rack. Allow to cool completely before icing.

**6** For the icing, put the chocolate and milk in a medium microwave-safe bowl and microwave on high power 1 minute (or melt in a heatproof bowl over a pan of gently simmering water). Stir until smooth. Whisk in remaining cocoa powder until smooth. Whisk in soft cheese and remaining vanilla extract. Stir in icing sugar until combined.

**7** Place one cake layer on a serving plate. Spread with jam and about a third of the icing mixture. Place second layer on top. Spread the rest of the icing over top and side of cake.

**PER SERVING** 364Kcals, 5g protein, 10g fat, 3g saturated fat, 67g carbohydrates, 1g fibre, 0.5g salt

¼ of your 5 a day

## helpful **hints**

• For a square cake, use two 20 x 5cm square tins in place of the two 23cm rounds. To make a single-layer cake, substitute a 33 x 23 x 5cm tin. Start checking that the cake is sufficiently well cooked about 10 minutes before the baking time recommended in the recipe given here.
• For cakes with a lighter texture, separate the eggs before adding them. Add the yolks to the creamed sugar and oil (or butter) mixture. Whisk the whites separately until stiff peaks form and gently fold into the batter.
• To prevent cake layers from sticking to the wire racks while cooling, first spray the racks lightly with non-stick cooking spray.

• MAKE AHEAD

# whisky-squash cake

The addition of butternut squash gives a wicked-looking cake essential nutrients, including B vitamins, beta carotene, vitamin C, iron and magnesium.

**SERVES** 16 **PREPARATION** 15 minutes
**COOKING** 50 minutes, plus cooling

non-stick cooking spray
280g plain flour
2 teaspoons baking powder
1 teaspoon bicarbonate of soda
1 teaspoon salt
2 teaspoons ground cinnamon
300g caster sugar
250ml vegetable oil
4 large eggs
450g butternut squash,
   cooked and mashed
60ml whisky
icing sugar, for dusting (optional)
strawberries, to serve (optional)

**1** Preheat oven to 180°C (160°C fan oven), gas 4. Coat a 2.25 litre fluted ring tin with non-stick cooking spray.

**2** Stir flour, baking powder, bicarbonate of soda, salt and cinnamon in a small bowl.

**3** Beat sugar, oil, eggs and squash in a large bowl until well combined. Beat in flour mixture until evenly moistened. Beat in whisky. Using a rubber spatula, scrape batter into tin.

**4** Bake until a skewer inserted into the cake comes out clean, 45 to 50 minutes. Transfer tin to a wire rack. Leave cake to cool in tin for 15 minutes. Run a thin-bladed knife around the edge and centre ring of the tin. Turn out cake on to rack and leave to cool completely. Dust with icing sugar and serve with strawberries, if you like.

**PER SERVING** 280Kcals, 4g protein, 14g fat, 2g saturated fat, 36g carbohydrates, 1g fibre, 0.6g salt

**½** of your **5 a day**

• MAKE AHEAD

# carrot-pineapple cake

This cake is one of the most delightful ways to get your quota of vitamin A, with 80 per cent of the daily requirement contained in each slice.

**SERVES** 16   **PREPARATION** 20 minutes
**COOKING** 50 minutes, plus cooling

non-stick cooking spray
350g plain flour
2 teaspoons ground cinnamon
1 teaspoon baking powder
1½ teaspoons bicarbonate of soda
½ teaspoon salt
300g caster sugar
125ml vegetable oil
4 large eggs
135g unsweetened apple sauce
500g carrots, peeled and grated
225g canned crushed pineapple in natural juice
80g seedless raisins
50g walnuts, chopped
250g low-fat soft cheese, softened
620g icing sugar, sifted
1 teaspoon vanilla extract

**1** Preheat oven to 180°C (160°C fan oven), gas 4. Coat two 23cm round sandwich tins with non-stick cooking spray.

**2** Sift together flour, cinnamon, baking powder, bicarbonate of soda and salt in a medium bowl.

**3** Beat sugar, oil, eggs and apple sauce in a large bowl until thoroughly combined. Beat in flour mixture just until evenly moistened. Stir in the carrots, pineapple and juice, raisins and walnuts. Divide batter between prepared tins.

**4** Bake until a skewer inserted into the centre of each cake comes out clean, 45 to 50 minutes. Transfer the tins to a wire rack. Leave to cool for 30 minutes. Turn cakes out on to racks. Leave to cool completely.

**5** For the icing, beat soft cheese in a large bowl on low speed for 1 minute. Add icing sugar and vanilla; beat until smooth.

**6** Place a cake layer on a serving plate. Spread with a third of the icing. Place second layer on top. Spread remaining icing over the top and side of cake.

**PER SERVING** 458Kcals, 6g protein, 12g fat, 3g saturated fat, 87g carbohydrates, 2g fibre, 0.6g salt

**½** of your **5 a day**

## did you **know...**

...that pineapple contains an enzyme called bromelian that acts as a natural meat and poultry tenderiser when it is added to marinades or stews? Bromelian is also an anti-inflammatory and may help to reduce the risk of blood clots.

# ruby mincemeat tarts

Carrot and beetroot give the dried fruits in this mincemeat a rich flavour and colour, and add nutritional value too.

**SERVES** 6  **PREPARATION** 15 minutes  **SOAKING** 1 hour
**COOKING** 25 minutes

1 carrot, peeled and finely grated to
   give 60g prepared weight
1 cooked beetroot, peeled and finely grated
   to give 60g prepared weight
½ small eating apple, peeled, cored and finely grated
75g traditional dried apricots, chopped
60g glacé cherries, chopped
25g sweet dried cranberries
grated zest and juice of ½ orange and ½ lemon
2 tablespoons brandy or rum (optional)
1 teaspoon ground cinnamon
375g ready-rolled puff pastry
250g mascarpone or low-fat soft cheese, to serve

**1** Mix the carrot, beetroot, apple, apricots, cherries and cranberries. Stir in the orange and lemon zest, juice, brandy or rum, if using, and cinnamon until thoroughly combined. Cover and set aside at room temperature for 1 hour.

**2** Preheat oven to 190°C (170°C fan oven), gas 5. Use a 7.5cm round cutter to stamp out 12 circles of puff pastry and press them into 12 deep patty tins. Prick the bases of the pastry tarts. Stir the mincemeat and use a teaspoon to fill the tarts generously.

**3** Bake until the pastry rims are puffed and browned around the edges, 20 to 25 minutes. Transfer to a wire rack to cool slightly. Serve warm with dollops of mascarpone or low-fat soft cheese.

**PER TART**  488Kcals, 6g protein, 32g fat, 19g saturated fat, 40g carbohydrate, 2g fibre, 0.6g salt

**¼**
of your
**5 a day**

---

• MAKE AHEAD

# no-bake pumpkin pie with gingery crust

This is a quick-fix but impressive-looking dessert that's packed with beta carotene and fibre.

**SERVES** 8  **PREPARATION** 10 minutes  **CHILL** 5 hours

330g gingernut biscuits
50g butter, melted
2 packets (100g each) instant
   vanilla pudding mix
375ml milk
430g pumpkin or squash,
   cooked and puréed
1¼ teaspoons ground cinnamon
¾ teaspoon ground ginger
¼ teaspoon freshly grated nutmeg
pecan nut halves, to decorate (optional)

**1** Put the biscuits into a food processor and whiz to make fine crumbs. (Alternatively, put them in a plastic bag and crush with a rolling pin.) Put in a bowl and stir in the melted butter until the crumbs are evenly coated. Lightly press crumb mixture over base and side of a 23cm pie dish.

**2** Whisk pudding mixes and milk in a medium bowl until thick and blended. Stir in pumpkin or squash purée, cinnamon, ginger and nutmeg. Spread evenly over gingernut crust. Garnish top with pecan nut halves, if you like. Cover and chill for at least 5 hours or overnight.

**PER SLICE**  364Kcals, 6g protein, 24g fat, 14g saturated fat, 74g carbohydrate, 2g fibre, 1.4g salt

**½**
of your
**5 a day**

## helpful hint

Instead of a whisk, you can use a food processor or blender to combine the filling ingredients for this pie. If you're short on time, make the pie even faster by using a shop-bought, sweet pastry crust.

# sweet & spicy carrot pie with nut crust

• MAKE AHEAD

A mixture of toasted nuts add healthy fats and a rich flavour to the crust of this rich and filling pie.

**SERVES** 8   **PREPARATION** 25 minutes   **COOKING** 1 hour 10 minutes

500g carrots, peeled and cut into chunks
125g marie or digestive biscuits
50g walnuts, lightly toasted
70g hazelnuts, lightly toasted
60g soft light brown sugar
1¼ teaspoons ground cinnamon
1¼ teaspoons ground ginger
3 tablespoons vegetable oil or
   light olive oil
25g butter, melted
200g caster sugar
1 tablespoon plain flour
½ teaspoon salt
¼ teaspoon freshly grated nutmeg
pinch of ground cloves
4 large eggs, lightly beaten
185ml semi-skimmed milk
whipped cream, to serve (optional)

**1** Place carrots in a large pan of boiling water to cover; cook until tender, about 20 minutes. Drain well. Purée in a food processor, or mash. Leave to cool slightly.

**2** Preheat oven to 200°C (180°C fan oven), gas 6. Put the biscuits into a food processor and whiz to make fine crumbs. (Alternatively, put them in a plastic bag and crush with a rolling pin.) Toast the nuts in a small pan over medium heat, stirring often, until browned, about 3 minutes.

**3** Coarsely chop the nuts and put into a bowl. Add biscuit crumbs, brown sugar, ¼ tsp cinnamon and ¼ tsp ground ginger. Stir to combine. Stir in the oil and melted butter until crumbs are evenly moistened. Press crumb mixture over base and side of a 23cm deep pie dish.

**4** Stir together sugar, flour, remaining ginger and cinnamon, salt, nutmeg and cloves in a small bowl. Stir into carrot purée. Add the eggs and milk; stir until smooth and thoroughly blended. Pour mixture into crust.

**5** Bake until a skewer inserted in the centre of the pie comes out clean, about 45 minutes. Serve warm or chilled with cream, if you like.

**PER SERVING** 453Kcals, 9g protein, 25g fat, 6g saturated fat, 52g carbohydrates, 2.5g fibre, 0.6g salt

½ of your 5 a day

## helpful **hint**

Custard-type pies made with eggs and milk may develop a crack across the top during baking or cooling due to moisture loss. To minimise cracks, try putting a shallow dish of hot water on the bottom shelf of the oven.

# sweet potato pie
## with cranberry-
## pecan marmalade

A fresh cranberry and nut layer lightens the texture and gives contrasting flavour to this classic dessert as well as adding a special blend of antioxidants. Cranberries provide fibre along with some vitamin C.

**SERVES** 8  **PREPARATION** 20 minutes
**COOKING** 1 hour 5 minutes, plus cooling and chilling

85g pecan nuts
175g whole frozen cranberries,
   plus extra to decorate
240g caster sugar, plus extra for dusting
375g shortcrust pastry, thawed if frozen
flour, for dusting
500g orange sweet potatoes,
   cooked and mashed
375ml light evaporated milk
1 large egg, lightly beaten
2 large egg whites, lightly whisked
½ teaspoon vanilla extract
½ teaspoon ground cinnamon
¼ teaspoon freshly grated nutmeg
¼ teaspoon ground allspice
pinch of salt

**1** Toast the nuts in a small pan over medium heat, stirring often, until browned, about 3 minutes. Chop. For the cranberry-pecan marmalade, place the cranberries, 100g sugar and 120ml water in a small pan. Bring to the boil. Reduce heat; simmer until the cranberries pop and are softened, about 10 minutes. Remove from heat. Stir in pecan nuts. Cool.

**2** Preheat oven to 220°C (200°C fan oven), gas 7. Roll out pastry on a floured surface and use to line a 25cm pie dish. Crimp edges.

**3** Thoroughly combine the mashed sweet potato, evaporated milk, remaining sugar, egg, egg whites, vanilla extract, cinnamon, nutmeg, allspice and salt in a large bowl.

**4** Spread cooled marmalade over base of pie shell. Pour the sweet potato mixture on top.

**5** Bake for 10 minutes. Lower temperature to 180°C (160°C fan oven), gas 4. Bake until the centre is set, about 40 minutes. Transfer pie to a wire rack. Cool for 30 minutes. Chill. Decorate with cranberries, dusted with sugar.

**PER SERVING** 561Kcals, 10g protein, 26g fat, 7g saturated fat, 77g carbohydrate, 4g fibre, 0.9 salt

**1** of your **5 a day**

**fresh ideas**
If whole cranberries are unavailable, substitute 400g whole-berry cranberry sauce. Heat gently to soften. Stir in pecans and cool mixture before using.

# on the **menu**

Sweet teacakes keep well if they are stored in a cool place in an airtight container. However, if they become a little dry, try lightly toasting slices and spreading them with butter or fruit preserve.

# carrot-courgette
## sweet teacake

You'll get A, B and C vitamins from the vegetables, omega-3 fatty acids from the walnuts, plus fibre from the wheat bran in the wholemeal flour.

**MAKES** 12 slices  **PREPARATION** 15 minutes
**COOKING** 1 hour, plus cooling

non-stick cooking spray
210g plain flour, plus extra for dusting
70g wholemeal flour
1¼ teaspoons bicarbonate of soda
1 teaspoon baking powder
1 teaspoon ground cinnamon
½ teaspoon salt
¼ teaspoon freshly grated nutmeg
260g caster sugar
185ml vegetable oil
3 large eggs
1 teaspoon vanilla extract
250g grated carrots, blotted dry
300g grated courgettes, blotted dry
50g walnuts, chopped (optional)
70g icing sugar
1½ tablespoons orange juice
1¼ teaspoons grated orange zest

**1** Preheat oven to 180°C (160°C fan oven), gas 4. Coat a 23 x 13cm loaf tin with non-stick cooking spray and dust with flour.

**2** Mix both flours, bicarbonate of soda, baking powder, cinnamon, salt and nutmeg in a medium bowl. Beat sugar, oil, eggs and vanilla extract in a large bowl until well blended. Stir in carrots and courgettes. Beat in flour mixture until evenly moistened. Stir in walnuts, if using. Spread batter in tin.

**3** Bake until a skewer inserted into the centre comes out clean, 55 to 60 minutes. Transfer tin to a wire rack. Leave cake to cool for 10 minutes. Loosen edges of loaf with a thin-bladed knife. Turn on to a rack. Cool completely before glazing.

**4** Mix the icing sugar, orange juice and zest in a small bowl. Add another 1 to 2 tsp orange juice to thin, if necessary. Pour half the glaze over the cooled cake, spreading it evenly. Leave to set for 5 minutes. Pour on the remaining glaze.

**PER SLICE** 353Kcals, 6g protein, 17g fat, 2.5g saturated fat, 49g carbohydrates, 2g fibre, 0.6g salt

½ of your 5 a day

# summer
## cucumber sorbet

A magically easy, refreshing and healthy dessert.

**SERVES** 4  **PREPARATION** 10 minutes, plus 6 hours freezing

1 cucumber, very thinly peeled and
    cut into chunks
250ml elderflower cordial
450g strawberries
about 2 tablespoons icing sugar
8 strawberries for decoration
small strawberry leaves, washed,
    for decoration (optional)

**1** Turn the freezer to the fast-freeze setting. Purée the cucumber in a food processor or blender until smooth. Turn the purée into a freezer container and stir in the cordial. Freeze until three-quarters frozen, but still slightly sludgy in the middle, 3 to 4 hours.

**2** Whiz the frozen mixture in a food processor or use an electric whisk to break up the ice crystals, until the sorbet is opaque and smooth. Freeze until firm, 2 to 3 hours.

**3** Cut the 8 reserved strawberries into quarters for decoration. Purée the remaining strawberries until smooth, then stir in the icing sugar to taste. Divide the strawberry sauce among four dishes. Use an ice-cream scoop to serve the sorbet on the sauce. Decorate with strawberry slices and leaves, if you like. Serve immediately.

**PER SERVING** 217Kcals, 1.5g protein, 0g fat, 0g saturated fat, 53g carbohydrate, 1.5g fibre, Trace salt

2 of your 5 a day

# homemade pumpkin spice ice cream

• MAKE AHEAD
• HEART HEALTHY

For fibre and protective antioxidant vitamins along with a lovely fresh flavour and creamy texture, this ice cream is hard to beat.

**SERVES** 6   **PREPARATION** 20 minutes, plus freezing

310ml light evaporated milk
1 large egg
120g soft light brown sugar
175g pumpkin or squash, cooked and puréed
1 teaspoon vanilla extract
½ teaspoon ground ginger
½ teaspoon ground cinnamon
large pinch of freshly grated nutmeg
pinch of salt
biscuits, to serve (optional)

**1** Bring evaporated milk to the boil in a medium pan. Whisk egg and sugar in a large bowl. Gradually whisk in the boiling milk. Stir in pumpkin or squash, vanilla extract, ginger, cinnamon, nutmeg and salt. Chill well.

**2** Churn in an ice-cream maker, following manufacturer's instructions, or put into a freezerproof container and freeze for 4 hours beating once or twice with an electric whisk to break up the ice crystals. Soften slightly before serving. Serve with biscuits, if you like.

**PER 120ml** 152Kcals, 5.5g protein, 3g fat, 1.5g saturated fat, 27g carbohydrates, 0.3g fibre, 0.2g salt

½ of your 5 a day

# soft pumpkin biscuits

• MAKE AHEAD
• HEART HEALTHY

These moist and chewy pumpkin biscuits are packed with beta-carotene and fibre.

**MAKES** 24 biscuits   **PREPARATION** 15 minutes
**COOKING** 15 minutes, plus cooling

non-stick cooking spray
70g plain flour
70g wholemeal flour
½ teaspoon ground cinnamon
¼ teaspoon salt
¼ teaspoon bicarbonate of soda
¼ teaspoon ground allspice
60g soft light brown sugar
3 tablespoons honey
60ml vegetable oil
1 large egg white
260g pumpkin or squash, cooked and puréed
60g sweet dried cranberries or seedless raisins
35g walnuts, chopped (optional)

**1** Preheat oven to 180°C (160°C fan oven), gas 4. Coat two large baking sheets with non-stick cooking spray. Sift flours, cinnamon, salt, bicarbonate of soda and allspice into a bowl. Beat the brown sugar, honey, oil and egg white in a large bowl to combine. Stir in puréed pumpkin or squash. Stir in flour mixture until evenly moistened. Fold in dried cranberries or raisins and the walnuts, if using.

**2** Drop heaped teaspoons of biscuit dough on to the baking sheets, spacing them about 2.5cm apart. Bake until a skewer inserted into the centre of a biscuit comes out clean, about 15 minutes. Leave the biscuits on the sheets for 1 minute. Use a metal spatula to transfer them to a wire rack to cool. Store in an airtight container for up to a week.

**PER COOKIE** 70Kcals, 1g protein, 3g fat, 0.5g saturated fat, 8g carbohydrates, 0.7g fibre, 0.1g salt

# carrot & oat cookies

- MAKE AHEAD
- HEART HEALTHY

The oats in these fragrantly spiced cookies help to protect your heart by lowering cholesterol levels.

**MAKES** 48 cookies   **PREPARATION** 20 minutes
**COOKING** 10 to 12 minutes, plus cooling

non-stick cooking spray
140g plain flour
2½ teaspoons baking powder
½ teaspoon salt
½ teaspoon ground cinnamon
¼ teaspoon ground cloves
95g rolled porridge oats
1 large egg
125ml vegetable oil
1 teaspoon vanilla extract
230g soft light brown sugar
125g carrots, grated
120g seedless raisins

**1** Preheat oven to 190°C (170°C fan oven), gas 5. Coat two large baking sheets with non-stick cooking spray. Sift the flour, baking powder, salt, cinnamon and cloves into a medium bowl. Stir in the oats.

**2** Beat egg, oil and vanilla extract in a large bowl. Beat in sugar. Beat in flour mixture in batches until evenly moistened. Fold in carrots and raisins to make a stiff dough.

**3** Drop heaped teaspoons of dough on to the baking sheets, spacing them about 5cm apart.

**4** Bake until golden brown and slightly darker at the edges, 10 to 12 minutes. Leave cookies on baking sheets for 2 minutes. Use a metal spatula to transfer them to a wire rack to cool. Store in an airtight container for up to a week.

**PER COOKIE** 62Kcals, 0.8g protein, 2g fat, 0.5g saturated fat, 10g carbohydrates, 0.3g fibre, 0.1g salt

## helpful **hint**

To freeze the dough for drop cookies, spoon dough on to baking sheets. Place sheets in the freezer until dough is frozen solid. Transfer dough drops to a container. To bake, put frozen drops on prepared baking sheets. Thaw at room temperature. Bake as directed in the recipe.

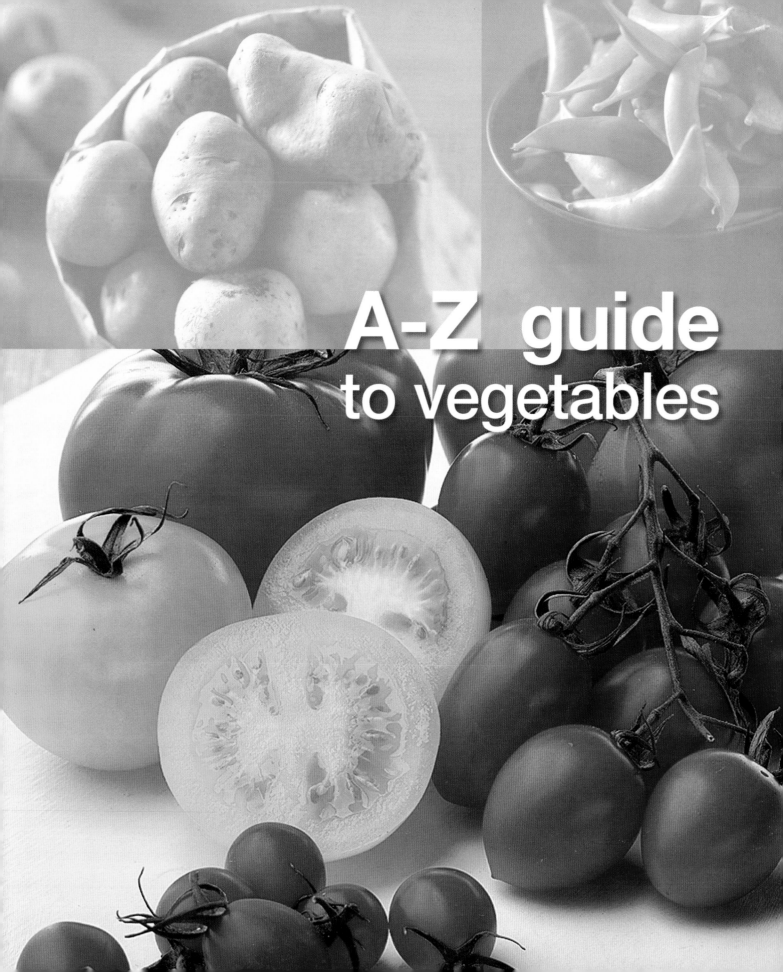

# A-Z guide
## to vegetables

## fresh **ideas**

**Classic dip** Pluck the leaves from just-cooked artichokes and arrange on a serving platter. Stir equal parts of olive oil and melted butter, and a few drops of lemon juice in a small bowl. Serve as a dip for the leaves.

**Tofu dip** Combine mashed roasted garlic, ground black pepper, soft silken tofu and lemon juice.

**Pasta and pizza** Cooked artichoke hearts work well in a pasta sauce and as a pizza topping with fresh tomato sauce, salami and Parmesan.

## getting **ready**

**1** Cut off the stem at base of globe.

**2** Snip off sharp tips from petals with a pair of scissors.

**3** Rub with lemon to stop discoloration.

# artichokes (globe)

The giant flower bud of a bushy thistle plant, the globe artichoke is high in fibre. The edible parts are the nutty flavoured heart and the base of the outer leaves.

**PACKED INTO** 1 LARGE STEAMED ARTICHOKE

**25 calories**
- high in **fibre**
- **iron, copper and magnesium** and other essential minerals
- 35 per cent of the daily **B vitamin folate** requirement

## at the market

**Season** From June to November; peak time June and July.

**What to look for** Artichokes should be heavy for their size. Choose those with a tight, compact head. Leaves should be green, purple or bronze. Avoid artichokes with opened out, curled or dry leaves.

## in the kitchen

**Storing** Store unwashed and with stems intact in the vegetable drawer of the fridge for one week.

**Preparation** Wash well under cold running water. Trimming techniques are shown at left.

**Basic cooking** **To steam,** place prepared whole artichokes in a steamer (non-aluminium to prevent discoloration) over boiling water. Cover and cook until an outer leaf is easily pulled out, 30 to 40 minutes. Drain upside down in a colander before serving. **To boil,** cook in a large pan of lightly salted boiling water with a few drops of lemon juice added, for 30 to 40 minutes.

**Best uses in recipes** Artichokes are usually served as a first course. Serve hot artichokes with melted butter or hollandaise sauce, or sprinkle with lemon juice and salt. Serve cold with a vinaigrette or a low-fat mayonnaise.

## at the table

Eat artichokes with your fingers. Pluck a leaf from the side and dip the free end into sauce. Bite down on that end and pull the leaf through your teeth, scraping off all the pulp. To get to the heart, remove the outer leaves, then pull out the pale centre petals and scrape off the choke (the fuzzy layer that sits on top of the heart). (See also Jerusalem artichokes on page 304.)

# asparagus

A member of the lily family, asparagus is a springtime delicacy either lightly boiled or steamed. It is low in calories, high in fibre and contains vitamins C and E.

**PACKED INTO** 100G COOKED ASPARAGUS

**26 calories**
- thiamine and other **B vitamins** necessary for energy metabolism
- 25 per cent of the daily requirement for **vitamin C**
- a phytochemical called **glutathione**, which is one of the most potent antioxidants for fighting the cell destruction that leads to disease

## at the market

**Season** Locally grown asparagus is available during May, June and July.

**What to look for** Asparagus should have firm round spears with tightly closed tips of deep green, purple or white. Purple spears are larger and less fibrous than green ones. It has a nutty flavour when cooked. White asparagus (grown shielded from sunlight) has a very delicate flavour, milder than either green or purple. Try to pick spears of uniform size to ensure even cooking.

## in the kitchen

**Storing** Asparagus should be eaten as soon as possible after being picked. Stored at room temperature, it can, for example, lose half its vitamin C in two days. If you must keep it overnight, wrap the bottom ends in damp kitchen paper, cover it with cling film, and put it in the fridge.

**Preparation** Wash carefully to remove any sand. Snap off and discard the tough ends (right).

**Basic cooking** Asparagus can be cooked many different ways.
**Steaming or boiling** It takes 3 to 5 minutes to cook asparagus either way. Do not overcook or spears will become soggy and limp. Remove from the pan when just crisp-tender; asparagus will continue to cook as it cools.
**Microwaving** Place spears, tips to the centre, in a shallow microwaveable dish. Add 60ml water, cover tightly and cook at full power for 4 to 7 minutes.
**Roasting** Preheat the oven to 190°C (170°C fan oven), gas 5. Lay the spears in a single layer in a shallow tin, sprinkle with olive oil and season with salt and pepper. Roast until spears are crisp-tender, about 20 minutes.
**Barbecuing** Brush spears with olive oil, sprinkle with salt and place crossways on the grill rack over medium coals. Cook, turning often, until tender, 4 to 6 minutes. Sprinkle with pepper and lemon juice just before serving.

## fresh ideas

**To top it off** Asparagus goes well with lemon or balsamic vinaigrette, mustard-mayonnaise, soy sauce and ginger, or grated Parmesan cheese.

**Party nibbles** Ham or prosciutto slices rolled around short spears of cold cooked asparagus – with or without a dab of mayonnaise.

**Soup plus** Leftover, cooked green asparagus can be puréed in a food processor and then gently heated with a little milk, chopped parsley and tarragon, and salt and pepper to taste, to make asparagus soup.

## trimming asparagus

**1** Feel along the lower stalk for a natural breaking place – a divide between tough and more tender parts.

**2** Snap off the end of the stalk. For a thick stem, peel the remaining part with a swivel-bladed peeler.

## fresh **ideas**

**Coat slices of small aubergines** in egg and breadcrumbs. Bake in a hot oven until tender. Top with chopped basil or oregano leaves and serve as an hors d'oeuvre.

**Grilling gives aubergine a meaty,** rich flavour. Halve a large aubergine lengthways; prick skin. Place cut side down on a barbecue or under a grill and cook until skin blisters and blackens. Place in a paper bag for a few minutes to loosen skin. Peel, then mash flesh. Drizzle with oil and season with salt and pepper.

## salting
## aubergine

**1** First slice the aubergine into uniform pieces with a sharp knife.

**2** Lay slices on kitchen paper and sprinkle with salt. Leave to stand 30 minutes to release moisture.

# aubergines

Like tomatoes and avocados, the aubergine is a fruit that is treated like a vegetable. Aubergine is a key ingredient in Middle Eastern and Asian recipes.

**PACKED INTO** 100G RAW AUBERGINE

about **15 calories**
• it also provides useful amounts of **vitamin B$_6$**
• dietary **fibre**
• phytochemicals called **anthyocyanins** which are believed to help protect against the build-up of cholesterol in the arteries.

## at the market

**Season** UK-grown aubergines are available from May to October, although most aubergines are imported.

**Varieties** Although there are many varieties available around the world, in the UK you are most likely to find the deep red or purplish-black aubergines. They can be long and narrow (Lebanese, Long Tom or Japanese) or short and plump, varying in size from large to very small.

**What to look for** Select fruit that is heavy for its size, with firm, glossy, unblemished skin and a healthy looking crown. The tastiest are firm with thin skins. Larger ones are more likely to be seedy, tough and bitter.

## in the kitchen

**Storing** Use an aubergine within a couple of days of purchase. If you must store it, keep it in a cool place but preferably not in the fridge because it's likely to soften and become bitter very quickly.

**Preparation** It's not necessary to peel an aubergine before cooking, unless the skin is especially thick or you simply prefer your vegetables peeled.

**Basic cooking** Aubergines soak up oil during cooking, which is one of the drawbacks from a health point of view. Nowadays most aubergines do not need salting to remove any bitter taste, but it's useful for reducing the amount of moisture in the vegetable, making it less oil-absorbent (left). When aubergine is used as the basis of a dip, such as Middle Eastern baba ghanoush, however, it is often baked whole or boiled until the flesh is soft enough to mash, avoiding the oil issue altogether.

To grill or barbecue aubergine for a side dish, cut crossways into 1cm slices and brush with oil and cook, oiled side facing the heat source, until browned on both sides. Brush with oil and turn slices twice during cooking. Sprinkle with salt, pepper and chopped fresh parsley or basil before serving. You will use less oil when grilling aubergine slices than if you fry them, and it's a healthier way to pre-cook them when making a moussaka.

# avocados

Healthy, unsaturated fats give this tropical fruit (it is not a vegetable) its creamy texture and nutty flavour. Called 'midshipman's butter' by English seafaring crews over a century ago, avocados taste delicious simply mashed on toast. Avocados are used mostly in appetisers and salads.

**PACKED INTO** 1 SMALL AVOCADO

about **190 calories**
- a significant amount of vitamin E, which slows the ageing process and protects against cancer
- monounsaturated fats, which help to lower blood levels of LDL (bad) cholesterol
- lutein, which protects against cancer and eye diseases
- folate to help protect against heart disease
- glutathione, an antioxidant that protects body cells from damage
- beta-sitosterol, which helps to block absorption of cholesterol in the intestine
- magnesium to help with muscle function and energy metabolism
- potassium to keep electrolytes in balance

## at the market

**Season** Avocados are not grown in the UK, so all are imported. Available all year in street markets and supermarkets. As they ripen once picked from the tree, avocados are often sold unripe for ripening at home.

**What to look for** Variations in size, colour and skin texture depend on the variety and where it is grown. No matter what type of avocado you buy, look for heavy fruit and avoid any that is bruised or has sunken spots in the skin. A ripe avocado will yield to gentle pressure from your hand.

## in the kitchen

**Storing** If you buy an unripe avocado, it will ripen at room temperature over the course of a few days. To speed up the ripening process, place the avocado in a brown paper bag. Store at warm room temperature for a day or two or until the avocado yields to gentle pressure from your hand. You can ripen a cut avocado this way, too. The cut surface will eventually discolour but this can be delayed by coating the cut surface with lemon juice and then covering it with cling film. Ripe avocados can be stored in the fridge for four or five days. Don't store unripe ones in the fridge because they will never ripen properly. If you find yourself with an excess of ripe avocados, peel and stone the fruit and purée it with a little lemon or lime juice to limit discoloration. You'll need about 2 teaspoons of juice for each avocado. Then pack the purée into a covered plastic container, label with the date and store in the freezer for up to four months.

## fresh ideas

**Use mashed avocado** to bind a sandwich of bean sprouts and chopped vegetables, seasoned with salt and pepper and tucked neatly into a wholewheat pitta pocket.

**For a creamy, tart salad dressing**, mash an avocado with low-fat plain yoghurt and add lime juice, salt and Tabasco sauce to taste.

**To make an avocado smoothie**, purée the flesh of an avocado with milk, a touch of honey and a couple of ice cubes.

**Avocado for dessert?** Well, it is a fruit! Purée fresh avocado with some sugar or honey and lemon juice for an easy mousse. Top with toasted almonds.

## The cocktail-stick test

You can feel an avocado to see if it's ripe, but if you're still not sure, use a cocktail stick. Push it into the stem end of the avocado, and if it moves in and out with ease, it's ripe and ready to eat.

# ...avocados

**Preparation**  To peel an avocado, first slice it into quarters (right) or halves lengthways, cutting to the large centre stone. You can twist the cut avocado to separate the halves. Remove the stone with a paring knife if it doesn't lift right out. If the avocado is ripe, use your fingers to peel back the skin (right). Otherwise, use a paring knife. Always rub or sprinkle cut avocado with lemon juice to prevent discoloration. This inevitable browning doesn't affect the flavour or nutritional value, but it does make the avocado look less appetising. Cover mashed or puréed avocado with two layers of cling film applied directly to the surface. The convenient belief that pressing the stone into mashed avocado will prevent browning is, unfortunately, not true.

## Best uses in recipes

Avocados are usually eaten raw. High heat causes them to turn bitter, so generally avocado should be added to hot dishes just at the end of cooking or after the heat has been turned off. Sliced or chopped avocado adds a richness to salads, wraps and sandwiches. Avocado is also a basis for many classic dishes such as avocado with crab or prawn salad, and avocado and grapefruit salad with a honey-mustard dressing.

**Best recipe**  Mashed avocado is traditionally used as the basis of the Mexican dip guacamole, now enjoyed around the world as an easy-to-make, light, nutritious starter. **To make guacamole,** you will need 2 ripe avocados, halved and stoned; 1 large tomato, peeled, cored, seeded and coarsely chopped; 1 small, finely chopped red onion, 15g chopped coriander leaves, 3 tablespoons lime juice, ¾ teaspoon ground cumin, ¾ teaspoon salt and ¾ teaspoon Tabasco sauce. Scoop the avocado flesh into a bowl and mash it with a fork until the texture is almost smooth. Add all the remaining ingredients and stir gently to combine. Cover with a double layer of cling film; place in the fridge until ready to use. Guacamole is usually served with tortilla chips for scooping, but a healthier option is to serve it with sliced raw vegetables, such as carrot, celery and pepper.

## varieties

Avocados are not grown in the UK but are available all year round.  The main types available are Fuerte and Hass. The Hass is a medium-sized avocado that weighs about 250g. It has a pebbly skin that turns from green to a purplish-black as it ripens. Fuerte has a smoother green skin. You can also buy organic avocados, if you prefer.

## cutting up an avocado

**1** Using a sharp knife, cut out a quarter of the avocado.

**2** Pull off the skin with your fingers; it is easily removed if the avocado is sufficiently ripe.

**3** Slice the flesh with a paring knife. Sprinkle with lemon juice to stop the fruit quickly discolouring.

# beans

Green beans, flat beans, broad beans or runner beans ... whatever your fancy, these edible pods add crunch and plenty of nutrients to your meals.

**PACKED INTO** AN 80G SERVING OF FRENCH BEANS

about **20 calories**
- phytochemicals called **saponins**, believed to stimulate the immune system
- the B vitamin **folate**, important in pregnancy and for normal growth

## at the market

**Season**  Broad beans are available from the end of June until early September. Locally grown French and green beans are available during July and August; runner beans from July to September. Beans lose their crunchy sweetness during prolonged storage; the sooner they make it from field to table, the better.

**What to look for**  Regardless of which variety you are shopping for, choose beans that snap rather than bend when folded over. Most pods should be straight with a 'peach fuzz' feel, except runner beans, which have a knobbly surface. There should be no blemishes or brown spots. Limp beans will be tough and bland. Try to select slender beans of a uniform size to ensure even cooking.

## in the kitchen

**Storing**  Keep beans in the vegetable drawer of the fridge, loosely wrapped in cling film, and use as soon as possible.

**Preparation**  To prepare fresh green or French beans, snap or trim off the stem end; the fine point at the tip is edible so there's no need to remove it. Beans can be left whole or cut to any length needed; they look good cut on the diagonal. To prepare runner beans, trim off the tops and tails then thinly slice lengthways with a knife or use a bean slicer. They can also be cut into short pieces if you prefer.

**Basic cooking**  Steam or simmer beans for 3 to 10 minutes, depending on their thickness, until they're cooked but still retain a bit of crunch – take a test bite to determine this. Beans also cook well and retain their colour in the microwave. Or, try blanching beans for 1 or 2 minutes in a large pan of lightly salted boiling water and then finishing them when needed by sautéing them in butter or olive oil just before serving. However you cook them, drain beans immediately. If you're planning to finish them later or use them chilled for a salad recipe, plunge the crisp-tender cooked beans into iced water to stop the cooking process and to retain their bright colour; drain and pat dry before chilling or adding to other ingredients.

## fresh ideas

**Cooked beans can be jazzed up** with various seasonings and other ingredients. Before adding them, toss cooked beans in a hot frying pan to rid them of moisture. This way, the beans will better absorb the additional flavours.

**To make garlic oil**, mix 2 tbsp olive oil per 500g beans with 2 cloves finely chopped garlic. Heat until just beginning to sizzle. Add beans and cook, tossing, until heated through. Season with salt and pepper.

**To make lemon butter**, toss 500g cooked beans with 1½ tbsp melted butter in a hot frying pan. Sprinkle lightly to taste with fresh lemon juice, salt and pepper.

**To add toasted almonds**, lightly brown flaked almonds in groundnut oil or butter. Mix with the cooked beans and season to taste.

**Thinly slice prosciutto or ham** and heat in a little olive oil or butter in a large frying pan. Add cooked beans and toss to mix.

**Add Parmesan cheese** after tossing beans in melted butter. Season with ground black pepper.

# ...beans

## varieties

The beans that we eat fresh are not different species from the dried beans that are cooked for hours to use in chilli con carne. Fresh beans are edible pods that are picked at a different time in the plant's growth cycle. Green beans, for example, are the immature pods of kidney beans. Here is a guide to some of the edible pods and beans

**borlotti beans** are grown not for the pods but for the mature beans inside the pods. The beans are also sold in dried form.

**flat beans** Also known as Helda beans, flat beans are a popular variety of stringless bean, a little like a runner bean but with a smooth skin.

**green beans, dwarf beans, French beans (haricots verts)** are other common names for green beans which range in length from 10 to 20cm. Baby green beans are picked young when their carbohydrate content is present in the form of sugar and they are the

sweetest of all the types. Green beans can be served whole or cut into pieces. As well as being served hot as a side vegetable they can be added to risottos and vegetable dishes and taste delicious cold in salads.

**runner beans** are long beans with a coarse-textured skin. Older beans have a string down each side, which needs to be removed before cooking. Tender young beans have the best texture and flavour.

**yellow wax beans** Colour and nutrition separate wax beans from green beans, which they resemble in both size and flavour. Green beans have eight times as much beta carotene as the paler yellow beans.

## Best uses in recipes

Fresh green beans, sautéed in butter and seasoned with salt and pepper, make a refreshing accompaniment to almost any main dish. Any fresh bean, cut to a manageable length, is a good addition to a stir-fry or a hot pasta dish, adding texture and bulk. Cold cooked green beans add colour and texture to potato and pasta salads.

### shell beans

Broad beans and soya beans fall nutritionally between fresh green beans and dried beans. They have high protein and carbohydrate counts and low vitamin counts. Used much in the same way as dried beans (except that they don't need to be soaked), shell beans contain protein, potassium, vitamin C and iron in different degrees. Broad beans are rich in folate and vitamin C. Use them cold in salads and hot as a side dish alone or in soups or stews. Soya beans are a staple of Asian cuisine. The fresh beans are unique among beans in that they have high amounts of complete protein and also contain unsaturated fat. They are now available frozen in many supermarkets and their mild flavour makes them suitable for adding to all kinds of dishes, such as stir-fries, vegetable sautés and curries.

*broad beans*

## did you **know...**

...that broad beans were an important part of the diet in Britain during the Middle Ages? Eaten with grains the beans provided valuable protein, especially for poorer people who had little meat. It is believed the beans were brought here by the Romans.

# beetroot

Ruby-red beetroot tastes sweet because it contains more natural sugar than any other vegetable that we eat. They are still low in calories, very low in fat and packed with important vitamins and minerals.

**PACKED INTO** 50G COOKED BEETROOT

about **23 calories**
- 25 per cent of the recommended daily allowance of **folate**
- some **vitamin C**
- **potassium** and **magnesium**

## at the market

**Season**  Local beetroots can be bought from July to January, but are at their best during the summer months, when baby beetroots are also available.

**What to look for**  If possible, choose roots with their tops on; those that have been clipped have most likely been in storage. The leafy tops should look fresh and the roots should be firm, smooth and unbruised. Pick uniform-sized beetroots up to 7cm in diameter. If you shop at a farmers' market, you may also see golden beetroots. They can be cooked and used the same way as the red variety, but their roots and greens are milder in flavour.

## in the kitchen

**Storing**  First twist off the leafy tops, leaving about 3cm of the stem attached to the bulbous root. Leave the long, stringy root intact. Store the greens and beetroot in separate plastic bags in the vegetable drawer of your fridge. The greens should be used within a couple of days. The roots will keep for up to a couple of weeks. Preparation  Gently scrub beetroots under cold running water and dry on kitchen paper. Leave the 3cm of stem attached to the unpeeled whole root to prevent colour (and nutrients) from 'bleeding out' during cooking.

**Basic cooking**  To preserve their colour and nutrients, beetroots should not be peeled or cut before cooking. Baking, microwaving and steaming are the best methods of cooking. To bake, wrap in foil, place in a baking tin, and cook at 180°C (160°C fan oven), gas 4 for 1½ to 2 hours. To steam, put in a steamer pan and cook for 40 minutes to 1 hour. Leave to cool in the pan. Peel when cool enough to handle. Serve hot, or cool and chill for salads.

## Best uses in recipes

Cooked beetroots are eaten hot as a side dish and cold in salads. They are used in a borscht, a soup which can be served hot or cold. They are also pickled. Raw grated beetroot adds crunch to a salad.

## fresh ideas

**Young beetroots** up to 3cm in diameter have tender, edible skin that doesn't require peeling. Baby beetroots also have the sweetest greens. The leaves and roots can be cooked separately and then served together. Steam the roots for about 15 minutes. Meanwhile, sauté the greens in olive oil and butter. Drain the beetroots. Cut them in half and sprinkle with salt and pepper. Place sautéed greens on a plate and top with the warm beetroot.

**Sprinkle hot beetroot** with lemon juice, salt and pepper and dot with little pieces of butter.

**Serve hot or cold beetroot** with a yoghurt and horseradish sauce.

**Team cooked beetroot, sliced and chilled**, with orange segments, thin slices of red onion and a handful of toasted walnuts. Add vinaigrette.

## did you know...

...that betalains, the bright red pigments in beetroot, can be extracted for use as a natural food colouring and dye?

## fresh **ideas**

**Broccoli stalks**, are tender and tasty. Blanch, steam or stir-fry sliced stems, or grate coarsely and serve in salads.

**Purée cooked broccoli** with a little chicken stock, milk or cream, dried marjoram, cayenne pepper and salt to make a quick, creamy soup.

**Sauté chopped onion and garlic in olive oil**, add steamed purple sprouting broccoli and halved cherry tomatoes. Heat through. Add to pasta and top with Parmesan.

## cutting up broccoli

**1** Cut off stem and side shoots but don't discard. They're tender and delicious when cooked.

--------------------------------------------------

**2** Remove individual florets for use in a stir-fry or include them in a raw vegetable platter for dips.

# broccoli

Super-high in vitamins, and jam-packed with phytochemicals that help to fight off disease, broccoli is one of the healthiest stars of the vegetable world.

**PACKED INTO** 80G COOKED BROCCOLI

about **19 calories**
• around 75 per cent of the recommended daily allowance for **vitamin C**
• 26 per cent of the requirement for **folate**
• useful amounts of **vitamin B$_6$** and **fibre**
• cancer-fighting **indoles**

## at the market

**Season**  Local broccoli is available from the end of July until October. Purple sprouting broccoli is available from March to May.

**What to look for**  Select dark green heads and leaves, and bright green stems for broccoli. Purple sprouting broccoli has purple heads about 2.5cm wide, on stems about 10cm long with the leaves attached. The stalks holding the florets for both types should be slender and crisp and the florets themselves tightly closed. Yellowed, flowering buds are a sign of old age.

## in the kitchen

**Storing**  Keep in a plastic bag in the vegetable drawer of the fridge for three or four days.

**Preparation**  Wash well. Peel tough skin from broccoli stalks, if you like. If cooking long spears with florets attached, slice spears lengthways up to the florets. The leaves are full of vitamins and flavour and can be cooked. Add to soups or stir-fries. Tenderstem broccoli has a tender asparagus-like stem so you can cook and eat it attached to the floret.

**Basic cooking**  Short cooking time brings out the best flavour and colour, and helps to prevent broccoli's valuable vitamins from leaching into the cooking water. It also prevents the breakdown of chemicals in broccoli that release strong-smelling sulphur compounds that smell like rotten eggs. Blanch, steam, sauté or stir-fry florets and chopped-up stems and leaves with a little added liquid for just 3 to 5 minutes.

## Best uses in recipes

Raw broccoli often features on vegetable platters for dips or in salads. Broccoli florets can be sautéed with olive oil and garlic, added at the beginning of a vegetable stir-fry, or steamed and topped with cheese sauce, white sauce or a squeeze of fresh lemon juice. Tender purple sprouting broccoli makes a good side vegetable with just seasoning and a little butter, or quickly stir-fry with toasted sunflower and sesame seeds.

# brussels sprouts

Thanks to generations of overcooking, Brussels sprouts may be the most maligned vegetable in the world. But these mini cabbages have a delicious, earthy flavour if they are treated well in the kitchen.

**PACKED INTO** 80G BRUSSELS SPROUTS

**28 calories**
- 100 per cent of the recommended daily requirement of vitamin C
- around 44 per cent of the recommended daily requirement of the B vitamin folate
- fibre
- phytochemicals called indoles and isothiocyanates, which help to protect against cancer

## at the market

**Season**  UK-grown Brussels sprouts are in season from the end of November until February.

**What to look for**  Look for bright green, tightly packed leaves. Avoid any whose leaves have begun to yellow and unfurl or whose stem ends are dry and browned. A strong off-flavour and aroma develops in those that have been stored too long. If serving sprouts whole, choose ones roughly of uniform size so that they will cook evenly. Smaller sprouts are generally milder and sweeter than larger ones. Also look out for Brussels tops.

## in the kitchen

**Storing**  Store unwashed in a paper bag in the fridge for two days.

**Preparation**  Before cooking, proceed as shown (right). Sprouts that are more than 2cm thick are best halved or quartered to make them easier to cook and eat. To prepare Brussels tops, cut into two through the heart.

**Basic cooking**  Boil sprouts, uncovered, in lightly salted water for 5 to 10 minutes, depending on thickness; they should be just tender enough to be pierced by a skewer. Avoid overcooking, which will render the sprouts mushy, pale and strongly flavoured. Brussels sprouts can also be steamed or microwaved. Sauté Brussels tops briefly in a frying pan, then add a little stock, pepper and a pinch of dried herbs. Braise until just cooked, about 5 minutes.

## Best uses in recipes

Thinly sliced sprouts can be used in stir-fries and sautés, more easily absorbing savoury sauces and dressings than whole ones.

## fresh ideas

**Team Brussels sprouts** with one or several of the following: butter and lemon, caraway seeds, apple slices, crushed juniper berries, balsamic vinegar, dill, toasted walnuts, ham, Cheddar cheese.

**Loose leaves from Brussels sprouts** make a nutritious garnish for soups, stews, salads or any dish that could use a little colour. Peel off the outer leaves and steam them over boiling water for about 3 minutes, or until they are crisp-tender.

## to prepare brussels sprouts

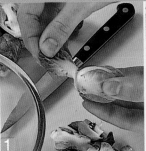

**1**  Trim stems and discard discoloured or wilted outer leaves.

**2**  To bring heat to the centre when cooking sprouts whole, score an X into the base of each one.

## fresh **ideas**

**Use cabbage leaves** as steamer wrappers. Sprinkle thick fish fillets with fresh herbs such as tarragon or dill, and wrap in cabbage leaves. Steam over stock to which more of the same herbs have been added. The whole parcel can be eaten.

**Steam cabbage or pak choi leaves** and wrap them around matchsticks of carrot and peppers. Serve the packets with a spicy dipping sauce.

**Stir-fry sliced cabbage and onions** and add to coarsely mashed potato. Use as a stuffing for chicken or turkey for roasting.

## did you **know...**

...that sauerkraut is simply pickled cabbage?

# cabbages

Now that more is known about the health benefits of this once-humble vegetable, cabbage has become a nutritional superstar. There are hundreds of different types.

**PACKED INTO** 80G COOKED CABBAGE

13 calories
• 40 per cent of the daily requirement for vitamin C
• useful amounts of folate, vitamin B$_6$, magnesium and fibre
• sulforaphane, isothiocyanates and dithiolethiones, all phytochemicals which have known disease-fighting capabilities
• phytochemicals called indoles, which help to protect against breast, prostate and colon cancers

## at the market

**Season** Available all year. Savoy cabbage is available in the cooler months.

**What to look for** When choosing red or green cabbage, select firm heads that are quite heavy for their size. Looser-leafed, elongated varieties such as Chinese leaves will also be heavy for their size. Choose heads with fresh-looking cores and no wilted leaves or yellowing. A head weighing about 1kg serves four to six people for a side dish.

## in the kitchen

**Storing** All varieties of cabbage should be stored, unwashed, in a paper bag or wrapped in a damp tea towel, in the vegetable drawer of the fridge. Green or red cabbages with tight heads will keep for up to two weeks; loose-leafed Chinese leaves will keep for up to one week.

**Preparation** Remove and discard any damaged or wilted outer leaves and trim away any brown spots. Remove and discard tough outer leaves from the larger heads of cabbage. Rinse cabbage in cold water just before cooking. Use a knife, grater, mandolin or food processor to shred heads of green or red cabbage. First, cut the head into quarters with a large, heavy knife. Then remove the core. You can then shred the cabbage by slicing it vertically, or using a hand-held grater, a mandolin or a food processor with the grating disk attached.

**Basic cooking** Whatever the type of cabbage, always cook it very briefly and drain it well. Cabbage has a bad name simply because it has a history of being overcooked. The simplest technique for cooking all types of cabbage is to first slice or chop it and then steam it over boiling water until it is barely tender, about 5 minutes.

**Drain well**. Just before serving, sauté in butter or olive oil to heat through, and season with salt and pepper.

## Best uses in recipes

Grated raw cabbage is used to make salads and coleslaws. Crisp cabbage leaves can be cut up and substituted in any recipe that calls for lettuce, including sandwiches. Whole raw cabbage leaves, especially savoy cabbage leaves, can be used in place of tortillas for a flavoursome, low-calorie wrap for sandwich fillings. Cooked cabbage is served as a side dish with meat, poultry and sausages. It is also used as a filling for small pastry cases, such as the Russian peroshki, and for dumplings. Cabbage is a useful ingredient in a wide variety of soups, stews, salads and stir-fries.

**Best recipe** One of the most popular and easy-to-make recipes for cabbage is coleslaw, a mixture of shredded cabbage, carrots and an almost sweet creamy dressing, traditionally made from mayonnaise, but increasingly made from soured cream and/or yoghurt. **To make coleslaw,** In a medium bowl, whip 3 tablespoons low-fat, plain yoghurt, 2 tablespoons light soured cream, 1 teaspoon prepared mustard, ½ teaspoon sugar, ½ teaspoon cider vinegar, ¼ teaspoon celery seeds, a pinch of salt and black pepper to taste. For the salad, add 225g coarsely shredded cabbage and 2 coarsely grated carrots. Mix well, then chill for 3 hours, tossing occasionally. Serves 4.

## cutting up pak choi

**1** Use a sharp knife to separate the leaves from the white base.

**2** Chop the leaves evenly into 5cm pieces.

**3** Slice base into slivers along ribs, perpendicular to the base.

## varieties

**chinese leaves** have long white ribs and tender, pale green leaves. They have a relatively mild taste that works well raw in salads as it does not dominate. Chinese leaves are also good cooked in soups and stir-fries.

**green cabbage** is an all-purpose vegetable. It is the most common cabbage. The head is tight and has pale-to medium-green very crisp leaves.

**pak choi** is a variety of Chinese cabbage; it is used extensively in Asian cooking. It does not form a head and looks more like a leafy green vegetable than a cabbage. It is richer in beta carotene and calcium than green cabbage.

**red cabbage**, with its distinctive purplish red leaves, can be teamed with sweet ingredients in soups such as borscht and side dishes such as sweet-and-sour cabbage with apples. It is much used in Central European cuisines.

**savoy cabbage** has tender, crinkled, pale green leaves. It has a milder flavour than that of green cabbage, with which it can be interchanged in recipes. It is used extensively in European cuisines.

## fresh **ideas**

**Use carrot juice** instead of water in homemade bread or pizza dough to add extra nutrients.

**Sauce barbecued chicken** with a carrot-based gravy: sauté sliced carrots with olive oil and garlic until very soft and then purée with carrot juice and lemon juice to taste.

**Substitute carrot juice** for stock in soups, stews and sauces.

**Use grated carrot** as a substitute for coconut in biscuits and cakes to cut calories and boost nutrition.

## making **matchsticks**

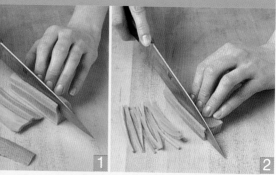

**1** Section peeled carrots into 5cm lengths; then cut into broad slices.

**2** Put several broad slices in a pile and cut off matchstick slices in bunches.

# carrots

If one vegetable gets top prize for nutritional value and versatility, it is the carrot, which features in the cookbooks of just about every country and cuisine in the world.

**PACKED INTO** 80G COOKED CARROTS

**19 calories**
- more than 100 per cent of the daily requirement for **vitamin A**, in the form of **beta carotene**
- a good supply of **vitamin B$_6$**
- **fibre** to keep the digestive tract healthy

## at the market

**Season** UK-grown carrots are available from May to October, but with many growers using polytunnels the season is beginning to be lengthened.

**What to look for** Whether you buy them long and tapered or short and stubby, in bunches or in plastic bags, choose smooth, firm, evenly coloured and evenly shaped carrots. Avoid carrots that are soft, withered, oversized or green around the shoulders. For carrots sold in bunches, look for ones with bright green, fresh-looking feathery tops. Small, slender carrots are usually the sweetest.

## in the kitchen

**Storing** Discard the leafy green tops because they steal nutrients from the roots. Keep carrots, loosely wrapped, in the vegetable drawer of the fridge. Tiny, early carrots keep only a day or two, whereas large carrots keep for at least a week. Small, bagged carrots are usually good for a couple of weeks.

**Preparation** Many of a carrot's nutrients are concentrated just below the skin's surface. For this reason, scrub tender young carrots rather than peel them. Large not-so-young carrots may require peeling.

**Basic cooking** Carrots can be boiled, steamed, roasted, grilled and added to soups and stews. Raw carrot sticks and raw baby carrots are a nutritious snack. Grated carrots add colour and nutrients to salads and sweets. Sliced carrots can be steamed, stir-fried or roasted to serve with or without other vegetables as a side dish. Turn freshly cooked carrots in butter, dill, salt and pepper to coat. To glaze carrots, combine brown sugar, salt, ginger and a little cornflour in a small pan. Add orange juice. Cook, stirring, until the mixture thickens. Stir in butter and spoon over hot roasted carrots. To braise, place carrots in a pan with butter, orange juice and zest, sugar, salt and pepper. Bring to the boil, cover, lower heat and cook for 5 minutes. Uncover, raise heat, and stir until liquid has evaporated and carrots are tender.

# cauliflower

Creamy white, purple or a brilliant chartreuse – these are the colours of today's cauliflower. A close relative of broccoli, cauliflower has the nutritional attributes of its cousin, but a milder flavour.

**PACKED INTO** 80G COOKED CAULIFLOWER

**22 calories**
• it is an excellent source of **vitamin C**
• provides useful amounts of **folate** and **vitamin B$_6$** and cancer-fighting **phytochemicals**

## at the market

**Season**  Local cauliflowers are available from October until early May.

**What to look for**  Choose a head with a fresh, crisp, creamy-white curd. The size of the head has no bearing on quality. Avoid cauliflower that is turning brown or with curd that appears to have been trimmed. These are indicators of old age. Old cauliflower has an unpleasant odour when cooked and has a strong taste. Try to buy cauliflower with some or all of its leaves intact; they protect the curd from damage and help to retain its freshness.

## in the kitchen

**Storing**  Cauliflower generally does not keep well, especially if it has been trimmed of its leaves. If you can't use a head of cauliflower the day you buy it, place it, unwashed, in a perforated or open plastic bag and chill for no more than a day or two. The same goes for leftover cooked cauliflower. Rather than reheat it as a side dish or serve it cold as a salad vegetable, it's best to purée leftovers with a little stock and use it for soup the next day.

**Preparation**  Wash cauliflower just before cooking or eating raw. Use a sharp knife to separate the florets into bite-sized pieces, retaining a bit of stem. To keep florets crisp and white until serving, place in a bowl of iced water, stir in a squeeze of lemon juice and chill. Drain the florets and pat dry just before serving.

**Basic cooking**  Cook cauliflower carefully, checking it often, because it goes from undercooked to overcooked in a flash. Florets are cooked as soon as the stem end is tender. Cauliflower will discolour if cooked in aluminium or iron pans.

## Best uses in recipes

Serve raw cauliflower with dips. Cooked, it can be served with a sauce, made into soup or added to combinations of vegetables for use in curries.

## fresh ideas

**Top cauliflower with sauces,** add seasonings and dressings. Try some of the following with either cooked or raw cauliflower:

• **Cheese sauce**
• **Vinaigrette dressing**
• **Mustard-mayonnaise sauce**
• **Curry sauce**
• **Yoghurt with fresh or dried herbs**

## did you know...

...that purple cauliflower is a cross between broccoli and cauliflower? It has more beta carotene than white cauliflower and turns white when cooked. The acid-green, romanesco cauliflower retains its colour on cooking. It has a relatively mild flavour.

## fresh **ideas**

**For finger food,** fill 5cm lengths of celery stalk with:

- **Cream cheese** with chopped onions and chives or chopped peppers
- **Curried** egg salad
- **Chicken salad** combined with dill mayonnaise
- **A blend of cottage and blue cheeses**
- **Peanut butter**

## to **julienne** celery

**1** Trim off top and bottom of stalks.

**2** Cut into 5cm pieces; line up cut pieces as guides.

**3** Sliver each piece into matchsticks.

# celery

Although celery will never win a star for its nutritional properties, it's an excellent snacking vegetable with a low calorie count that comes from its water content.

**PACKED INTO** 2 MEDIUM CELERY STICKS (60G)

**4 calories**
- **polyacetylene**, a medicinal substance that helps to reduce inflammation
- **potassium** to maintain blood pressure
- **vitamin C** for healthy gums and teeth
- useful amounts of dietary **fibre**

## at the market

**Season** UK celery is available from late September until mid January.

**What to look for** Choose firm stalks that are pale to medium green, with crisp, fresh-looking leaves. The greener the stalk, the more intense the celery flavour. Celery can be sweet or bitter and it's hard to tell just by looking at it which it is. Scratch the base of a head with your fingernail. If it smells bitter, it will taste bitter.

## in the kitchen

**Storing** Wrap in layers of damp kitchen paper or a damp tea towel and store in the vegetable drawer of the fridge for up to two weeks. Keep away from the coldest parts of the fridge (the back and side walls) because it freezes easily and then becomes limp and unusable.

**Preparation** After trimming celery, cut into either end of the stalk with a small, sharp knife and pull down and out to remove stringy fibres.

**Basic cooking** To cook as a side dish, slice stalks and sauté in groundnut oil. Alternatively, cut stalks into 5cm lengths and simmer in stock. Eat as is, or sprinkle with grated cheese and place under the grill until lightly browned.

## Best uses in recipes

Every part of the celery plant is usable. Add the strongly flavoured leaves to soups and stews for seasoning. Cut up the outer ribs and sauté, braise or stir-fry with other vegetables. Tender inner stalks can be included on raw vegetable platters or to snack on. Along with onions, chopped celery is an essential seasoning in many traditional soups, stews, casseroles and other mixed dishes, such as the stuffing for poultry.

# chillies

Mild to fiery, chillies spice up many cuisines, in particular those of Mexico and the Asian countries.

**PACKED INTO** 1 MEDIUM-SIZED RAW CHILLI (15G)

about **4 calories**
• useful amounts of **vitamin C**
• contains the antioxidant **capsaicin** which is thought to inhibit the growth of cancer cells

## at the market

**Season**  Most chillies are imported. Asian markets are usually the best source. UK-grown chillies are available between July and September.

**What to look for**  Fresh chillies should be well shaped, firm and glossy, with no wrinkles, and with fresh-looking green stems. Dried hot chillies should be glossy and unbroken.

## in the kitchen

**Storing**  Wrap unwashed chillies in kitchen paper. Don't use plastic bags because moisture causes chillies to decompose. Keep fresh chillies in the vegetable drawer of the fridge for up to three weeks. Dried chillies can be stored in an airtight container at room temperature; they will last as long as four months. In the fridge, they'll last even longer.

**Preparation**  Take care when handling chillies. The membranes and seeds harbour capsaicin, the substance that makes chillies hot. It can badly irritate the skin and cause considerable discomfort if it gets into your eyes or an open cut. You might want to

## Putting out the fire

Although they all go under the name of capsaicin, several different substances give a chilli its characteristic 'heat' and have varying effects when they reach your mouth. Some give the back of your throat a quick burn; others seem to explode on your tongue and linger on the roof of your mouth. If you bite into an unbearably hot chilli, the best way to extinguish the fire is by eating or drinking a food that's high in fat, such as whole milk, ice cream, avocado, peanut butter or buttered bread. Water just won't do it!

## fresh ideas

**Add finely chopped chilli** to stir-fries and vegetable sautés.

**Make a hot chilli and sweet pepper salsa** by finely chopping red, green and orange peppers and jalapeño and chipotle chillies. Add finely chopped red onion and coriander and vinegar. Serve with meat, poultry or fish.

**A sprinkling of chopped chillies** adds a kick to burgers, tomato sauce or a cheese sauce.

## deseeding chillies

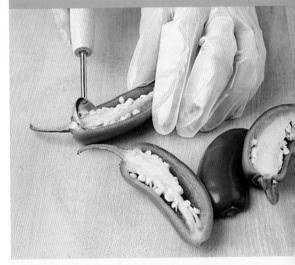

Wear plastic gloves to protect you from the heat. Remove seeds and ribs with a mellon baller or a sharp knife.

# ...chillies

wear rubber gloves while you prepare them. Wash chillies, cut them open and remove the membranes and seeds if you prefer a milder flavour in your dish. After chopping chillies, wash the cutting board and the utensils, as well as your gloves. If you grind dried chillies to use in powder form, be careful not to inhale the fumes or expose your eyes to them. To minimise discomfort, try soaking chillies in hot water for 30 minutes, then puréeing them with a little of the soaking liquid. Then proceed with your recipe.

**Basic cooking**  Just a sprinkling of chopped chilli adds zing to all kinds of dishes from burgers to salad dressings. Roast and peel large mild chillies just as you do peppers (page 291), then stuff them with cheese or meat and deep-fry. Remove the ribs and seeds when you peel them.

# varieties

Most chillies have a predictable heat level, depending on what kind they are. A chilli's pungency is determined not only by its variety, but also by its growing conditions. Some of the milder varieties are eaten as low-calorie snacks. Others have a searing heat. Chillies are a good source of beta-carotene and vitamin C. They may help to relieve nasal congestion.

**anaheim or bullhorn chillies** range from mild to medium hot. These long, slender red or green chillies are among the most popular. Roasting improves their flavour. They are large and mildly flavoured and are good for stuffing.

**bird's eye or Thai chillies** are thin-fleshed with a deep fiery heat. Flavour varies from mild to sweet. Colours range from red to cream, yellow or orange. Use in Thai salads and noodle dishes.

**cayenne chillies** have long, thin red pods that can grow as long as 20cm. They are fiery hot with a tangy flavour. Use in salsas, sauces and soups. Used to make dried ground cayenne pepper, a staple seasoning in North American cooking.

**habanero (meaning Havana) or Scotch bonnet chillies** have a fiercely hot and fruity flavour. They may be as much as 30 times hotter than jalapeños. Use to flavour oils, vinegars and salsas.

**jalapeño chillies** are thick-fleshed and very hot. They are sold fresh as well as canned, sliced and pickled. Usually, they are found in their mature green stage, not the fully ripe red stage. Chipotles are smoked jalapeños.

**pasilla chillies** are long, dark and greenish-red. Moderately hot, they are usually used in dried form.

**poblano/ancho chillies** (poblano refers to the fresh chilli, ancho to the dried one) are mild to medium hot. One of Mexico's most popular chillies, it is often roasted to intensify the flavour. Poblanos can be stuffed with other ingredients, or blended and added to soups.

**serrano chillies** range from bright green to red (the sweeter of the two). They have thick flesh and a biting heat. A favourite in Tex-Mex cooking, they often feature in hot salsas. They can also be pickled and roasted.

# courgettes & squash

Summer squash include yellow and green courgettes, marrows, the dainty patty pan squash and spaghetti squash. Unlike winter squash – pumpkins – summer squash have thin skins and cannot be stored over winter.

**PACKED INTO** 80G SLICED COOKED COURGETTE

**15 calories**
- 22 per cent of the daily requirement for **vitamin C**
- useful amounts of **folate**
- several **B vitamins** used in energy production
- **magnesium**

## at the market

**Season** UK-grown courgettes are available between June and early October. Another bonus of the summer harvest is the availability of courgette flowers – a true delicacy. Marrows, being overgrown courgettes, are available in late summer: towards the end of August through to October.

**What to look for** Courgettes and summer squash are best when young and small. Choose courgettes that are between 10 and 15cm in length. Choose squash, courgettes and marrows with bright, shiny skins and a firm texture. Don't be put off by a few light scratches – the skins are so tender and thin that they are practically unavoidable.

## in the kitchen

**Storing** Store courgettes, marrows and other summer squash in a perforated plastic bag in the fridge for up to four days.

**Preparation** Give courgettes and squash a good rinse and trim their ends. Small and medium-sized squash have edible skin. Peel marrows and scoop out the seeds. Discard any dry, pulpy parts. Squash can be precut for later use, covered with a damp tea towel, and chilled for several hours. To use squash in breads and muffins, grate the raw vegetable and blot with kitchen paper to remove as much of the excess liquid as possible.

**Basic cooking** Courgettes and patty pan squash can be steamed, sautéed, stir-fried or barbecued. An easy way to prepare courgettes is to cut green and yellow varieties into thin slices, and sauté in a little olive oil until they just begin to soften and brown. Add chopped garlic, fresh herbs, salt and pepper, and cook for another minute or two. Drizzle with lemon juice and serve. To barbecue, cut patty pan squash in half lengthways and lightly oil the cut surface. Place cut side down on the grill just until lightly charred and tender. Marrow can be stuffed and baked or cut into pieces and steamed.

## fresh ideas

**Sticks of courgette**, resembling fat French fries, can be briefly roasted, then used for dipping into savoury sauces and spicy dips.

**Blanch courgettes** Slice lengthways, stuff with crumbled feta cheese and top with breadcrumbs. Place under the grill until cheese starts to melt and crumbs begin to brown.

**Add small cubes** of cooked summer squash to pasta sauces.

**Make ribbons** to garnish salads by running a cheese grater lengthways down the sides of a raw courgette.

**Add cooked squash** to an omelette with tomato, herbs and onion for a Mediterranean-style brunch.

**Marrow with tomato** Fry chopped onion and garlic in olive oil, then add chopped tomatoes and thyme, add peeled and cubed marrow. Simmer until tender.

# ...courgettes & squash

## Best uses in recipes

**Best recipe**  To make **Potato and Courgette Cakes**, grate 1 large potato and rinse well, squeezing out excess moisture. Grate 1 large courgette. Combine with 1 large egg white, 1 tablespoon plain flour, black pepper to taste, 1 tablespoon sesame seeds and 2 crushed garlic cloves. Shape into eight cakes. Grease a large frying pan and fry cakes on both sides over a medium heat until lightly browned. Keep warm. Meanwhile, poach 24 peeled raw prawns lightly in fish stock until pink. Drain and set aside. Place two cakes on each serving plate and arrange 3 prawns on each. Sprinkle with finely chopped chives and serve. Serves 4.

## squash varieties

**marrow**  These large vegetables are actually matured courgettes with tough skins that need to be peeled. They have a more watery flavour and are suitable for stuffing with a meat or a mushroom and vegetable filling, or can be cut into pieces and sautéed with flavourings such as ginger and garlic, or in a sauce.

**patty pan squash**  come in several varieties: green, white, bright yellow or orange. Their name comes from the French name 'pâtisson' which is the Provençal word for a cake made in a scalloped mould. Picked young, the flesh of these squash is firm and sweet. They can be steamed whole and served as a side vegetable.

**spaghetti squash**  is a medium-sized oval vegetable, with smooth yellow skin. After boiling or baking the squash whole, halve it and pull the flesh out with a fork into spaghetti-like strands. Toss with olive oil and some chopped fresh herbs. Alternatively, top with a fresh tomato sauce and sprinkle with grated Parmesan or another hard cheese. Spaghetti squash provides fibre and is low in calories, making it useful for a light meal.

## courgette flowers

can be stuffed and cooked to serve as an attractive appetiser. Male flowers – those without the tiny squash attached – are the best to cook. Fill the flowers with goat's cheese and fresh herbs, then pinch them shut and sauté briefly in hot oil. Drain on kitchen paper. Pumpkins and okra also have edible flowers. Okra flowers are ivory or yellow with a funnel shape. Pumpkin flowers are similar to courgettes.

courgette flowers

# cucumber

Cool to the tongue and refreshing to the palate, cucumbers are a good foil for hot foods such as curries, and also add crunch and fibre to salads and salsas.

**PACKED INTO** 50G CUCUMBER

about **5 calories**

• cucumber provides plenty of **water** which will help keep the body hydrated plus small amounts of **vitamin C**

## at the market

**Season**  UK-grown cucumber is available from January to November.

**Varieties**  Cucumbers belong to the same plant family as pumpkins and melons. Varieties include common (green skin, white flesh), ridge or Lebanese (small with green skin and greenish flesh) and telegraph (long with green skin and white flesh).

**What to look for**  Select firm cucumbers that are heavy for their size, with no soft spots or shrivelled skin.

## in the kitchen

**Storing**  Cucumbers that are plastic wrapped will keep for up to a week in the vegetable drawer of the fridge. Cut cucumbers must be tightly wrapped and checked daily for signs of decay – soft spots develop quickly.

**Preparation**  Some people prefer to remove the seeds from cucumbers before eating. Peel the cucumber, if you wish, then cut lengthways in half. Use the tip of a spoon to scoop out the centre row of seeds from each half. Discard seeds. Chop, slice or fill the cucumber as directed in a recipe.

**Basic cooking**  Cucumbers aren't just for eating raw in salads. Sliced or chopped, they can be steamed, sautéed or stir-fried in a little oil, sprinkled with salt and chopped fresh dill and served warm as a side dish.

## Best uses in recipes

Cucumbers are most commonly eaten in salads and mixed vegetable platters, as snacks, and as part of chilled, uncooked soups such as gazpacho. They are also the basis for many types of pickles. To make a speedy sweet-and-sour cucumber salad without pickling, simply marinate thinly sliced cucumber and onion in vinegar, sugar, salt and pepper for several hours in the fridge. Serve chilled with meat or fish.

## fresh ideas

**Add slices of chilled cucumber** to almost any sandwich.

**Stir grated or diced cucumber** into plain yoghurt and add chopped mint, ground cumin and pepper to make the Indian condiment raita – a cooling accompaniment to curries.

**Slice a cucumber** lengthways, scoop out seeds, poach in water to cover for 5 minutes and fill with hot, seasoned rice.

**Sauté cucumber slices** in butter or oil and sprinkle with dill.

**Purée peeled cucumber** in a food processor with yoghurt, a peeled garlic clove, fresh dill, lemon juice, salt and pepper for a chilled soup.

## did you know...

...that scoring the skin of a cucumber gives slices a green and white edge that looks attractive in salads? Trim the ends, stand the cucumber on one of them, and, pressing gently, run the tines of a fork down its length. Repeat the process around the circumference of the cucumber.

## fresh **ideas**

**Sprinkle chopped fresh fennel** leaves on cooked prawns or clams.

**Use halved fennel stalks** similar to celery sticks, for carrying fillings such as cream cheese or tuna salad.

**Add fennel stalks with celery** to flavour chicken and fish stocks.

**Add chopped fennel stalks** to the other seasoning vegetables (onion, garlic and carrot) when making a fresh tomato sauce.

## preparing **fennel**

**1** Cut feathery fronds from fennel.

**2** Peel with a vegetable peeler.

**3** Remove core, then cut bulb vertically.

# fennel

From seed to stem, the entire fennel plant is edible and used in many different ways to impart a mild, aniseed flavour to foods. Fennel's unusual liquorice taste goes especially well with tomato and fish dishes.

**PACKED INTO** 80G COOKED FENNEL

about **9 calories**
- it provides useful amounts of **vitamins B$_6$** and **folate**
- dietary **fibre**

## at the market

**Season** UK-grown fennel is available from June until October.

**What to look for** Choose stalks with fresh-looking feathery fronds and smooth whitish-green bulbs and stems with no cracks.

## in the kitchen

**Storing** Separate fennel stems from the bulb before storing. Wrap stalks and bulb separately in plastic bags and put in the vegetable drawer of the fridge for up to four days. Use the stalks first, because they don't keep as well. Fennel loses its flavour with longer storage; it dries out and starts to turn brown.

**Preparation** To prepare fennel for cooking or eating raw, trim the base and remove any tough outer ribs. Trim off stalks with feathery leaves. Halve, core and slice the bulb. Raw fennel will turn brown soon after slicing so, to prevent discolouring, drop sliced fennel into a bowl of water with a little lemon juice and chill until ready to cook or serve.

**Basic cooking** Fennel can be steamed, boiled, braised, stir-fried or eaten raw. To braise, combine 2 sliced fennel bulbs and 125ml chicken stock or white wine in a large frying pan. Bring to the boil over medium heat. Reduce heat, cover and simmer until fennel is tender when pierced with a fork, about 20 minutes. Sprinkle with salt and pepper. Makes four servings. The stalks and feathery leaves can be used as a seasoning or garnish for soups, salads and seafood.

## Best uses in recipes

Fennel has an affinity for fish. In French cuisine, for example, fish is often baked on a bed of sliced fennel. Try barbecuing fish over fennel stalks or add leaves to the poaching stock for a large salmon.

# garlic

In addition to its culinary virtues, garlic has a long history of healing and curing. It has antibacterial and antifungal qualities that help to keep the immune system in good shape.

**PACKED INTO** ONE CLOVE OF COOKED GARLIC

about **3 calories**
• the phytochemical **allicin** which may help to lower cholesterol and reduce the risk of cancer

## at the market

**Season** Local garlic is available from July to early October.

**What to look for** Select firm garlic with dry, tight-fitting skin. A head of garlic should feel heavy and firm in your hand and the cloves appear plump and well formed. Garlic can be a creamy white or tinged a pinkish purple.

## in the kitchen

**Storing** Depending on how fresh it is when purchased, garlic will keep in a cool, dark, dry place for up to three months. Vented and lidded garlic jars made of a porous material, such as terracotta, make ideal storage containers. Do not chill.

**Preparation** To peel a garlic clove, lay it under the flat side of a large knife and then hit the side of the knife with your fist, sufficiently hard to split the clove so that the skin is easily removed.

**Basic cooking** Garlic is a basic seasoning in dishes worldwide. Rub a wooden serving bowl with a cut garlic clove to season a salad. For roasts and braises, the longer garlic cooks, the more mellow its flavour. When sautéing or stir-frying garlic, however, take care not to burn it or it will taste bitter.

**Roast garlic cloves** to a soft paste to make a low-fat spread for bread and grilled meats. Add sliced roasted garlic to soups, stews and pasta sauces.
**To roast a whole bulb of garlic,** preheat oven to 190°C (170°C fan oven), gas 5. Cut across the top of the bulb with a sharp knife to expose all the cloves. Brush the tops of the cloves with olive oil and season with salt. Wrap the bulb in foil and bake until very soft, 30 minutes to 1 hour. When cool enough to handle, push the softened garlic cloves from their skins.
**To roast individual cloves,** separate them from a bulb and toss, unpeeled, with 1 tablespoon olive oil in a small baking dish. Roast until tender when pierced with a knife, about 15 minutes. Serve with roast meats, stir through mashed potatoes or use to season stir-fried vegetables.

## fresh ideas

**For the maximum health benefits,** chop or crush garlic and let it stand for 10 minutes before using. This allows allicin, associated with anticancer and cholesterol-lowering effects, to be activated.

**Cook garlic** slowly in olive oil over a low heat, then discard. Use the oil to impart a mild flavour to foods.

**Tuck slivers of raw garlic** into lamb, beef and veal for roasting.

**Make garlic bread** with olive oil (no saturated fats), not butter.

## roasted garlic

**1** Cut 5mm off the top of garlic head.

**2** Roast as directed (see text). Push out the roasted cloves.

**3** Mash garlic with a fork until smooth.

## fresh ideas

**Purée steamed greens** with garlic and plain yoghurt. Top with sliced spring onions and serve cold as a summer soup.

**For a quick pasta sauce,** purée steamed spinach with parsley and lemon juice.

**Make a salad dressing** in a food processor or blender with steamed Swiss chard and a handful of parsley and basil. Add olive oil, lemon juice, crushed garlic, salt and black pepper.

**Some simple seasonings** for cooked greens:

- **Balsamic vinegar**
- **Fresh lemon juice**
- **Sesame oil and soy sauce**
- **Finely chopped fresh dill**
- **Toasted sesame seeds**

# greens

Leafy green vegetables that are used in cooking rather than salad making (although there is some overlap) are a large and diverse group.

**PACKED INTO** ONE 80G SERVING OF COOKED MIXED GREENS

about **15 calories**

- **beta-carotene** that is converted into vitamin A in the body
- half the daily requirement for **vitamin C**
- antioxidant **vitamin E** to protect the heart
- phytonutrients called **organosulphur compounds** that detoxify potential carcinogens
- **carotenoids** to reduce the risk of age-related eye disease and certain kinds of cancer

## at the market

**Season** A variety of greens is always available.

**What to look for** Regardless of the variety, pick brightly coloured, crisp leaves. Avoid bruised or excessively dirty leaves as well as limp or yellowing specimens – both are sure signs of age. Woody stems and coarse veins in the leaves practically guarantee that the vegetable will be tough and bitter.

**Where to buy the best** At a local farmers' market, greens will be newly picked. In a supermarket, greens that are displayed in a chilled section of the produce department are likely to stay fresh, as cool temperatures discourage decay and bacteria.

## in the kitchen

**Storing** Do not wash greens before storing them – too much moisture encourages the leaves to rot. Use perforated plastic storage bags or boxes, which allow air to circulate around the leaves and maintain just enough moisture to preserve their crispness.

**Preparation** Soak in cold water and then rinse thoroughly immediately before cooking to release any dirt trapped in stems or crinkly leaves. Trim any bruised outer leaves and cut off tough stems. Stems can be used in stock or soups. Swiss chard stems taste good sautéed briefly in olive oil and garlic, although they do not retain their bright appearance.

**Basic cooking** Greens are frequently the victim of overcooking, which leaves them soggy, bland and an unappetising shade of grey. Brief, gentle cooking or quick cooking over a high heat brings out their subtle flavours without ruining the delicate texture of the leaves. Cavolo nero is the exception (opposite). There is one general rule that applies to all greens, which is that they cook down to about a third of their original volume. Greens can be simply tossed in butter over a high heat until just wilted and then sprinkled with a

## cutting up greens

**1** To chop greens quickly, roll a bundle of leaves together into a cigar shape.

**2** Slice across the cigar to reduce the greens to shreds for fast cooking or to add to soups.

## cavolo nero

Literally means black cabbage. It is also known as black-leaf kale. This leafy, dark green vegetable can be prepared in many of the same ways as spinach and cabbage. Cavolo nero features widely in Italian cuisine, especially in recipes from Tuscany. It has a good, strong flavour. While leafy greens are often ruined through overcooking, cavolo nero is unique in that it benefits from long, slow cooking. One of the most famous recipes showcasing this type of greens is the classic soup, ribollita. After it is made, it is traditionally left for a day before serving to allow it to thicken and the flavours to develop. Cavolo nero also tastes delicious fried in good-quality olive oil with garlic and finely chopped chilli.

cavolo nero

little grated nutmeg, which takes the edge off any coarseness in the flavour. Finely chopped greens are a good addition to egg dishes such as soufflés, omelettes and quiches and to stuffings for roasts. The classic dish eggs Florentine comprises two soft poached eggs on a bed of cooked spinach, topped with mornay (cheese) sauce and grated cheese such as Cheddar or Parmesan.

**Best recipe** **To make ribollita**, the traditional hearty Tuscan soup, soak 300g cannellini (or other white beans) in water for at least 8 hours, or overnight. Drain and then boil in 2 litres of water until cooked. Drain, reserving the cooking liquid. Slice an onion and sauté in olive oil in a large, deep frying pan. Meanwhile, coarsely chop a head of cavolo nero, a quarter of a savoy cabbage, 1 bunch of Swiss chard, 1 leek, 2 potatoes, 2 carrots, 2 courgettes, 2 celery sticks and 2 peeled plum tomatoes. Add the vegetables to the pan and allow to soften slowly over a medium heat, about 10 minutes. Add the reserved cooking liquid with half the cooked beans. Purée the remaining beans in a food processor and add to the pan. Season with salt and pepper to taste. Simmer, partially covered, for 2 hours. Add 8 slices stale Italian bread such as ciabatta, stir well and boil for 10 minutes. Turn off the heat and leave to stand for a day to allow the flavours to develop and the soup to thicken. Reheat just before serving. Spoon into large bowls; drizzle with olive oil.

## did you know...

...that a pinch of bicarbonate of soda added during cooking makes greens even greener? However, it also breaks down the plant tissues, making the texture mushy and destroying many of the vitamins. Flavour and nutrients should be the major issues, not looks. If you cook greens briefly, they will be a lovely fresh green anyway.

# ...greens

## getting children to eat their greens

There's no doubt that leafy greens are probably the group of vegetables most disliked by children, but because greens are so good for growing bodies it's worth finding different ways to serve them. Finely sliced leaves, quickly stir-fried, will make greens more appealing, and you could also try bubble and squeak by adding some grated cheese or chopped grilled bacon to mashed potato and finely sliced cooked greens. Season well and form into cakes, then fry in a little oil. Serve with a poached egg on top for a light meal.

## varieties

**beetroot leaves** Like fresh spinach, beetroot leaves are tender and cook quickly. They have a mild flavour. Cook them in a covered frying pan using just the water that clings to the rinsed leaves. Add butter or olive oil. Other ingredients to add to give the greens more flavour include crushed garlic, ground cumin or a good dash of Tabasco sauce.

**kale** is available in several varieties with leaves that are crinkly, serrated, or feathery, in tones of blue-green, grey-green, light green or reddish purple. All but the season's first tender leaves tend to be quite tough and need braising for 12 to 15 minutes. Kale has a full flavour and is good chopped and added to hearty winter soups near the end of cooking.

**spinach** The best known of all the cooking greens, spinach has dark green, crisp, crinkly leaves. The young leaves, often called baby spinach, can be used in salads. Trimmed spinach leaves can be cooked in a pan with just the water left clinging to the leaves from rinsing. Cover and steam for 1 or 2 minutes. Do not overcook.

**spring greens** are loose-leafed greens. The leaves often have a hard central stem, which can be cut out if you prefer. Better still, slice the stems thinly and cook with the leaves, as they have a sweet flavour. Slice the leaves thickly and steam or briefly stir-fry to retain their crispness and colour. Grated ginger, garlic, soy sauce, chopped chilli and sesame seeds all taste good with stir-fried spring greens.

**swiss chard** is sometimes confused with spinach, with which it is interchangeable. However, chard has an earthier taste. The leaves can be blanched, sautéed, steamed or stir-fried. The wide stem, or rib, which can be a vivid red, yellow or a bright white, can be chopped and sautéed in oil or butter. The stems take a little longer to cook than the tender leaves.

# kohlrabi

The bulb-like stem of kohlrabi tastes like a mild, sweet turnip with traces of its cruciferous cousins, cabbage and Brussels sprouts, and a bit of radish. It has edible greens that are rich in iron.

**PACKED INTO** 80G COOKED KOHLRABI

about **14 calories**
- 50 per cent of the daily requirement for **vitamin C**
- vitamin A precursor **beta carotene** to protect eyes and aid in normal cell division and growth
- **antioxidant bioflavonoids** to prevent cell damage by free radicals
- plenty of **fibre**
- good amounts of **potassium** to maintain fluid balance and proper metabolism and muscle function

## at the market

**Season**  UK-grown kohlrabi, is vailable from July until mid November.

**What to look for**  Choose fresh-looking deep-coloured green leaves with no yellowing, and firm bulbs with smooth skin and no soft spots. Bulbs should be heavy for their size. Bulbs less than 7cm in diameter are the most tender; larger ones tend to be tough and woody. Kohlrabi bulb and stem colour can run from white to pale green and from red to purple, depending on variety. The flesh is always white and the flavour is essentially the same.

## in the kitchen

**Storing**  You can keep fresh kohlrabi in a ventilated plastic bag in the vegetable drawer of the fridge for up to two weeks.

**Preparation**  Kohlrabi leaves are even more nutritious than the bulb, which is an argument for cutting them up and cooking them with the bulb. Discard the leaf stalks. The bulb can be easily peeled with a small, sharp knife, but some cooks think the flavour is better if the vegetable is cooked with its peel still in place. Once cut, kohlrabi flesh is quick to discolour, so you may want to put slices or cut up pieces in a bowl of water with a little lemon juice until ready to cook.

**Basic cooking**  Kohlrabi is usually peeled, sliced or chopped, and steamed until tender, then buttered and seasoned with salt and pepper. It is also delicious braised in a beef or chicken stock, seasoned with onions and herbs. Many cooks steam or microwave kohlrabi pieces and then mash them with butter and seasonings. Sliced kohlrabi is often used in Asian stir-fries as a substitute for the more expensive water chestnuts – it has the same crispness with a little more flavour.

## fresh ideas

**Add small amounts** of grated raw kohlrabi to salads to give a sweet, pungent accent.

**To pickle kohlrabi,** soak slices of kohlrabi and onion for several hours in 1 litre iced water to which 4 tablespoons pickling salt have been added. Drain the vegetables and place in a medium bowl. Put 475ml vinegar in a pan with 150g sugar, 1 tablespoon mustard seed, 1½ teaspoons celery seed, and ¼ teaspoon turmeric. Boil for several minutes, stirring to make sure sugar is dissolved. Pour mixture over the vegetables and leave to cool. Cover and chill for three days.

**If the leaves attached to the bulb** are fresh and green, wash them and remove the ribs. Blanch the leaves until just wilted. Drain thoroughly and chop. Sauté in butter or olive oil and season with salt and pepper.

## did you know...

...that kohlrabi may look like a root vegetable but is actually a bulbous stem with leaf stalks sprouting from one end?

## fresh **ideas**

**Brush cleaned and trimmed leeks** lightly with olive oil and grill as an accompaniment for steak.

**Stir sautéed leeks** into mashed potatoes for a comfort-food treat.

**Thinly sliced, raw young leeks** add flavour and crunch to salads.

**Braise leeks** and fresh carrots together in stock. Sprinkle the tender vegetables with dill and serve as a side dish for fish.

**Bundle baby leeks,** cook them as you would asparagus, and serve with lemon juice, salt and pepper.

## did you **know...**

...that Welsh people still wear leeks on St David's Day in memory of King Cadwallader's victory over the Saxons in 640? The Welsh avoided friendly fire by identifying themselves to each other with leeks worn in their caps.

# leeks

With a milder, sweeter flavour than onions and a crunchy bite when cooked, leeks are a great vegetable for savoury, nutritious side dishes, and to add to soups and stews.

**PACKED INTO** 160G COOKED LEEKS

about **34 calories**
- 28 per cent of the daily **vitamin C** requirement to fight infection
- 32 per cent of the daily requirement for **folate** to regulate growth
- the phytochemical **diallyl sulphide** that is thought to lower the risk of stomach cancer
- **kaempferol**, a substance that may block cancer-causing compounds
- **quercetin**, another phytochemical that helps to fight cancer and heart disease
- **fibre** for protection against high cholesterol

## at the market

**Season** Available from September through to March.

**What to look for** Fresh leeks look like giant spring onions with straight root ends. Check both ends – the tops should be a healthy looking dark green and the root end should be white for several centimetres with unblemished skin that gives a little when you press it. The root end shouldn't be larger than 4cm in diameter with a bush of small roots still attached.

## in the kitchen

**Storing** Loosely wrap unwashed, untrimmed leeks in plastic and store in the vegetable drawer of the fridge for up to a week.

**Preparation** Leeks need careful cleaning (they are grown in furrows that are filled in with soil as they grow to keep the bottoms white). Trim off tough outer leaves and the roots at the base. Slit a leek lengthways from the base to the top and fan out the leaves under water, checking every layer for grit.

**Basic cooking** Whole leeks are often braised in stock or wine (you'll need 475 to 750ml liquid for 8 medium leeks) for 20 minutes or more. Be careful not to overcook them or they will lose their crispness and turn slimy. Cut-up leeks cook more quickly: steam or microwave them for 5 to 8 minutes. Sliced leeks add texture and flavour to soups and stews. Vichyssoise is the classic cold leek-and-potato soup: in a medium pan, sauté 2 sliced leeks and 1 chopped onion in butter until tender, about 5 minutes. Add 2 peeled and sliced potatoes and 550ml chicken stock. Simmer until potatoes are tender, 10 to 20 minutes. Cool, then purée in batches in a food processor. Stir in a little light soured cream, and salt and pepper to taste. Chill before serving.

# lettuces

There is an astonishing diversity of lettuces and salad leaves. Round lettuces are soft loose-hearted varieties, icebergs are large dense and crunchy, cos types have upright, crisp leaves. Loose-leaf varieties are harvested either as dense heads or individual leaves.

**PACKED INTO** 50G COS LETTUCE

**6 calories**
• all leaves contain small amounts of vitamin C and the B vitamins. The darker, strongly flavoured leaves such as rocket, spinach, watercress and radiccio tend to have higher levels of vitamins and phytochemicals than paler, sweeter leaves. The darker outer leaves of lettuce have up to 50 times more carotenoids than the paler inner leaves.

## at the market

**Season** UK-grown lettuces are available for most of the year, but you will find a greater variety during the summer months.

**What to look for** Regardless of the variety, lettuce should always look clean and fresh, with no wilted leaves or rust-coloured spots. Avoid large heads of lettuce with tough outer leaves and ribs.

## in the kitchen

**Storing** Wash lettuce before storing, and dry well. Discard any wilted or discoloured outer leaves. Wrap loosely in kitchen paper, then overwrap in plastic. Store in the vegetable section of the fridge. Tender-leaf lettuces will keep for a day or two; sturdier ones, such as cos and iceberg, will keep well for up to four days.

**Preparation** Tear small, tender lettuce leaves by hand. To shred large lettuce leaves, stack several of them on a cutting board. Roll the leaves up tightly from one long end. Slice the roll crossways. Shredded lettuce makes an attractive, edible bed for grilled seafood and marinated cooked meats.

**Serving** Never toss a green salad with dressing until it's time to eat or you'll end up with a soggy heap. To be well prepared ahead of time and to save on cleaning up, mix the salad dressing in the bottom of the salad bowl, top with salad greens, then chill up to 2 hours ahead of time. Toss the greens and dressing together just before serving. Be careful not to drown lettuce leaves in dressing – a little goes a long way.

**Dressing** The classic vinaigrette blends one part vinegar to three parts olive oil. Beating them together with a fork or a whisk will emulsify them. Experiment with seasonings such as garlic, herbs, mustard or lemon juice.

## new salads

Salad leaves have become so popular that other tender varieties are being added all the time, such as mizuna, purslane, salad burnet and sorrel. The growing tips of pea plants – pea shoots – are now available in some supermarkets. Crisp, sweet and

## fresh ideas

**Coarsely shred a mix** of sturdy, spicy lettuces, with some rocket or watercress, to use as a bed for grilled lamb chops or slices of steak.

**Use individual leaves** of endive to hold a savoury dip such as herbed goat's cheese as an hors d'oeuvre.

**Wrap sandwich fillings** such as egg or tuna salad, in lettuce leaves instead of bread to cut down on calories and carbohydrates.

**Grill fish in a generous covering of lettuce** to keep it moist. Spicier lettuces will add some flavour, too.

## did you know...

...that lettuce was originally regarded as a weed? Today, it is cultivated in many varieties all around the world.

# ...lettuces

tender, the shoots really do taste delightfully of peas. If you visit farmers' markets or buy organic salad leaves, you may find your salad selection includes some edible flowers. Popular ones are nasturtium, viola, thyme and chive flowers, and the petals of calendula. Not only do the flowers make a salad pretty but they add their own distinctive flavours as well.

# varieties

**cos,** or romaine, is a loose-head lettuce with sturdy, rich-green outer leaves, paler green inner leaves, and crisp ribs. It has a mild tangy flavour.

**endive,** or chicory, is a bullet-shaped, tightly closed head of smooth leaves with a slightly bitter taste. The characteristic whitish creamy leaves are the result of it not being exposed to sunlight during growing. Use raw in salads or steam, and serve with a cheese sauce or simply seasoned.

**frisée** has leaves tapering to sharp points. Outer leaves are lacy and green-rimmed; inner leaves are pale yellow and form a compact heart. The flavour is slightly bitter.

**iceberg** is a crisp, tightly packed lettuce that looks like a type of cabbage. It has pale green leaves and a mild flavour.

**lamb's lettuce,** or mache, is high in beta-carotene, with tender, round leaves and a mild flavour. Sold with its roots still attached, it is highly perishable and should be used right away.

**lollo rosso** is dark copper-red fading to bright green. The leaves are crisp and finely crinkled, with jagged edges resembling lace, and often used as a garnish. It has a mildy bitter flavour.

**mignonette** is a loose-head lettuce with small, soft-textured leaves that have a mild flavour. It is available in green and red varieties that look attractive mixed in a salad.

**oak leaf** is a loose lettuce with thin, tender reddish-brown or green scalloped leaves. It has a distinctive mild, nutty flavour.

**radicchio** comprises a tight head of crisp leaves which are a vibrant red or reddish-purple with white veins. The very bitter flavour works well in a salad of mixed leaves.

**rocket** comprises several rounded and spiked tender leaves jutting from slender stems. The delicious peppery flavour becomes more pungent with age. Rocket can be eaten raw and can also be added at the last minute to dishes.

**round** is a category of generally available lettuces that form small heads with soft, tender leaves. The heart is tender and the leaves have a mild flavour.

# mushrooms

Thousands of varieties of fungi, including edible mushrooms, cover the planet. Many wild mushrooms are toxic, even deadly, so unless you're an expert, it's best to pick your exotic mushrooms at a supermarket or farmers' market.

**PACKED INTO** 100G RAW COMMON MUSHROOMS

**13 calories**
- a variety of **B vitamins** for energy
- **copper** to support thyroid activity
- **potassium** to regulate blood pressure

## at the market

**Season** Farm-raised: available all year; wild mushrooms: in autumn.

**What to look for** Choose mushrooms that have smooth, dry skin and stems with no bruises. Buy only as many as you will use within a day or two. When mushrooms are cooked, they reduce in size by about a half.

## in the kitchen

**Storing** Keep mushrooms in a paper bag, or layered between sheets of kitchen paper, in the fridge for up to a two days.

**Preparation** Clean mushrooms just before using with damp kitchen paper or a soft vegetable brush to remove dirt. Trim stems as desired.

## fresh ideas

**When you want to add flavour** to button mushrooms, try using a few reconstituted dried mushrooms. These have a rich, intense flavour, while the buttons give the dish the texture you expect of mushrooms.

**To flavour soups and stews,** use the liquid from the reconstituted dried mushrooms, strained through cheesecloth. Add to sauces, too.

**Brush large flat mushrooms** with olive oil, salt and pepper, then barbecue or grill them as you would burgers. Serve sprinkled with chopped fresh thyme.

## varieties

**button** are white or off-white mushrooms with round caps and a very subtle flavour and fine texture. Larger, open, field mushrooms have a stronger flavour.

**chanterelles** are golden-coloured trumpet-shaped mushrooms with pale yellow gills and a distinctive flavour. They are one of the most popular exotic mushrooms.

**chestnut** are similar in shape to button mushrooms but have a tan-coloured cap and darker stalk, and a stronger, richer flavour than the white variety.

**oyster** have no stalk and are creamy white to grey with a very delicate texture. They actually do have an oyster-like flavour, and it intensifies with cooking.

**portobello** are older, larger, flatter chestnut mushrooms and come in a variety of sizes from average to extra-large. They have a rich, earthy flavour.

**shiitake** are quite strongly flavoured, with a meaty texture. The tough stems are usually discarded. They are often used in Asian cooking.

## fresh **ideas**

**Barbecue okra** Thread four or five pods onto two parallel skewers, to create a vegetable 'ladder'. Brush the pods with olive oil and sprinkle with salt. Barbecue on both sides until lightly charred. Sprinkle with vinegar or lemon juice. Serve hot.

**Serve raw okra** on a vegetable platter with a dip.

**Okra and stewed tomatoes** make a great combination. Okra keeps the tomato from becoming too watery, and the acid in the tomato keeps okra from becoming too gelatinous.

**Add slices of raw okra** to a salad for an extra crunch.

## did you **know...**

...that okra releases sticky, gelatinous juices as it cooks, which thicken whatever liquid it is in? That's why it is such an important ingredient in gumbos and other Creole dishes that don't use a roux of flour and fat for thickening.

# okra

Also known as lady's fingers, okra has long been a staple in Creole and Cajun cooking and is a popular Middle Eastern dish. You can buy it fresh, frozen, dried and in cans.

**PACKED INTO** 80G OKRA

about **22 calories**
• 32 per cent the daily requirement for **vitamin C**
• 19 per cent the daily requirement for **folate**, which prevents birth defects and promotes normal growth
• fibrous **pectin**, which reduces cholesterol in the blood and protects against stomach ulcers and other intestinal disorders
• **lutein** and **carotenoids**, phytochemicals that help to prevent blindness due to macular degeneration and cataracts

## at the market

**Season** Okra is imported and available all year.

**What to look for** Choose bright green pods no more than 7cm long, avoiding any oversized okra, which will be fibrous and tough. Pods should be firm with no browning or discoloration at the tips.

## in the kitchen

**Storing** Okra is quite perishable; if you must store it, spread the unwashed pods in a single layer in a perforated plastic bag and chill for a day or two. If kept longer, the okra will lose its texture and colour.

**Preparation** Wash okra just before using it. Some cooks prefer to gently scrub the pods with a soft brush or towel to remove the fine fuzz on the surface, while others contend that this is not necessary, because the fuzz is imperceptible after cooking. In any case, do cut off and discard the stem end. Avoid cutting into the okra's interior flesh – except when chopping the okra for stews or sautés – or its slippery juice will be released. The juice makes a good thickener for stews but you do not want this when cooking the okra as a side vegetable.

**Basic cooking** Okra can be steamed, stewed, cooked in the microwave, or fried. One of the most popular ways to cook okra as a side dish is to fry it. For 500g trimmed whole okra, you'll need some flour and cornmeal in separate bowls for coating, 2 eggs lightly beaten in a bowl, plus vegetable oil for deep-frying. Once the oil is hot (about 190°C), toss the okra in the flour, dip it into the eggs, and then roll it in cornmeal. Fry in batches, without overcrowding, until well browned, about 3 minutes. Drain on kitchen paper. Serve, sprinkled with salt.

# onions

There are very few kitchens where onions are not a staple food. White, brown and red onions, which are left in the ground to mature and have a tough outer skin for longer storage, are used almost daily. Spring onions, with their papery skin, should be purchased as needed.

**PACKED INTO** 1 MEDIUM YELLOW ONION

**36 calories**
- **vitamin C** to fight infection
- a phytochemical known as **diallyl sulfide** that is thought to lower the risk of stomach cancer
- **quercetin**, another phytochemical that fights cancer and heart disease

## at the market

**Season** Onions are available all year round. Spring onions are also available all year, but best in early summer.

**What to look for** Choose firm, evenly shaped onions and spring onions with smooth, brittle, papery skin. Avoid onions that have soft spots or wet, discoloured skin. Spring onions should be a bright white, with deep green leaves and fresh-looking roots.

## in the kitchen

**Storing** Store onions in a mesh bag in a cool, dry open space away from bright light. Don't store them with potatoes; the potatoes give off moisture and a gas that causes onions to spoil more quickly. They should keep up to a month. Milder, sweeter onions such as Spanish onions and shallots often don't keep as long as sharper-tasting onions. Spring onions should not be stored for long periods. Wrap them in plastic, chill and use within a few days of purchase.

**Preparation** Onions contain a substance called a lachrymator, which is released into the air when the vegetable is peeled or cut. When the vapours combine with moisture from your eyes, sulphuric acid is formed, leading to a painful burning sensation and tears. To minimise this, try peeling the onion while holding it under cold running water. Some people suggest chewing on a piece of bread while you chop, to stop tears forming. If you use a sharp knife and make quick work of chopping (overleaf), tears won't be too much of a problem. Onions are best chopped by hand. If you use a food processor, pulse gently off and on to avoid mashing the onion.

**Basic cooking** Onions can be steamed, microwaved, battered and deep-fried or roasted on their own to be served with meat, poultry or fish as a side dish. But onions are most often used – raw or sautéed – to season soups, stews, sauces, cooked vegetables, casseroles, stir-fries and stocks. Caramelising is a popular way to cook onions to accompany meat. To serve four, thinly slice 3 onions. Heat 1 tablespoon olive oil in a heavy pan over medium heat. Add onions and cook, covered, for 10 minutes, stirring often. Remove lid; cook for 10 more minutes, stirring occasionally. A pinch of sugar speeds up the caramelising process, producing browned, soft, aromatic onions to complement any dish.

## fresh ideas

**Cook sliced red or sweet white onions** in olive oil over low heat until they are very tender and golden brown. Serve them with meat, fish or poultry, or as a hamburger relish.

**Stuff large sweet onions** that have been cored with a seasoned rice mixture. Bake in the same way as you would stuffed peppers.

**Add sautéed onions** and chopped fresh dill to bread doughs.

**Stuff cored apples** with sautéed red onions and bake until tender. Serve with sausages and scrambled eggs for brunch or a light lunch, or poultry, or as a hamburger relish.

## did you know...

...that in Ancient Egypt, onions were seen as a symbol of the universe, and were represented in carvings in pyramids built between in 2500 and 2200 BC?

## cutting up
an onion

**1** Halve onion lengthways. Make several horizontal cuts, stopping about 10mm from the root.

**2** Make vertical cuts from top to bottom, keeping root intact.

**3** Hold onion by the root end, slice crossways, letting onion fall apart into small, even pieces.

## ...onions

## varieties

**pickling onions** are tiny, immature onions that are lifted in autumn. For pickling they are soaked in brine before peeling, and then peeled and pickled in a spiced vinegar. They can also be roasted whole, added whole to casseroles or stews or braised in a wine and tomato sauce.

**red onions** are mild enough to eat raw in salads, salsas and sandwiches, but they are often added to cooked dishes as well and are good for roasting. They have red to purplish-red flesh, which makes them especially attractive when used raw.

**shallots** grow in bunches, similar to cloves of garlic. They have light brown skin and white or purplish flesh. Shallots have a delicate but distinctive and delicious flavour that defines many French sauces and braised dishes. The shallot is not the same as a pickling onion.

**spanish onions** are very large onions with a tan skin and a mild flavour. They can be eaten raw in salads and sandwiches.

**spring onions** are small and delicate onions with a white bulb and bright green tops. They are the first choice as a salad onion but are also a regular ingredient in stir-fries and other Asian cookery. Spring onions can also be chopped or finely sliced lengthways and used as a garnish.

**yellow and brown onions** are the most commonly available onion. Their strong flavour makes them ideal as the basis for a wide number of dishes, from casseroles to sauces, although their flavour can change depending on the season and the particular variety.

**white onions** are medium to large in size, with white papery skin. They have a firey flavour, which is good for spicy dishes, and can also be stuffed and baked.

# parsnips

Related to carrots but lacking the orange colour (and beta carotene), parsnips look like pale versions of their cousins. They have a sweet, herby and slightly nutty flavour – and are high in fibre and nutrients.

**PACKED INTO** 80G COOKED PARSNIPS

about **56 calories**
• about one-fifth of the daily **vitamin C** requirement for heart health
• **folate** for making red blood cells
• **magnesium** for bone growth and metabolism

## at the market

**Season** Parsnips are available from the end of October until February and at their best from December to February. Frost improves their flavour, making them sweeter, so parsnips that are available in winter tend to have the sweetest taste.

**What to look for** Choose firm, medium-sized roots that are uniformly shaped and free from bruises or soft spots. Parsnips more than 20cm long may have a woody core. Young parsnips are high in natural sugars, so they caramelise well when baked.

## in the kitchen

**Storing** Keep parsnips – without their greens – in a perforated plastic bag in the vegetable drawer of the fridge for up to four weeks.

**Preparation** For most uses, trim the tops and bottoms of parsnips and peel with a vegetable peeler (right). Cut into large chunks for roasting or small pieces for boiling or steaming. If you are intending to purée parsnips, you can cook them first, and peel them easily afterwards by hand.

**Basic cooking** Parsnips are best when they are cooked until just tender. Steaming is a good method to use, as is microwaving. They taste good roasted and you can also braise them in stock and season them with herbs or bake them as you would sweet potatoes. Purée cooked parsnips in a blender or food processor and serve with butter, and salt and pepper. Or, combine puréed parsnips with puréed swede, pumpkin or sweet potatoes. Parsnip enriches the nutritional value and the flavour of soups and stews; be careful not to put them in to cook too early or they will become mushy.

## fresh ideas

**Grate tender young raw parsnips** into salads to add flavour, texture and vitamin C.

**Puréed parsnip** can be used as the basis for delicious pancakes. Add 1 medium grated carrot, 2 sliced spring onions, 1 egg, 1 tablespoon flour and a pinch of salt. Cook pancakes in batches in a non-stick frying pan with a little groundnut oil. Serve warm topped with apple sauce or a dollop of soured cream.

## cutting up parsnips

**1** Trim top and bottom from parsnips. Then use a vegetable peeler to trim away a thin layer of peel.

**2** To dice, cut parsnip in two along the length and remove any woody core. Then cut across each piece.

## fresh **ideas**

**Toss a handful of blanched peas** into fresh salads.

**Pluck a handful** of fresh green peas from their pods and eat them straightaway for a nutritious snack.

**Add raw shelled peas** to stews, soups and vegetable sautés during the last minutes of cooking.

**Add peas** to plain grains such as rice, couscous and pasta.

**Garnish a platter** of sliced roasted meat with a handful of blanched shelled peas.

**For a smoky taste** to complement their sweetness, sauté sugar snap peas with a little chopped bacon.

**Cut blanched mange-touts** into small pieces and add them to egg or tuna salad to provide texture.

## did you **know...**

...that a 75g serving of fresh green peas has more protein than an egg?

...that mange-touts, so closely associated with Chinese stir-fries, were actually developed in Holland in the 1500s?

# peas

Thanks to the popularity of mange-touts and sugar snap peas – both peas with edible pods that require little preparation – more people are enjoying the benefits of fresh peas today than ever before.

**PACKED INTO** 80G COOKED GREEN PEAS

about **55 calories**
- **B vitamins** for energy production
- **vitamin C** for resistance to infection
- **folate** to promote normal growth
- **iron** to carry oxygen through your body
- plenty of **fibre** to maintain digestive health

## at the market

**Season**  Because mange-touts and sugar snap peas have become so popular they are imported all year round, but for sweetness you can't beat home-grown varieties in season. UK-grown peas are available from June to August; mange-touts and sugar snap peas from June to September.

**What to look for**  The freshest pea pods at the market will look shiny and firm; if rubbed together they squeak a little. Avoid any pale green or yellow pods, an indicator that their sugars have begun to turn to starch. If possible, taste one to test. The sweetest peas are small to medium sized. They should fit snugly inside their pods without looking swollen or crowded. Large, heavy,  pea pods usually signal that the peas will be tough and starchy. On the other hand, light, thin pods are an indication that the peas will be bland-tasting.

## in the kitchen

**Storing**  Like sweetcorn, time is of the essence when it comes to serving fresh peas, so storage is not recommended. If you must, store peas briefly in cling film in the coldest part of the fridge.

**Preparation**  To shell peas, snap off the top of the pod and pull the string down the side, opening the pod in the process. The peas will pop right out. Sugar snap pods are edible, but you may encounter some varieties that need stringing. To string sugar snaps, bend the stem tip toward the flat side of the pod to snap it, then gently pull downward, removing the string with the stem. Mange-touts need only the stem tip trimmed or can be left as they are.

**Basic cooking**  Nothing could be simpler than cooking fresh peas. Boil water, add a good pinch of salt and stir in the peas. Sugar snap peas and mange-touts will be crisp-tender in 1 to 2 minutes; shelled peas, depending on their size and freshness, will cook in 2 to 4 minutes. A pinch of sugar in the cooking water boosts the flavour of peas that are not perfectly sweet.

# peppers

Red, yellow, purple, orange and green peppers are available. Bursting with goodness they taste good both raw and cooked, and add flavour and colour to a huge range of dishes.

**PACKED INTO** 80G RAW RED PEPPER

about **26 calories**
- the antioxidant **beta carotene** to fight chronic disease
- **folate** for normal growth
- more than twice the daily requirement for **vitamin C**

## at the market

**Season** Peppers are mostly imported and are available all year.

**What to look for** Choose well-shaped globes with firm, glossy skin and no cuts, blisters or bruises. Reject any with mouldy stems, which might be a sign of rot on the inside. Peppers should feel heavy for their size and look crisp, not limp or spongy.

## in the kitchen

**Storing** Store, unwrapped, in the vegetable drawer of the fridge. Green peppers keep for about a week. Yellow, orange and red ones keep for up to five days.

**Preparation** Cut pepper in half through the stem end and remove the stem, seed pods and white ribs. Cut the pepper into flat panels for slicing and chopping. To peel a pepper, you must first char it over a gas flame, under a grill or over a barbecue, turning it often for even blackening. Steam the charred peppers in a paper bag or under an upturned bowl for 15 minutes. Scrape off the skin, cut out the stem and core, and discard the seeds.

**Basic cooking** Barbecue whole peppers for 20 minutes or slow-roast them at 190°C (170°C fan oven), gas 5 for 30 minutes. Use raw purple peppers in salads; they turn an unpleasant colour when cooked. Whole peppers, tops cut through to make a lid, can be stuffed with meat or grain mixtures. First microwave the shells for 2 minutes or steam for 5, then stuff and cook the whole dish.

## Best uses in recipes

Raw or cooked, red, yellow and orange peppers are sweeter than green ones. Raw peppers, chopped or sliced, are good additions to all kinds of salsas as well as salads – pasta, potato, rice or mixed salad leaves. Chopped and sautéed in oil, peppers enhance pilafs, pasta sauces, soups, stews and stir-fries.

## peeling peppers

**1** Roast peppers under a grill or on a barbecue lined with foil. Cook until the skins are charred and blistered.

**2** Place in a paper bag and seal tightly. Allow to steam for 10 minutes.

**3** Peel away the skin, then remove the stem and seeds.

**4** Cut pepper into bite-sized chunks.

# potatoes

It's hard to believe that the ever-popular and highly nutritious potato was once thought to be poisonous. Today, there are many different varieties to choose from – waxy or floury fleshed and with a wide range of skin colours.

**PACKED INTO** 1 MEDIUM BOILED POTATO

about **88 calories**
- good amounts of **potassium** to maintain normal blood pressure
- more than half the daily requirement for **vitamin C**
- flavonoids and other protective **phytochemicals**, especially in its skin
- insoluble **fibre** for better digestion

## fresh ideas

**Add potatoes to soups** and, once cooked, remove some of them, mash and return to the pan to thicken the soup without adding extra flour.

**Make a colourful potato salad** with unpeeled red, white and yellow-skinned potatoes.

**Substitute mashed potato** for some of the oil in a salad dressing. Then add chopped garlic and lemon juice or vinegar and whisk until smooth. The potato will give the dressing a creamy texture.

**Bind burgers** with cubes of cooked potato instead of using fresh **breadcrumbs.**

**Top a baked potato** with low-fat cream cheese and chopped fresh herbs such as parsley, chives or dill. Season with salt and pepper.

## at the market

**Season**  Since most mature potatoes store well, they are available all year.

**What to look for**  Choose potatoes that are firm, dry and well formed, with no bruises, cuts, cracks or sprouted eyes. Avoid potatoes with green spots, which indicates the presence of a toxin that develops when potatoes are exposed to light.

## in the kitchen

**Storing**  Keep potatoes loosely wrapped in brown paper or netting in a cool, dark, dry place with good air circulation. Under the best conditions, potatoes will keep for several months. New potatoes (see below) are the exception; they should be eaten within a week of purchase.

**Preparation**  Scrub potatoes well before cooking. Cut off and discard any sprouted areas. Peel, if you prefer, for mashed potatoes.

**Basic cooking**  will vary according to type. The varieties box (right) is a guide to the best uses of some of the most commonly available types. New varieties are regularly appearing on the market. Try some of the following:

**Anya potatoes** have smooth, firm flesh and an elongated shape. They are a cross between a Pink Fir Apple and a Desirée potato. Bake or use in salads.

**Estima potatoes** are oval with firm, moist and yellow flesh and are good for baking and roasting as potato wedges.

**Pink Fir Apple** is a knobbly speciality potato with a waxy texture. Ideal for boiling and serving with salads.

**New potatoes** that truly live up to that name are dug while the top of the plant is still green, rather than waiting for the foliage to die down. Be aware that the label 'new' may sometimes be given to washed small potatoes from a regular crop. Ask your supplier for information. True new potatoes are small with a waxy skin and intense flavour, such as **Jersey New Royals** (right). They do not store well and should be eaten within a week of purchase.

Also try **Maris Bard** and **Rocket** new potatoes, **Wilja** for mashing, **Sante** for roasting in wedges or deep-frying as chips.

**Best recipe** To make **Potatoes with Hazelnut Sauce** as a side salad, boil 1kg small potatoes until tender; drain. In a small bowl, whisk together 4 egg yolks, 1 teaspoon Dijon mustard, 2 teaspoons wine vinegar, a pinch of sugar and salt, and a generous grinding of black pepper. Place the bowl over a pan of simmering water and whisk until the egg mixture begins to thicken. Cut 125g unsalted butter into cubes. Whisk into the mixture, a cube at a time, then whisk in 100ml hazelnut oil. Adjust seasoning, if necessary. Spoon sauce over potatoes and scatter with 50g lightly toasted hazelnuts.

## did you **know...**

...that potato skins are richer in B vitamins, fibre, calcium, iron, phosphorus, potassium and zinc than potato flesh?

...that all the best flavour in a potato is close to the skin?
Use a potato peeler instead of a knife to pare off the skin as thinly as possible, in order to preserve the maximum taste.

# varieties

The range of potatoes on offer can be quite bewildering to the consumer. Basically, potatoes are either waxy or floury and it is these qualities that determine their suitability for certain cooking methods. Skin and flesh colours are numerous, as the following guide reveals.

**cara** are oval or round waxy potatoes with a white skin and creamy flesh. They are good for baking, mashing, boiling and roasting.

**charlotte** are waxy with a nutty flavour and yellow skin and flesh. Suitable for boiling, baking and salads.

**desirée** have pink skin and golden flesh. The pink shade will vary in intensity depending on the soil in which it has been grown. Midway between waxy and floury, Desirée are good for boiling, mashing, baking, roasting, slicing or making into chips.

**jersey new royals** are much loved for their small size and waxy texture. Available in May. Boil and serve as an accompaniment.

**king edward** are pink-skinned floury potatoes and are particularly good for baking and roasting as well as deep-frying as chips, as their texture is soft and dry when cooked. If you make potato gnocchi, floury potatoes will give you the best results and they should be peeled after they have been boiled to avoid the flesh becoming too wet. As floury potatoes disintegrate when cooked they are not suitable for serving boiled in pieces.

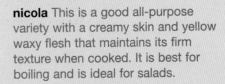

**maris piper** are cream-skinned potatoes with a texture that is fairly floury, making them a good all-purpose potato for baking, roasting and boiling. Maris Piper are also available as new potatoes.

**nicola** This is a good all-purpose variety with a creamy skin and yellow waxy flesh that maintains its firm texture when cooked. It is best for boiling and is ideal for salads.

## fresh ideas

**Combine mashed white beans** with tuna, chopped onion and dill to make a sandwich spread or dip.

**Mash chickpeas with parsley**, garlic, lemon juice, salt and pepper to make a low-calorie, low-fat hummous. Serve with small triangles of pitta bread.

**Mix types of beans** (black, red, pinto, for example) in a vegetarian chilli dish.

**Toss warm lentils** in a vinaigrette dressing and stir through chopped onion, cherry tomatoes, rocket and coarsely chopped cos lettuce to make a warm side salad.

## sprouting beans

Rinse, then soak 2 tablespoons mung beans or green lentils overnight in cold water. Rinse and put into a large jar. Cover the top with muslin and secure with an elastic band. Put in a warm, well-ventilated dark place. Rinse and drain well through the muslin twice a day. When sprouts are about 2.5cm long put them near a bright window for a few hours to boost their nutrient content. Rinse and use.

# pulses

The edible dried seeds of certain leguminous plants, pulses include peas, beans and lentils. Black, white, pink, green and yellow, pulses are an important ingredient in cuisines around the world. In this age of fusion cooking, pulses can be mixed and matched in a variety of exciting and nutritious dishes.

**PACKED INTO** 3 HEAPED TBSP RED KIDNEY BEANS

about **80 calories**
• a third of the daily requirement for **fibre**
• three heaped tbsp of cooked beans will count as one of the five servings of fruit and vegetables that we are supposed to eat each day
• all varieties of beans provide good amounts of **protein** and **fibre** as well as a selection of the **B vitamins**, **magnesium**, **iron** and **zinc**

## at the market

**Season** Pulses are available dried or canned all year.

**What to look for** Name-brand products are usually better quality than generic or store-brand products, but the nutritional value is the same. Generically labelled cans might contain more broken or squashed beans. When buying dried beans in bags or bulk, look for clean, smooth, evenly shaped beans with little or no debris.

**Where to buy the best** A good health-food shop or natural foods market may be best for buying dried beans in bulk. Health-food shops are also the best source for dried and canned organic beans and lentils. All supermarkets carry packaged dried beans and canned beans; some carry organic brands.

## in the kitchen

**Storing** Canned beans keep indefinitely. Store dried beans in a sealed package or container and cook by the use-by date, as beans toughen when old. Once cooked, store, covered, for up to five days in the fridge.

**Preparation** Dried legumes should be well rinsed before using and picked over to remove any foreign particles such as pebbles or pieces of grit that may have slipped through. With the exception of lentils, all dried beans should be soaked before cooking. Place in a large bowl with plenty of cold water to cover. Leave to stand at room temperature for at least 8 hours or overnight. Or, combine the beans with water to cover in a large pan. Heat to boiling, and boil for 2 minutes. Remove from heat, cover, and leave to stand for 1 hour. Whichever pre-soaking method you use, discard the soaking water, then add fresh water before cooking.

**Basic cooking** All pulses can be cooked using a ratio of 1 part beans to 3 parts water. Combine beans and water in a pan. Do not add salt; it hardens the skins. Boil beans and peas over medium-high heat for 10 minutes. Reduce heat to low, cover, and simmer until tender, 1 to 2 hours. Simmer red lentils for 20 minutes; about 25 to 40 minutes for other types.

# varieties

 **aduki beans** These small red-brown beans with a white stripe have a sweet flavour and are particularly popular in Japanese cooking.

 **black-eyed beans** Medium-sized, creamy white beans with a black spot, they are used in Cajun and Caribbean cuisines.

 **black kidney beans** A staple in Latin American dishes, these earthy beans are lower in folate than red kidney beans but are still high in nutritional value.

 **borlotti beans** Medium-sized and oval, these are pink and beige in colour, smooth and creamy in texture and nutty in flavour – a good addition to soups and stews.

 **broad (fava) beans** Large and brown when dried, broad beans, also known as fava beans, are staples in Middle Eastern and Mediterranean cooking.

 **butter beans** Starchy and filling, butter beans come in two sizes: a large variety and the smaller lima beans. They are popular in casseroles and soups.

 **cannellini** Large white Italian kidney beans, available canned and dried, cannellinis are used in salads and soups.

 **chickpeas** Medium-sized, tan coloured and nut-shaped, these beans are the main ingredient in hummous and often featured in Mediterranean and Middle Eastern dishes.

 **flageolets** These pale green kidney beans are traditionally served with lamb, but can also be used with other meats, and in soups, stews and salads.

 **haricot beans** These small, white rounded beans have a mild flavour. Use in traditional recipes for baked beans.

 **kidney beans** Large pink or red kidney-shaped beans, this variety is often served with rice and is a favourite for chilli con carne, stews and soups.

 **lentils** Very small brown, green, orange, or yellow legumes, lentils are featured in Middle Eastern and Central European cuisines in soups, stews, salads and side dishes.

 **mung beans (moong dhal)** Greenish-brown, yellow or black, these small beans cook quickly and have a sweet, fresh flavour. Use in Asian recipes.

 **pigeon peas** These small, creamy white beans with orange mottling are used in Caribbean, African and Indian cooking. They contain high levels of protein.

 **pinto beans** Medium-sized, mottled pinkish-tan, kidney-shaped beans, pinto beans are used in Latin American cooking and are one of the most nutritious types.

 **puy lentils** These small, black lentils have an excellent rich and peppery flavour and retain their shape during cooking.

 **soya beans** Medium-sized, round and green when fresh, soya beans are yellow when dried. Highly nutritious, they are processed into tofu, soya drinks and flour.

 **split peas** Made from fresh green peas, these legumes split when dried. They are a favourite ingredient in soups and a good thickening agent in stews and curries.

 **split red lentils** These are the fastest of all lentils to cook. They are good for soups, pasta sauces or mixed with butter, seasoning and herbs to make a sandwich spread.

## fresh ideas

**Add peeled and diced** butternut squash to soups, stews, pies and casseroles.

**Add peeled, grated pumpkin** to pancake batter.

**Make a sauce** of puréed pumpkin and grated Parmesan cheese to serve with pasta.

**Cook chunks** of pumpkin with sugar, sultanas, red pepper and spices until tender. Serve as a chutney with meats or poultry.

**A little olive oil or butter** will enhance the flavour of cooked pumpkin. You can also add any of the following seasonings:

- Brown sugar
- Curry powder
- Honey and sage
- Honey, ginger and cinnamon
- Jalapeño chilli and fresh coriander

# pumpkins & squash

There are many types of pumpkin, also known as winter squash. Each is a powerhouse of good nutrition, to fight heart disease, cancer and depression.

**PACKED INTO** 100G COOKED BUTTERNUT SQUASH

**32 calories**
- 35 per cent of the daily requirement for vitamin C
- excellent amounts of beta carotene which the body converts to vitamin A
- B vitamins for energy production
- fibre to help to maintain digestive health
- eye-protective lutein
- heart-helping magnesium and potassium

## at the market

**Season** Butternut squash is available all year round, but is not grown in the UK. Local pumpkins are available from late autumn throughout winter.

**What to look for** The large pumpkins on sale for Halloween at most supermarkets do not have the best flavour and tend to have watery flesh. When choosing pumpkins for cooking, look for dry, hard, tough-looking skin with no soft spots or bruises. Pick smaller pumpkins for their sweeter flavour and more tender flesh. Make sure they still have their stalks attached.

## in the kitchen

**Storing** At home, store cut pumpkin in a paper bag in the fridge for up to a week. For the best flavour, use the same day. Whole pumpkins can be stored at room temperature for up to three months.

**Preparation** To prepare pumpkin, use a large cook's knife or cleaver to split the vegetable in half. You can use a sharp paring knife or heavy-duty vegetable peeler to remove the skin on smooth pumpkins, if necessary. It's nearly impossible to peel acorn squash and other ridged varieties. Remove seeds and fibrous pulp. Cut flesh into small pieces.

**Basic cooking** Pumpkin can be baked, steamed, boiled, stewed or cooked in a microwave oven. A quick way to prepare pumpkin is to bake it. Halve the pumpkin, scoop out and discard the seeds, and place, flesh side down, in a lightly greased baking tin. Bake at 200°C (180°C fan oven), gas 6 until very tender (a fork inserted into the flesh through the skin moves easily in and out), about 45 minutes to 1 hour, depending on the size of the pumpkin. Cut into smaller pieces to serve. To boil, place pumpkin pieces in lightly salted water to cover. Bring to the boil, cook until tender, about 20 to 25 minutes. Add butter, salt and pepper, and mash or purée, if you like.

# varieties

There are many varieties of pumpkin to choose from, each with a different shape, size, marking and flavour. The hulless or semi-hulless seeds can be roasted like sunflower seeds. They are a good source of essential fatty acids, potassium and magnesium. Look out for locally grown varieties in late autumn. You will find that most pumpkins are versatile so can be used for a variety of recipes.

**baby bear** is a small squash with firm and sweet flesh, suitable for sweet and savoury recipes. It can be stuffed and baked as a single serving.

**butternut** This medium-sized, pear-shaped squash has dry-textured, bright orange flesh and the skin is easy to remove with a swivel peeler. It has a mildly sweet, nutty flavour. It is an ideal variety for puréeing and making into a rich winter soup.

**crown prince** This large, pale blue pumpkin has a tough skin and stores well. Although difficult to peel, the flesh tastes very good. Can be roasted unpeeled in segments, or peeled and cubed for adding to risottos and used for pumpkin soup.

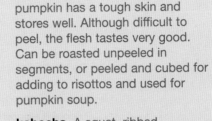

**kabocha** A squat, ribbed pumpkin, kabocha has grey-green skin with paler stripes. Its orange flesh is sweet and nutty. Having a sweeter taste than most varieties, it is particularly good for roasting. It also suits boiling, steaming and stir-frying.

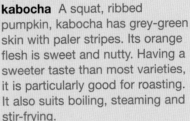

**onion** With bright orange skin and flesh, this distinctive onion-shaped squash is good for making into soups and for roasting and cubing for vegetable stews.

**sweet mama** A small kabocha-type fruit that can be cooked as a single serving.

## preparing pumpkin

**1** With a knife, cut off stem and halve lengthways. Scoop out all the seeds with a spoon.

**2** Cut the halves lengthways into quarters and then cut the flesh into chunks.

## did you **know...**

...that pumpkins are heavy consumers of nutrients in the soil, so if you grow your own it's best to grow a different vegetable, such as lettuce or cabbage, in the same spot the following year.

## fresh **ideas**

**If you like a little spiciness** but can't take the heat of chillies, try garnishing dips, salads, hot or cold soups, stir-fries and other dishes with slivered or grated radishes.

**Simmer mooli slices** in stock and then glaze with orange juice, just as you do carrots.

**For an easy side salad**, combine any of the following pairings with a well-seasoned vinaigrette dressing: orange segments and radishes; cucumber slices and radishes; peas or mange-touts and radishes.

## **matchstick** radishes

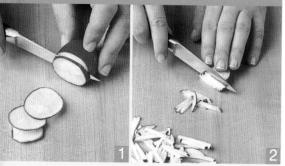

**1** With a paring knife, cut radishes into disks about 1cm thick.

**2** Stack three or four discs and cut crossways into 1cm sticks.

# radishes

A bunch of round red radishes or tapered white radishes can go a long way towards enlivening a salad or a plate of appetisers. Radishes add a pleasant crunch as well as a hint of heat without the burn.

**PACKED INTO** 3 MEDIUM RADISHES

about **5 calories**
• 10 per cent of the daily requirement for **vitamin C**
• cancer-fighting phytochemicals known as **flavonoids**

## at the market

**Season**  Radishes are available from April until early October; mooli from May to November. Horseradish is available in the autumn.

**Varieties**  Although red radishes are the best known, in most vegetable markets, you can now find long, tapered **white radishes**, called **mooli** or **daikon**, which are large, white and carrot-shaped, native to Asia, and have a sharper flavour than red radishes. **Horseradish** is a long and tapered root with a brown skin. As it is fiery hot, it is usually sold prepared as a sauce, but can also be bought fresh and grated.

**What to look for**  Choose firm red radishes with taut, brightly coloured skin and fresh-looking leaves. White radishes and horseradish should be firm, unblemished and smooth.

## in the kitchen

**Storing**  Remove and discard any leaves before storing. Wrap red and white radishes and horseradish in cling film and store in the fridge for a week.

**Preparation**  Scrub radishes and trim the ends. Peel mooli and horseradish. Protect your eyes when peeling horseradish, perhaps by wearing glasses, as fumes from the skin of the vegetable can badly irritate your eyes. If radishes have started to wither, it is possible to revive them by soaking them in iced water for an hour before serving.

**Basic cooking**  Although red radishes are most often eaten raw in salads, they can also be steamed or sautéed until tender and served as a side dish. The flavour of all radishes mellows with cooking. Steam whole, trimmed red or white radishes for about 10 minutes. Sauté sliced radishes for 4 minutes. The simplest seasoning is a sprinkling of salt and a little butter. Horseradish is finely grated and can be mixed with soured cream, a little mustard and seasoning to make a sauce to serve with beef. A little horseradish goes a long way, so it is always used as a condiment and not as a vegetable.

# sweetcorn

In late summer the first corn on the cobs appear. Barbecue or steam them for the sweetest flavour. At other times, use frozen sweetcorn and baby corn in recipes.

**PACKED INTO** A MEDIUM COB OF CORN

about **80 calories**
• sweetcorn is a useful source of **vitamin C**, **vitamin B$_1$**, **vitamin B$_6$**, **niacin**, **folate**, **phosphorus** and dietary **fibre**
• it contains the phytochemical **zeaxanthin** which helps to reduce the risk of age-related macular degeneration.

## at the market

**Season**  Sweetcorn is available from the end of August until the beginning of October.

**Varieties**  Sweetcorn has a high sugar content – up to 6 per cent of its weight – and is picked at an immature stage to be eaten on the cob. Field corn is picked at a more mature, starchier stage and is used as livestock feed and, after refining, for a number of products, from whisky to plastics.

**What to look for**  Always buy corn on the cob with the husks intact, as the sugar in the kernels transforms into starch as soon as the husk is removed. Pull back the husk to inspect the kernels; there should be evenly formed straight rows of plump, smooth, shiny kernels. Check the silky end to make sure there is no decay or any worm holes.

## in the kitchen

**Storing**  The sooner you use it, the sweeter corn on the cob will be. If you must store it, place the cobs in a plastic bag and keep them in the vegetable drawer of your fridge for a day or two. Store baby corn in the same way.

**Preparation**  Remove the husk and silk from corn just before cooking. For barbecuing or roasting, you may want to keep the husks attached (right) to protect the kernels during cooking.

**Basic cooking**  Corn on the cob can be steamed or boiled for 5 to 10 minutes, or barbecued, roasted, or cooked in the microwave. Keep cooking times brief. You can barbecue corn on the grill rack or nestled in the coals. Either way, pull back the husks and brush the kernels with vegetable oil or melted butter. Refit the husks back over the corn and put the cobs in iced water until you are ready to cook them. Grill over medium-hot coals for 10 to 20 minutes, turning often.

## fresh **ideas**

**Sweetcorn** isn't just for eating off the cob. Try using it in or with some of the following:

• **Cheese sauce**
• **Tomato salsa**, with red onion and finely chopped coriander
• **Carrots, pepper, stock and leftover chicken** to make a soup
• **Add baby corn** to stir-fries

## for the **barbecue**

**1**  Shuck corn from tip to stem; husk must not be removed all the way.

**2**  Remove the corn silk by hand.

**3**  Pull husks back up over kernels. Soak corn in iced water.

## fresh ideas

**Make a salad** with chunks of cooked sweet potato. Dress with lime juice, olive oil, curry powder and salt, and sprinkle with finely chopped spring onions.

**Mash cooked sweet potatoes** with grated Parmesan cheese. Use in place of half the cheese in your favourite lasagna recipe.

**Make sweet potato chips** by thinly slicing sweet potatoes and drizzling them with olive oil. Bake in a 200°C (180°C fan oven), gas 6 oven until tender and crisp.

## did you know...

...that sweet potatoes are called yams in some countries, although the two vegetables are unrelated? Yams grow on vines whereas sweet potatoes grow under the ground.

# sweet potatoes

These orange tubers belong to a select group of power vegetables loaded with important nutrients. Beta-carotene, the carotenoid that gives the colour to sweet potatoes, is a powerful antioxidant linked to lowered risk of certain cancers and heart disease.

**PACKED INTO** 200G BAKED SWEET POTATOES

about **230 calories**
- 100 per cent of the daily requirement for **vitamin C**
- 20 per cent of the recommended daily amount of **vitamin B$_6$**
- excellent amounts of **beta carotene** which the body converts to **vitamin A**
- **magnesium**, **fibre** and **potassium**

## at the market

**Season**  As sweet potatoes are not grown in the UK, they are imported and are available all year round.

**Varieties**  Sweet potatoes can be white, purple or orange/red/gold. The white skinned sweet potatoes have white flesh, and the purple sweet potato has a creamy-white flesh.

**What to look for**  Choose firm sweet potatoes with smooth, dry skin and no cracks or blemishes. Check the tips of the potatoes, which is where decay usually begins.

## in the kitchen

**Storing**  Keep sweet potatoes in a cool, preferably 12°C, dark place for up to a month. At normal room temperature, they will last up to a week. Don't put raw sweet potatoes in the fridge; they tend to harden and develop an 'off' taste. You can freeze cooked sweet potatoes for longer storage.

**Preparation**  Scrub unpeeled potatoes well before baking. Potatoes to be cut up for cooking can be peeled with a swivel-blade peeler. Alternatively, peel whole potatoes after cooking.

**Basic cooking**  To bake whole sweet potatoes, preheat oven to 220°C (200°C fan oven), gas 7. Pierce each potato in several places with a fork or knife tip. Arrange potatoes in a foil-lined baking tin. Bake until very tender, about 1 hour.

## Best uses in recipes

Baked sweet potatoes are served split and mashed with butter as a side dish. Their sweetness can be enhanced by cooking them with pear, apple or orange juice. For a different taste, season sweet potatoes with lime juice and fresh coriander, or mash with roasted garlic, salt and pepper. Mash boiled sweet potatoes to use as a side dish.

# tomatoes

Although Italy and other Mediterranean countries are probably best known for dishes that feature tomatoes, they are, in fact, native to Central America.

**PACKED INTO** 1 MEDIUM RAW TOMATO

about **14 calories**
- 36 per cent of the daily requirement for **vitamin C**
- useful amounts of **vitamin B$_6$** and **folate**
- sight-protective **lutein** and **zeaxanthin** that help to stave off vision loss
- **beta carotene** that is converted to **vitamin A** in the body
- a phytochemical called **lycopene** that fights prostate cancer
- anti-cancer chemicals **caffeic**, **ferulic** and **chlorogenic acids**

## at the market

**Season**  There are British tomatoes available at the market from March to November, but summer is the best time to buy and enjoy fresh tomatoes from local growers – or your own garden.

**What to look for**  Choose firm, ripe, evenly shaped, deeply coloured tomatoes with no tears or bruises in the skin. Ripe tomatoes have a very distinctive earthy fragrance.

**Where to buy the best**  Farmers' markets and shops that specialise in organically grown produce are most likely to have the sweetest, juiciest fruits (tomatoes are technically a fruit, not a vegetable).

## in the kitchen

**Storing**  Always store tomatoes at room temperature. Store any slightly underripe tomatoes in a brown paper bag to ripen them and improve their flavour. Chilling destroys a tomato's taste and texture.

**Preparation**  Use a sharp, serrated knife to slice tomatoes. To remove seeds, cut the tomato in half and gently squeeze out seeds and liquid. To peel tomatoes, follow instructions and photographs (right).

**Basic cooking**  Tomatoes can be halved and barbecued, grilled, or roasted in a hot oven until they start to shrivel, 10 to 15 minutes. Do not overcook them or they will collapse. Large varieties can be stuffed.

## fresh **ideas**

**Cook fresh tomatoes** with sugar, cinnamon, and orange zest to make a savoury jam.

**Combine tomato juice** with an equal amount of carrot juice and chill. Garnished with chopped fresh tomato and a dollop of yoghurt, the mixture serves as a refreshing summer soup.

**To give a nutritional boost** to savoury soups, replace half the water with tomato juice.

**Make a quick sauce** for pasta salad by combining tomato purée, tomato juice, olive oil, balsamic vinegar and chopped fresh basil.

## peeling a tomato

**1**  Cut a shallow X in the base of each tomato.

**2**  Blanch in boiling water for about 1 minute. Skin will shrivel. Place in cold water.

**3**  Remove skin with a paring knife or with your fingers.

# ...tomatoes

## Best use in recipes

Most tomatoes are used to make sauce. They are also used in soups, stews, casseroles and sautés and eaten raw in salads. Cherry and baby plum tomatoes are served on vegetable appetiser platters and eaten as they are as snacks.

**Best recipe**  One of the most useful recipes is a **basic tomato sauce**, which can form the base of a pasta sauce, to add to lasagne or to top pizzas. You can use canned tomatoes for speed or fresh tomatoes for a fresher flavour. Heat 1 tablespoon olive oil in a large pan over medium heat and fry 1 finely chopped onion and 1 crushed garlic clove until soft, about 5 minutes. Peel, core and chop 450g tomatoes, or use 400g can chopped tomatoes. Add to the pan with 1 tablespoon tomato purée, 1 teaspoon mixed herbs, 1 teaspoon sugar, salt and pepper to taste. Stir well, bring to the boil, then reduce the heat. Cover and simmer until the tomatoes have thickened and cooked to a pulp, 20 to 30 minutes.

## varieties

**baby plum tomatoes**  are small, red or yellow, grape-shaped, and, like cherry tomatoes, can be eaten just as they are.

**beef tomatoes**  are very large, deeply ridged, dark red tomatoes that are wonderful for salads and sliced in sandwiches.

**cherry tomatoes**  are small red or yellow tomatoes that are often sweeter and lower in acid than round tomatoes.

**green tomatoes**  are merely tomatoes that were picked from the vine prior to ripening. If they are wrapped in paper and left at room temperature, they'll slowly ripen and turn red, but don't expect them to be sweet. Firm and tart, green tomatoes are commonly used for pickling or frying.

**plum tomatoes**  are a red, egg-shaped, fleshy variety that is especially good for sauces, soups, and other cooked dishes. Plum tomatoes can also be eaten raw in salads and can be used to make dried tomatoes. They are a useful storecupboard ingredient in cans.

**round, or salad, tomatoes**  These are the most common tomatoes. Medium sized, they can be eaten raw or cooked. As they can be acidic, a little sugar can be added to tomato sauces when cooking with them. Also available in yellow and orange.

**vine-ripened tomatoes**  are smaller than round tomatoes and are ripened to have a deep red colour. They have a much sweeter flavour than round and although more expensive are preferable, especially for eating raw. Vine-ripened cherry tomatoes are also available.

# turnips & other root vegetables

A member of the cabbage family, turnips are prized for their roots as well as their greens. A staple vegetable since early Roman times, they grow easily in poor soil and are high in nutrients and low in calories.

**PACKED INTO** 80G COOKED TURNIP

about **10 calories**
• 20 per cent of the daily recommendation for **vitamin C**
• **indoles** to fight cancer
• **lysine** to prevent cold sores
• **soluble and insoluble fibre** to lower cholesterol and prevent constipation

## at the market

**Season**  Available all year, but local turnips are best in June and July, and from September to January.

**What to look for**  Choose smooth, heavy, firm turnips, preferably on the small side – closer to a golf ball than a tennis ball – with a minimum of fibrous root hairs at the base. Large turnips can develop a strong flavour that's too assertive for most tastes. If greens are attached, they should be crisp and a vibrant green.

## in the kitchen

**Storing**  Keep turnips in a plastic bag in the vegetable drawer of the fridge for up to a week. Detach and store turnip greens separately and use within a few days.

**Preparation**  Trim a slice from the top and bottom of each turnip and peel as thinly as possible with a swivel vegetable peeler to save nutrients.

**Basic cooking**  Before cooking, place cut-up turnip in cold water with lemon or vinegar added to prevent the flesh from darkening. For the same reason, do not cook turnips in aluminium or iron pans. To preserve the mild, peppery flavour, do not cook turnips beyond the crisp-tender stage because overcooking intensifies the flavour.

Turnip chunks can be roasted with meat or poultry or in a shallow roasting pan by themselves (30 to 45 minutes at 190°C (170°C fan oven), gas 5). Turnips can be boiled, steamed, microwaved or braised, whole or in pieces. Cooking turnips whole takes longer – up to 30 minutes. Sliced or matchstick turnips can be successfully stir-fried or sautéed. Turnip chunks add a sweet, peppery note to soups and stews. Mashing boiled, steamed or microwaved turnips with butter, salt and pepper is a classic way to serve the vegetable. But mashed turnip also goes well with other mashed vegetables, such as potatoes, spiced with some onion or roasted cloves of garlic and fresh herbs such as chives or parsley.

Puréed turnips on their own are deliciously sweet, but their bulk and texture tends to be a little on the thin side. Adding one medium potato for every three turnips makes a creamier, richer purée.

## fresh **ideas**

**Steam sliced turnips,** carrots and potatoes and mash them together with seasoning. The combination is smoky and delicious.

**Sauté cubes of turnip** in olive oil with garlic and shredded turnip greens as a side dish.

**Add shredded turnips** and dill to shredded potatoes to make potato rösti with a fresh new taste. Fry in a little butter.

**Make a slaw** of shredded turnips and shredded apples; dress with a combination of cider, apple cider vinegar and Dijon mustard.

## did you **know...**

...in the late 4th century BC, when King Nicomedes of Bithynia (now part of northern Turkey) was travelling far from the sea and craved anchovies, his cook served him thin slices of turnip sprinkled with poppy seeds and salt?

# ...turnips & other root vegetables

## varieties

**celeriac** is a knobby root that tastes like celery and has a crisp texture. It is low in calories and rich in phosphorus, potassium and vitamin C. Grate it fresh for salads or braise it in stock as a side dish. Alternatively, dice it and add to soups. Scrub the root well and peel before cutting up for cooking or raw vegetable platters. Roast celeriac in its skin and peel afterwards. Celeriac goes well with pork.

**jerusalem artichoke** is a gnarled root packed with vitamin C, iron, fibre and calcium, and has a nutty taste and a crisp texture. Grated or sliced fresh jerusalem artichoke adds a smoky flavour and lots of crunch to salads and slaws. Put cut-up or peeled jerusalem artichokes in cold water with lemon juice to keep the flesh from turning brown. Do not use iron or aluminium cookware. Bake the vegetable for 30 to 60 minutes or boil for 10 to 20 minutes. Mash or purée the artichokes with parsley and other fresh herbs and a little butter or oil. For a side dish to accompany roasts or grilled meats or chicken, braise with potatoes, carrots and celery in beef or chicken stock. Use slices in place of water chestnuts in stir-fries for both their flavour and crunchy

texture. Despite the name this vegetable is no relation of the spiky-leaved globe artichoke.

**salsify** is a long root vegetable that is often called the vegetable oyster because the flesh tastes faintly of oyster when cooked. The root is usually covered in soil, which must be washed off before the skin is peeled. Rinse then cut into short pieces. Cook in water with a teaspoon of lemon juice. Toss the cooked salsify in butter and seasoning and serve with a little grated Parmesan cheese, if you like.

**scorzonera** is similar in appearance to salsify although the skin is darker. It has a delicate flavour, a little like artichokes. Prepare and cook as salsify. Serve tossed in butter and seasoning with some chopped fresh rosemary or sage.

**swede** is a sweet-flavoured vegetable that is often served boiled and mashed with a little butter. It goes well with roast duck because both have strong flavours that complement one another. Smaller, firm specimens have the sweetest flavour. Store uncovered in the fridge for up to two weeks. Peel and cut into chunks then boil or

steam. Add grated swede to a traditional Cornish pasty filling of finely shredded beef, grated potato and lots of black pepper.

## did you know...

...that turnips are one of the only vegetables that you can plant near potatoes, because potatoes tend to need lots of space to spread and grow and are poor garden companions?

# watercress

Hot and peppery watercress is a wonder-vegetable full of vitamins A and C, iron, calcium and folic acid. Just a little will perk up a salad or add a piquant flavour as a garnish.

**PACKED INTO** 100G WATERCRESS

about **31 calories**
- nearly a day's requirement for vitamin C
- indoles to help to fight cancer
- sulforaphane, a phytochemical that helps to fight cancer
- 2.7mg of beta carotene

## at the market

**Season** UK-grown watercress is in season from April until November, but particularly good in April and May, and from September to early November.

**What to look for** Watercress should have dark crisp leaves and no signs of yellowing or wilting. It is often sold in sealed packs but also available in bundles. Check that the leaves look fresh and bright.

## in the kitchen

**Storing** Keep watercress that is sealed in a pack in the salad drawer for two to three days. Put the stems of watercress when bought in a bundle into a small container of water and cover with a plastic bag. Store in the fridge for up to two days.

**Preparation** Trim off any tough stems or yellow leaves and divide into small sprigs. Put into a bowl of water and wash gently, then lift out and drain in a colander. Rinse under running water. Drain and pat dry with kitchen paper or spin briefly in a salad spinner.

**Basic cooking** Watercress is usually eaten raw or added at the last minute to sauces. It is not suitable for cooking as a side vegetable, although it makes a lovely soup.

## Best uses in recipes

Roughly chop watercress to mix into salads or stir into a seasoned white sauce or wine and cream sauce to serve with poultry or fish. For a creamy and mild soup, sauté with onion, potatoes and garlic in olive oil and a little butter, then add enough vegetable or chicken stock to make a soup. Cook until the potatoes are soft. Blend, then stir in a little cream or crème fraîche. Serve hot or chilled. Watercress can also be used as a garnish for fish and poultry dishes or soups.

## fresh ideas

**For a refreshing salad**, finely grate the zest from 1 orange. Using a knife, cut the segments from 2 oranges. Lay watercress leaves on a serving plate and arrange the orange segments over the top. Add the grated orange zest to a salad dressing of oil and vinegar, season then sprinkle over the orange segments and watercress.

**Add crunch to pasta** Dry-fry chopped bacon in a pan, remove and drain. Clean pan and fry chopped onion and diced red pepper with crushed garlic in olive oil. Add the bacon and roughly chopped watercress, then toss into cooked pasta. Serve sprinkled with Parmesan cheese.

## did you know...

...that the best watercress is grown in areas where the water is mineral-rich, such as Dorset and Somerset. The minerals are drawn up into the stem, making watercress an exceptionally healthy food.

# glossary
## of good nutrition

Refer to this mini-dictionary when you come across diet and nutrition terms in this book that require explanation.

**antioxidant** This term refers to certain vitamins and other substances in plant foods that help to prevent disease by fighting off toxic substances in the body known as free radicals, and repairing the cell damage that they cause.

**beta carotene** A member of a family of substances known as carotenoids, beta carotene is the pigment that gives the orange colour to sweet potatoes, carrots, pumpkins and other fruits and vegetables. It is also found in dark green vegetables, but its colour is obscured by the green colour of chlorophyll that is present in those vegetables. Beta-carotene is converted to vitamin A in your body and also functions as an antioxidant to help the body to fight cancer and other chronic disease.

**capsaicin** This phytochemical is found in all peppers and chillies but is most heavily concentrated in chillies. Capsaicin may protect against chronic diseases such as cancer and prevent blood clots.

**carbohydrates** The major components of foods are carbohydrates, protein and fat. Carbohydrates are either starches or sugars and are found in all plant foods – vegetables, grains, pulses and fruits. Foods that are high in carbohydrates are our main source of energy and, when carefully selected, can also be our best source of certain essential vitamins and minerals.

**carcinogen** A substance that causes the growth of cancer cells.

**carotenoids** This is a family of more than 600 phytochemicals responsible for the yellow, orange and red pigments found in vegetables and fruits. Some carotenoids, such as lutein and lycopene, function as antioxidants or have other disease-fighting properties. The antioxidant beta carotene is the best known of the carotenoid family.

cholesterol This waxy, fat-like substance is present in every cell in animals, including humans. Cholesterol is essential to many body functions, including the production of vitamin D, hormones and essential skin oils. Excess cholesterol in the blood can adhere to the walls of the arteries, forming a substance known as plaque that contributes to hardening of the arteries and, ultimately, to heart disease.

cruciferous vegetables This family of vegetables, including cabbage, cauliflower, broccoli, Brussels sprouts and leafy greens, contains phytochemicals known as indoles that help to protect against cancer.

flavonoids These phytochemicals are found in broccoli, carrots, onions, soya beans and other foods. They are the same phytochemicals that are thought to give red wine and tea their antioxidant potential to help to reduce the risk of heart disease.

free radicals These unstable compounds form in the body during normal metabolism and also result from other factors such as radiation, smoking cigarettes and drinking alcohol and environmental pollution. Free radicals set up a chain reaction of events that lead to cell destruction and potentially cause cancer. Antioxidants found in vegetables and fruit help the body to repair damage done by free radicals.

homocysteine People with elevated levels of this amino acid in their blood are at an increased risk of developing heart disease. Vitamins $B_6$, $B_{12}$ and folate help to convert homocysteine into a non-destructive form.

indoles Cruciferous vegetables such as cabbage varieties, cauliflower and Brussels sprouts contain this phytochemical, which is thought to be protective against hormone-sensitive diseases such as breast cancer.

isoflavones These are phytochemicals present in soya beans and other leguminous plants that are called phytoestrogens – plant substances that mimic oestrogen's action in the body and may protect against heart disease and hormone-sensitive cancers.

isothiocyanates These are phytochemicals found in cruciferous vegetables such as cauliflower and broccoli that stimulate the body's cancer-fighting enzymes.

legumes All beans, peas, lentils and peanuts are in the legume family. That makes them good plant sources of protein and iron, nutrients more often associated with animal foods. They are also good sources of B vitamins and fibre. Dried beans are referred to as pulses.

lutein This carotenoid is found in avocado, kale, spinach, parsley, red peppers and other vegetables and fruits. Lutein is thought to protect against age-related blindness resulting from macular degeneration.

lycopene This carotenoid is found in tomatoes, tomato products such as purée and sauce, watermelon, pink grapefruit and other fruits and vegetables. Studies have found that lycopene may be protective against prostate cancer and other chronic diseases.

pectin This soluble fibre, found in many fruits, vegetables and legumes, helps to lower cholesterol and regulate intestinal function.

phytochemicals These plant substances help to boost immunity and fight chronic disease such as cancer and heart disease.

phytoestrogens These phytochemicals, found in soya beans and other legumes, mimic the action of the oestrogen produced naturally by the human body. Because of this action, phytoestrogens may help to protect against heart disease and hormone-sensitive cancers such as breast cancer.

phytonutrients These phytochemicals have nutritional value in addition to disease-fighting capabilities.

resveratro This phytochemical helps lower cholesterol and protect against heart disease.

sulphoraphane Broccoli, cabbage and Brussels sprouts contain this phytochemical, which stimulates the production of anti-cancer enzymes.

zeaxanthin This carotenoid, found in broccoli and kale, helps to prevent age-related blindness which results from macular degeneration.

# vegetable **freezing chart**

Vegetables that are to be frozen must always be thoroughly cleaned and trimmed. Most need to be precooked by blanching in boiling water. Not all vegetables freeze successfully. Asparagus, for example, breaks down and becomes limp and watery when thawed. Other vegetables that freeze poorly include beetroots, whole or cut-up carrots, cauliflower, cucumber, aubergine, fennel, salad leaves, leeks, potatoes, radishes, courgettes and other summer squash. Here are instructions for handling those vegetables that freeze well.

| | | |
|---|---|---|
| **beans, green** | Blanch trimmed beans 3 minutes per 500g. Cool completely in iced water. Drain well and place in freezer container. | Use within 12 months |
| **broccoli** | Blanch bite-sized pieces of broccoli for 3 minutes. Cool completely in iced water. Drain well and place in freezer container. | Use within 12 months |
| **brussels sprouts** | Blanch trimmed sprouts for 3 to 5 minutes, depending on the size of the head. Cool completely in iced water. Drain well and pack into freezer container. | Use within 12 months |
| **greens** | Blanch whole leaves for 2 minutes. Cool completely in iced water. Drain well and pack into freezer container. | Use within 6 months |
| **okra** | Blanch trimmed, whole okra pods for 4 minutes. Cool completely in iced water. Drain well and pack into freezer container. | Use within 6 months |
| **onions** | Pack raw, finely chopped onions, spring onions or chives loosely in freezer container. | Use within 6 months |
| **peas** | Blanch shelled peas for 2 minutes. Cool completely in iced water. Drain well and loosely pack in freezer container. | Use within 12 months |
| | Blanch mange-touts and sugar snap peas for 2 minutes. Cool completely in iced water. Drain well. Place in single layer on a baking sheet or tray. Freeze, then pack frozen peas into freezer container. | Use within 9 months |
| **peppers** | Pack finely chopped, raw peppers in freezer container. | Use within 12 months |
| **pumpkin, squash & courgettes** | Cook pumpkin completely and purée before freezing. Cool completely before packing into freezer container. Cook squash completely and purée before freezing. Cool completely before packing into freezer container. | Use within 6 months |
| **root vegetables** | Cook carrots completely and purée before freezing. (Whole and cut-up carrots do not freeze well.) Cook parsnips completely and purée before freezing. (Whole and cut-up parsnips do not freeze well.) Cool completely before packing into freezer container. Cook turnips or swede completely and mash or purée before freezing. Cool completely before packing into freezer container. | Use within 6 months |
| **spinach** | Blanch whole leaves for 2 minutes. Cool completely in iced water. Drain well and pack in freezer container. | Use within 6 months |
| **sweet potatoes** | Cook sweet potatoes completely and purée before freezing. Cool completely before packing into freezer container. | Use within 6 months |
| **sweetcorn** | Blanch whole cobs for 4 to 8 minutes, depending on the size of the cob. Cool completely in iced water. Cut off kernels or leave cobs whole and pack into freezer container. | Use within 6 months |
| **tomatoes** | Blanch whole tomatoes for 2 minutes. Cool completely in iced water. Drain well and freeze for later use in cooking. Tomato sauce also freezes well. | Use within 12 months |

# index

All images are Reader's Digest copyright with the following exceptions:

5 Digital Vision/Getty Images 10 Pixtal 12 bottom right Pixtal 13 top Dallas Powell, Jr/ Dreamstime.com; bottom Pixtal 28 top Royalty-Free/Corbis; centre left Jules Frazier/Photodisc Green/Getty Images; bottom right Digital Vision/Getty Images 262 cr © Dorling Kindersley 267 (pak choi) C Squared Studios/Photodisc Green/Getty Images. 273 (habanero) C Squared Studios/Photodisc Blue/Getty Images 280 tr Stephen Oliver/© Dorling Kindersley 293 (cara, maris piper & King Edward) 2008 Agriculture and Horticultural Development Board. Source: The Potato Council 297 top left © Dorling Kindersley; centre right Lew Robertson/Jupiter 305 (bitter melon) Harris Shiffman/ Dreamstime.com.

- - - - - - - - - - - - - - - - - - - - - - - - - - - - - - -

The publishers would like to thank Sam and Steve Grima of Grima's Farm Fresh Produce

*Healthy & Delicious* is published by the Reader's Digest Association Limited, 11 Westferry Circus, Canary Wharf London E14 4HE

Copyright © 2008 The Reader's Digest Association Limited

This book was first published as *Vegetables for Vitality* in 2004 by The Reader's Digest Association, Inc., USA.

We are committed both to the quality of our products and the service we provide to our customers. we value your comments, so please do contact us on 08705 113366 or via our website at **www.readersdigest.co.uk**

If you have any comments or suggestions about the content of our books, email us at **gbeditorial@readersdigest.co.uk**

**Colour origination**
Colour Systems Limited

**Printed and bound** in China

## for Reader's Digest

**Project editor** Lisa Thomas
**Art editor** Julie Bennett
**Cookery editor** Jan Cutler
**Designer** Martin Bennett
**New recipes** Bridget Jones
**New photography** Sian Irvine (*assisted by* Joe Giacomet, *stylist* Katie Rogers)
**Photographers** Sang An, Martin Brigdale, Christine Bronico, Beatric Dacosta, Gus Filgate, Mark Ferri, Ian Hofstetter (*stylist* Katy Holder), William Lingwood, Steven Mays, Andrew McCul, David Murray, Sean Myers, Mark Needham, Alan Richardson, Jules Selmes, Lisa Koenig, Elizabeth Watt
**Editorial assistant** Jo Pickering
**Proofreader** Barry Gage
**Indexer** Diane Harriman

## Reader's Digest General Books

**Editorial director** Julian Browne
**Art director** Anne-Marie Bulat
**Managing editor** Nina Hathway
**Head of book development** Sarah Bloxham
**Picture research manager** Christine Hinze
**Pre-press account manager** Dean Russell
**Product production manager** Claudette Bramble
**Senior production controller** Katherine Bunn

**ISBN** 978 0 276 44502 6
**Concept code** US3905/IC
**Book code** 400-391 UP0000-1
**Oracle code** 250012595H.00.24